The Place of the Past

"This book is timely and needed in the current discourse among students and scholars of the Bible. In a comprehensive defense of historical criticism, the author skillfully shows what scholars of the past fifty years have gotten wrong about the past. Without ditching the newer methods developed since the mid- to late-twentieth century, Holland draws on a wealth of knowledge in philosophy, history, and biblical scholarship to show the necessity of historical criticism for biblical studies today. His 'principles' drawn from philosophy and the guild of historical studies broadly offer concrete suggestions by which historical criticism should move forward constructively. None of us working today in biblical studies can afford to ignore this important volume."

—**Bill T. Arnold**, Paul S. Amos Professor of Old Testament Interpretation, Asbury Theological Seminary

"This book is a useful overview of the methodological status quo of historical criticism vis-a-vis overtly synchronic and ideological approaches. It also offers a defense for the continuing value of historical criticism in dialogue and collaboration with other approaches. Well written and easily accessible. Recommended for all interested readers."

—**Steven L. McKenzie**, Spence L. Wilson Senior Research Fellow, Rhodes College , Memphis, Tennessee

"There's a generation of biblical scholars who have been taught to view historical criticism with either extreme skepticism or outright disdain. Truth be told, there are legitimate reasons for this. However, Holland's work clarifies just how much of an overcorrection this is. By beginning with the early church, and plotting developments across major intellectual eras, Holland shows how historical concerns have always existed and how they came to dominate. Yet the beauty of this work is that Holland plots a way forward, emphasizing that the valuable tools of historical criticism can be redeemed and utilized in an edifying manner. This is an insightful work, born out of Holland's own experiences and intellectual developments."

—**David B. Schreiner**, Associate Professor of Old Testament and Inductive Bible Studies, Asbury Theological Seminary

"As both a proponent and practitioner of historical critical approaches to biblical texts, I wholeheartedly appreciate Holland's nuanced treatment of the contributions and limits of historical criticism. Like any ancient text (biblical or otherwise), historical criticism itself has a history of transmission and development; and, as with any ancient text (biblical or otherwise), knowing the history of transmission and the worlds from which historical criticism arose is exceedingly beneficial—and necessary—if we, as Holland has capably argued, are to respect what ancient authors and communities have said about their experiences with God. Is there a place for historical criticism today? I believe there is, and I happily recommend Holland's fine book to those who think the study of the past is passé."

—**Kevin B. Burr**, Assistant Professor of Bible and Ministry, Harding University

The Place of the Past

Historical Criticism's Role in Biblical Studies

DREW S. HOLLAND

CASCADE *Books* • Eugene, Oregon

THE PLACE OF THE PAST
Historical Criticism's Role in Biblical Studies

Copyright © 2025 Drew S. Holland. All rights reserved. Except for brief quotations in critical publications or reviews, no part of this book may be reproduced in any manner without prior written permission from the publisher. Write: Permissions, Wipf and Stock Publishers, 199 W. 8th Ave., Suite 3, Eugene, OR 97401.

Cascade Books
An Imprint of Wipf and Stock Publishers
199 W. 8th Ave., Suite 3
Eugene, OR 97401

www.wipfandstock.com

PAPERBACK ISBN: 978-1-6667-8382-7
HARDCOVER ISBN: 978-1-6667-8383-4
EBOOK ISBN: 978-1-6667-8384-1

Cataloguing-in-Publication data:

Names: Holland, Drew S. [author].

Title: The place of the past : historical criticism's role in biblical studies / Drew S. Holland.

Description: Eugene, OR: Cascade Books, 2025 | Includes bibliographical references and index.

Identifiers: ISBN 978-1-6667-8382-7 (paperback) | ISBN 978-1-6667-8383-4 (hardcover) | ISBN 978-1-6667-8384-1 (ebook)

Subjects: LCSH: Historical criticism (Literature). | Bible—Hermeneutics. | Bible—Criticism, interpretation, etc.—History. | Bible.—Old Testament—Historiography. | Bible.—New Testament—Historiography.

Classification: BS500 H65 2025 (paperback) | BS500 (ebook)

VERSION NUMBER 07/16/25

Unless otherwise noted, Scripture quotations are from New Revised Standard Version Bible, copyright © 1989 National Council of the Churches of Christ in the United States of America. Used by permission. All rights reserved worldwide.

Dedicated to the glory of God in honor of my parents.

Contents

Preface | ix
Abbreviations | xiii

1. Introduction | 1
2. Historical Thinking in Antiquity Through the Medieval Period | 10
3. Sprouts of Historical Criticism in the Renaissance Through the Enlightenment | 40
4. The Normalization of Historical Criticism | 64
5. The Critique of Historical Criticism | 79
6. The State of Historical Criticism | 103
7. The Future of Historical Criticism | 128
8. Conclusion | 158

Bibliography | 165
Subject Index | 179
Author Index | 185
Scripture Index | 189

Preface

ONE OF THE PROMINENT topics of this book is the incessant wrangling among scholars concerning the meaning of a text. Aside from the text itself as an artifact of literary and historical curiosity, there are at least two more perspectives from which a text can be viewed. These are the intentions of the author and the effects the text has on its readers. In this space, I will offer some reflections on both of these, beginning with the latter.

I am grateful that you have picked up this book and chosen to give it a read. Much of this book is spent considering thousands of years of history. In particular, these portions deal with a "history of history," that is, how scholars over the years have studied the history of the Bible. If you have picked up this book, you continue this tradition of being compelled by the events and people of the Bible and its world and how we can effectively make sense of them. I hope that you will take the opportunity to correct and build on the arguments presented here. I release my work into the greater dialectics surrounding biblical exegesis and to you, the reader, to make of it what your insight and abilities can. My own knowledge and skills are limited, as I'm sure you will find, so please correct, reinforce, and add to what is here. As I suggest in the later chapters of this book, the grand conversations around these topics are crucial. Nothing less than human self-understanding is at stake.

So I have, in effect, not only addressed the dimension of the reader, for whom I am grateful, but I have also anticipated some of what I, the author of this text, intend to do with it. As much as I admire the many contributions around freeing the text from the author, this particular text comes with authorial intentions. It will likely be that my intentions do not always match the words on the page and that others may take more or different

Preface

meanings from what they read. Over these things I relinquish control. But it is important for me to express the intentions of this work as much as possible.

This work has its genesis in a personal journey. In the studies for my master's degree, I was introduced to how New Criticism, postmodernism, and the canonical approach could drastically alter the way readers understand the biblical text. I found these readings intriguing and carried them with me for several years of pastoral ministry and independent study. But, when I began a doctoral program in Old Testament at a different institution, another world opened to me. This was the world of biblical history, from reading Wellhausen in his own words, to studying the great finds of archaeology, to mining the nuances of linguistic changes in Northwest Semitic. From my first seminar, in which I realized I did not know how to correctly pronounce "Sennacherib," to a dissertation comparing regnal notices in 1–2 Kings to neo-Babylonian Chronicles, I matured, not only in my understanding of biblical history, but in my belief that knowledge of biblical history is important in order to read the Bible well.

What I did not have in these years was the guide that told me why it was important. What are sound principles for thinking historically about the Bible? In what ways is historical criticism science, and in what ways is it art? And, perhaps most important for me as a person of faith, how can biblical history inform theology? These kinds of questions drove me to dive into the available literature, research the philosophy of history, and produce a few articles as I worked out the issues found in this book. The extant literature, though excellent and cited in support many times throughout this work, was, for my tastes, too brief to encompass all the issues that concern historical criticism of the Bible. Ultimately, I wanted students to have access to a more comprehensive defense of historical criticism, albeit one with enough sympathies to other approaches, so I felt a full monograph was in order. I am grateful that Cascade Books has agreed. And I hope, once again, that what I offer here is worthy enough to larger conversations around biblical exegesis.

You will see that I find historical criticism important on many fronts. It sets boundaries in interpreting the text. It deepens the traditional plain sense of Scripture. It enables understanding and sympathy with biblical authors who sought to communicate their experiences about God. Is this all historical criticism does? Probably not, but I hope to stoke further conversation around this question. Is historical criticism the only way to read

Preface

the Bible? Absolutely not, and I urge exegetes to ask all kinds of questions of the text. But I do hope that what I write here provides a solid foundation for understanding why historical criticism is indispensable and how it can be done responsibly.

One final note on the critiques of the concept of an author. Michel Foucault argued that the modern obsession toward the author is due in part to our legal understandings of responsibility. An author, that is, is supposed to take accountability for her words. In this particular moment of history (and one point I make in this book is that we are all bound in history), I accept this for the words that follow. However poorly I may have done it, I wrote the following words and accept full responsibility for the strengths and weaknesses of their arguments.

Yet I also acknowledge, as I suppose Foucault would wish us to understand, that I did not write the following in a vacuum. I am a part of both an academic, social, and church community that formed my ideas and capabilities. There are so many in these communities I wish to thank, although I cannot thank them all. I am grateful to folks like Cochran Pruitt, Eli Fisher, David Schreiner, and Kevin Burr, who read and provided feedback on earlier drafts of different segments of this book. I am thankful to the staff at Cascade Books for accepting my proposal and for doing the necessary work to make this work accessible and more polished. My bosses at UT Southern offered me a gracious course-load reduction in the spring of 2024 so I could see this work to completion. The staff at UT Southern's Warden Memorial Library, especially Chris VanDoran, procured many of the resources you see in the bibliography. Many thanks to these and all of my beloved UT Southern colleagues. My wife, Vaughan, and my kids, Sam and Anne Yates, always provided the needed distraction of reminding me that I am loved no matter what comes of this book. I wish to offer my final thanks to my parents, David and Cathy Holland, in whose honor I dedicate this book. As students of history and nurturers of future generations, they have influenced me more than I can ever know.

Drew S. Holland
Fifth Week after Pentecost, 2024

Abbreviations

ABD	*Anchor Bible Dictionary.* Edited by David Noel Freedman. 6 vols. New York: Doubleday, 1992.
Ag. Ap.	Josephus, *Against Apion*
AIL	Ancient Israel and Its Literature
Ant.	Josephus, *Jewish Antiquities*
AsJT	*Asia Journal of Theology*
AsTJ	*Asbury Theological Journal*
BZAW	Beihefte zur Zeitschrift für die alttestamentiche Wissenschaft
BibInt	Biblical Interpretation Series
CBQ	*Catholic Biblical Quarterly*
civ.	Augustine, *De civitate Dei/The City of God*
ClQ	*Classical Quarterly*
COS	*The Context of Scripture.* Edited by William W. Hallo. 3 vols. Leiden: Brill, 1997–2002.
CPC	The Church and Postmodern Culture
CRINT	Copmendia Rerum Iudaicarum ad Novum Testamentum
Doctr. chr.	Augustine, *De Doctrina Christiana/On Christian Doctrine*
Her. Hist.	Herodotus, *The Histories*
Her. mal.	Plutarch, *De Heroditi malignitate*
Hist.	Polybius, *Histories*
Hist. eccl.	Eusebius, *Historia Ecclesiastica/Ecclesiastical History*
Hist. Pel.	Thucydides, *History of the Peloponnesian War*
HistTh	*History and Theory*
HTR	*Harvard Theological Review*

Abbreviations

HUCA	*Hebrew University College Annual*
IEJ	*Israel Exploration Journal*
IFT	Introductions in Feminist Theology
JBL	*Journal of Biblical Literature*
JCBS	Jews and Christians in Biblical Studies
JHebS	*Journal of Hebrew Studies*
JR	*Journal of Religion*
JRS	*Journal of Religion and Society*
JSOTSup	Journal for the Study of the Old Testament Supplement Series
JTISup	*Journal of Theological Interpretation, Supplements*
J.W.	Josephus, *Jewish War*
LAI	Library of Ancient Israel
OBT	Overtures to Biblical Theology
Princ.	Origen, *De principiis (Peri archōn)/First Principles*
RBL	*Review of Biblical Literature*
SBLRBS	Society of Biblical Literature Resources for Biblical Study
SBTS	Sources for Biblical and Theological Study
SocRes	*Social Research*
SSEA	Society for the Study of Egyptian Antiquities
ThTo	*Theology Today*
TynBul	*Tyndale Bulletin*
VTSup	Supplements to Vetus Testamentum
WTJ	*Wesleyan Theological Journal*
ZAW	*Zeitschrift für alttestamentliche Wissenschaft*

1

Introduction

IF YOU WERE TO visit the small town where I teach, you would likely be surprised that such a bustling settlement exists over an hour from the metropolitan limits of any major city. Not only does our town sport a public institution of higher learning, but it also boasts a busy town square with a picturesque county courthouse, several round-the-clock manufacturing facilities, some of the most unique restaurants you will ever visit, and immense pride in the local high school sports teams. As if plucked out of a Hallmark movie, Pulaski is as much as anyone could ask for in a rural, Southern county seat.

But there are a few overt signs of Pulaski's dark past. Many who may not have visited Pulaski know it best as the birthplace of the Ku Klux Klan. Pulaski became a bastion of the Southern "Lost Cause" movement in response to the Union army setting up a contraband camp[1] there, and conflicts over race continued for decades.

The pain of that past and the tension such pain produces are palpable when you look closer than Pulaski's quaint veneer. A historical marker noting Pulaski as the birthplace of the KKK has been turned around so that it cannot be read. Yet only a block away, the courthouse square hosts the statue of Sam Davis, a Confederate war hero who was hanged on a hill

---

1. A place where the families of black Union army soldiers settled while their family members were at war.

The Place of the Past

overlooking the county square after refusing to give up the name of a spy who assisted him. Davis's name is plastered on a bridge, a road, an apartment building, and a local park. Some will argue that these honorific names do not support his politics, only his courage. Some contend that the informant he protected was a runaway slave, thus easing the racial burden. For others, it is a stain.[2]

Even though the Civil War ended over 150 years ago, cities like Pulaski demonstrate the contemporary effects of racial tension, not only in the South, but throughout the United States. An hour to the southeast in Huntsville, AL and elsewhere throughout the U.S., memorials to Confederate soldiers (like that of Davis) have been recently moved and relocated in reaction to "Black Lives Matter" protests. Racial disparities and tensions still permeate cities across the country. Education, healthcare, and income lag behind for blacks in comparison to whites. In the years since the Civil War, the nation has failed to remedy the ills of systemic racism. One need look no further than Pulaski to see evidence of this, but one can look just about anywhere in the U.S.

The point is that the past matters. The way we construct the past in the present affects the stories we tell about our origins and how life got to be the way that it is. How we construct the past in the present shapes our identities, both as individuals and as communities. And how we construct the past can even tell us about the stodgy, and sometimes beautiful, aspects of human nature. In our pursuit of the truth, getting this past right also matters.

Such an example as the one I have given above, which concerns the past of only a few recent generations, proves this to be the case. But that is not the focus of this book. Instead, we reach back thousands of years to ask why it is important to study the past found in the Bible. Why does it matter to look into Bible's events and composition? After all, none of the nations it describes exist in the form they did then, and it is nearly impossible to trace any individual's origins to the people of two thousand or more years ago.

For one, the Bible still matters. As is often noted, it is the top-selling book of all time. It remains sacred Scripture for approximately a third of the world's population. And it has had an incalculable impact on the values we hold in western civilization.[3] Whether one subscribes to a religion based on

---

2. For a recent article on the efforts to remove Davis's name from the stadium, see McCall, "Equality March."

3. A recent and popular approach to this concept is seen in Tom Holland, *Dominion*.

Introduction

the Bible does not affect the fact that the Bible remains significant in our world. Consequently, studying the history the Bible tells should also mean something to us.

Further, the Bible, though not intended as a history book, is often our only source of some information about the past. In some cases, it provides an alternative testimony to events we know of from the ancient world. The Bible can be helpful in reconstructing more than our social values and religions in the West, providing testimonies to the histories of the ancient Near East and Greco-Roman world.

And, finally, the Bible does presume to speak to the human condition. As its many authors wrangle over the trajectory of humankind, the Israelites, the later Jews, and the early Christian church with the God of Israel, we never escape the characterization of humankind as being made in God's image (Gen 1:26–27) yet still marred by Adam and Eve's rebellion (Gen 3). For the writers of the Bible, such is not a primordial issue, but remains the human condition upon which we must reflect until history's end. The study of history gives us the tools to investigate the human condition of the Bible's characters, authors, and redactors.

The Problem

Perhaps what I have described thus far seems self-evident. After all, history is a part of the air we breathe. We are forced to study history as a part of our academic curricula. Roadsides bear historical markers waiting to inform us of what happened in the spot we now drive by. There are television channels, podcasts, and social media accounts dealing with nothing but history. But in the academic world, the traditional study of history has come under attack. In philosophy, postmodernism has challenged the normative means of studying the past. Philosophers such as Michel Foucault and Jean-Francois Lytotard have questioned the factual basis of any narratives we tell as a society, including history. The impact of postmodernism has shaken many academic disciplines, perhaps no more than the study of history. Many trained historians and history departments at colleges and universities have shied away from conventional modes of examining primary and secondary sources or constructing definitive critical narratives of the past to focus instead on meta-level questions of how history is told. For many historians, there is no solid foundation for studying the past, and we thus cannot be sure of the world that led us to the present.

The Place of the Past

In biblical studies, we find a similar predicament. "Historical criticism" is the blanket term used in biblical studies to describe diverse methodologies,[4] such as textual, source, redaction, and form criticisms, as well as comparison and general inquiries about historical veracity of traditional faith claims from the Bible. Whereas scholars of the late-nineteenth and early-twentieth centuries fixated on questions of historical criticism, many biblical scholars since the late-twentieth century have given up on these once-promising questions. Not only has postmodernism infiltrated the world of biblical studies,[5] many have wondered whether so-called "historical critics" have been asking the wrong questions about the biblical text to begin with. For instance, Brevard Childs, with his "canonical approach," wished for interpreters to view the Bible as primarily the repository of faith traditions.[6] Robert Alter encouraged scholars to turn away from the speculative, "excavative" approaches of historical criticism and focus on the literary genius of the biblical text.[7] Similarly, James Muilenburg promoted the study of a novel "rhetorical criticism" of the Bible to turn away from the speculative aspects of form criticism.[8] Within faith traditions in particular, a prominent emphasis has been placed on "theological exegesis" of the Bible, treating it as less as an artifact for scholars to dissect than a gem that the faithful can admire.[9]

These approaches did not appear out of thin air. Rather, they reflect a response to some futility on the part of the historical-critical methodologies. Very few consensuses have emerged from historical criticism, and it works with an underwhelming amount of historical data, given the antiquity of the world to which it refers. As a result, not a few biblical interpreters have found historical studies of the Bible speculative and thus unworthy of serious consideration. "If we can only discern so much about the Bible and

---

4. Because *many* methodologies are subsumed under the rubric of historical criticism, I resist the oft-used term "historical-critical method." For a recent study of the emergence of the term "historical-critical," which has forerunners in interdisciplinary Latin scholarship and is used in German-speaking biblical scholarship by the eighteenth century, see Brettler and Arakaky, "Historical-Critical," 206–18.

5. For classic treatments, see Adam, *Postmodern*; Aichele et al., *Postmodern Bible*.

6. We will continue to say more about Childs's work, but to see an example of how this approach is applied, see Childs, *Introduction*.

7. Alter, *Biblical Narrative*, 13–14.

8. Muilenburg, "Form Criticism and Beyond," 1–18.

9. For a recent understanding of this approach, see Reno, *End*.

its world," the thought goes, "are we not wasting our time debating over minutiae when there might be more important questions to ask?"

Furthermore, more recent approaches contend on firmer ground than a dubious past. Although it may be difficult to know what really happened when Sennacherib left Jerusalem (2 Kgs 19:35–37//Isa 37:36–38), we can be surer of the words on the page. One feature recent approaches to the Bible have in common is their focus on the final form of, as opposed to the world behind, the text. This echoes postmodern call to study the words in front of the reader. Conversations around the rise and fall of a plot, the characterization of God, or the existence of a chiasm are surely on firmer footing when scholars can agree to discuss a common text. Of course, this involves a tremendous amount of interpretation, which will depend on implicit understandings of the text. But at least the descriptive features of the interpreted subject, that is the words on the page, are present before us. The past is not, and this proves an epistemological crisis that is difficult for many scholars to overcome.

Consider the following recent summary of historical criticism from Keith D. Stanglin. He writes that historical criticism

> was and is academic and scientific. With modern readings of Scripture, interpretation came to mean accessing the one true meaning. The modern, historical-critical method sought only the truth of authorial intent. Whatever the original human author meant is the only thing a text can mean. Historical and cultural contextualization of the text is of utmost importance. Authorial intent entails reconstructing the psychology of the author and, because of increased skepticism about the text, the full history and previous authors behind the text. Although it is an impossible, conjectural task, it became the only criterion of meaning in the text. As a result of the Enlightenment, objectivity and detachment became prerequisites for interpreting a text. But the more the Protestant church focused its attention on Scripture as not only the primary—but the sole—source of truth and the deposit of the faith (explicitly excluding the voice of tradition), the more it focused on the literal reading. Both liberals and fundamentalists were united in their rejection of a fuller, spiritual sense. Authority for interpretation was decentralized, leading to a proliferation of individualistic, diverse, and contradictory interpretations.[10]

---

10. Stanglin, *Letter and Spirit*, 9–10.

As Stanglin suggests, historical criticism seems better suited for the academy than the church. Because of this, theological interpreters have turned, not only to literary approaches, but to traditional and "ruled" readings driven primarily by the confessions of the synagogue and church and only secondarily (if at all) by historical concerns. So, not only has historical criticism been challenged on its philosophical foundations, but on its theological footings as well.

Is There Any Room for History?

Regardless of the challenges leveled against historical criticism of the Bible, the many methodologies that are subsumed under the title "historical criticism" persevere. Historical-critical scholars remain concerned about the veracity of the Bible's historical witnesses. Archaeologists uncover finds and debate how these relate to the biblical text. Textual critics continue to learn numerous languages, grapple over barely legible manuscripts, and theorize about textual transmission based on their data. Source critics investigate whether a text was compiled in stages and redaction critics ask what the final compiler wished to achieve. Comparativists try to understand what the texts meant in their original cognitive, social, and political environments. Undeterred by the arguments of final-form critics against historical criticism, these popular approaches remain.

Thus, it seems there is an appeal to these practices, but this appeal has largely gone unstated. As we will see, many final-form readers of the Bible who trenchantly challenge the aims of historical criticism do not abandon it altogether, but leave an articulation of what historical criticism can genuinely contribute unresolved.[11] As a result, a firm divide still exists between those who contend for historical criticism's usefulness in exegesis and those who do not.[12] The approach of this book is to attempt to heal this divide, articulate historical criticism's appeal, and explain why historical criticism should keep its place in both the guild and the church. Again, for some, historical criticism does not need defending. But, for many, a defense is still

---

11. See, for example, Stanglin, *Letter and Spirit*, 213–14; Steinmetz, "Superiority," 38; Reno, *End*, 26, 28, 45, 75; Yeago, "New Testament," 163; Greenstein, "State," 22; Green, *Seized by Truth*, 112; Clines, "Historical Criticism," 9.

12. A description of this divide is found in several places, including the following: Strawn, "Docetism," 330–31; Barton, "Historical Criticism," 3; Joyce, "First Among Equals?," 17; Levenson, *Hebrew Bible*, 110; Baden, "Tower of Babel," 221.

necessary. The following is for those who need to understand a rationale for historical study of the Bible.

In this investigation, I do not wish to disparage those who have criticized historical criticism. Indeed, I was trained at one institution on theological interpretation and final-form approaches to the exclusion of historical criticism, and I gained there an enormous sympathy for these views. Moreover, I confess to primarily utilizing these approaches in my sermons. I sincerely hope I demonstrate sympathy for those who have turned from historical criticism in exegesis. Yet, I also wish to express a rational foundation for the excitement I felt when I truly engaged historical criticism for the first time at a later institution. I suppose I wish to have my exegetical cake and eat it, too. And I would be thrilled for readers of this book to have this joy in their exegetical ventures as well.

What this study will not do is claim one approach to studying the Bible as "best." Rather, one of the fundamental principles I assume is that interpreters of the Bible need many ways to encounter it. This is because we ask different questions of the text. Different questions require different approaches to address them. The question, "What does this text say about God for my church community?" requires a theological response. The question, "Why are there many different textual readings?" requires the answer of a text critic. The classic historical question, "How did it actually happen?" requires a host of historical queries. None of these questions is wrong in pursuit of knowing more about the Bible.

Final-form readings of the text are crucial for a "synchronic" (literally, "together-in-time," indicating the interpretation of the parts of a specific text taken together, united as a whole at the time the text was completed) reading of the Bible. Despite some objections we will discuss later on, it is legitimate to read the Bible as one would any piece of literature. It is legitimate for faith communities to read the final, received text as Scripture. It is legitimate for observers of religion and culture of the western world to read the final text as a repository of faith traditions that have shaped the world we live in.

It is also equally legitimate to read the Bible "diachronically," that is "through time." This is the work of the broad spectrum of historical-critical approaches. They look back from our present position to acknowledge that the Bible did not fall out of the sky. The text has a history, and it is important for historical critics—such as source, redaction, and textual critics—to understand that history. Moreover, the text is situated in a particular world.

Our understanding of a text, even for the most committed final-form reader, falls woefully short if we do not understand this world. Dare I say, readings divorced from such historical background are willfully ignorant. The efforts of comparativists, sociologists, archaeologists, and general historians are indispensable in this regard. We will have more to say about diachronic and synchronic readings in chapter 6. There is nuance to what I have thus far stated, but it is evident that the Bible should be able to withstand the myriad questions posed to it in the name of intellectual honesty.

The Path Ahead

Before we can expand further on these matters, we must explain how we arrived at this point of tension within the guild of biblical studies. The next three chapters begin our study with the origin of history writing, a much-debated theme. Although the Greeks are often supposed to be the progenitors of history writing, no small disagreement centers on whether we can speak of earlier authors as historians. The stakes for us here are twofold: (1) Did the biblical authors intend to convey history? If so, shouldn't we study it as such? (2) For how long has western society cared about historical questions? Is it anachronistic for us to force historical questions on the Bible? From these concerns, we will trace historical questions through to the Enlightenment and the larger renaissance of historical thinking that appeared in the nineteenth century. Finally, we follow this historical thinking in more specific applications of biblical studies to see how and why biblical interpreters have asked historical-critical questions.

In chapter 5, we will attempt to understand why the fashionable study of historical criticism became passé. Suddenly, in the mid-twentieth century, a confluence of arguments arose to contest not only the results but also the methodologies of traditional historical criticism. On the one hand, interpreters of the Bible debunked many of the confident conclusions of biblical theology in the late-nineteenth and early-twentieth centuries. This led to the need for a paradigm shift in understanding which questions were most important in studying the Bible and what historical criticism could even contribute to making sense of the Bible, particularly for communities of faith. On the other hand, the philosophical movement of postmodernism threatened the ability of academics in many disciplines to make sense of their work. Historians in general, and especially historians of the Bible, have scrambled to clarify their aims in light of such ideological menaces.

Introduction

Chapter 6 will provide a glimpse into how the various subdisciplines of historical criticism currently practice given the challenges they have faced over the preceding decades. We will see that no approach has ceased, but neither has any approach gone unscathed by the challenges to traditional modes of historical criticism. Further, we will discuss the promising emergence of memory studies and its impact on biblical interpretation.

The penultimate chapter suggests principles with which historical criticism may constructively move forward. Thankfully, biblical scholars have not been the only ones to wrestle with the meaning of the past. By leaning on conversations in philosophy and the historical guild at large, biblical scholars can learn much about the caution needed in drawing conclusions, the importance of a community of interpretation, the role of evidence, and the logic of speaking about the past.

Along the way, the reader will notice that this study is interdisciplinary. We will engage both Testaments of the Christian Bible, as well as the disciplines of philosophy and history. The reader will surely notice voids in my own knowledge and perspective, as I write this from the point of view of one trained primarily as an Old Testament interpreter. Thus, an invitation stands before the reader to contribute knowledge and correction where I fall short. I also write from the privileged position of a Western, middle-class, white, male academic who has benefited from the way history has been told in the modern period. As we will see, such a confession is crucial to the composition of history, as are both the willingness to absorb perspectives that are different and the attempt to speak as truthfully from my limited worldview as possible.

There are, of course, numerous fine books on biblical interpretation. This work can only at its most ambitious fill in gaps of these illuminating books, many of which I will engage with here. But what I hope emerges at the end of this study is what I feel has been lacking in recent discussions, namely clarity around the necessity of historical criticism for biblical studies. Although numerous attacks have been rightly leveled at its application in the past, I am confident there is a constructive future for historical criticism. I will recommend some foundational principles for this to occur, and I would be honored for the theme of this work to be expanded upon and improved. At the very least, I hope the following stimulates questions for serious interpreters of the Bible. There are many of us who believe historical criticism has its place because both history and the Bible matter. The challenge stands before us to claim why.

2

Historical Thinking in Antiquity Through the Medieval Period

HUMANS HAVE WRITTEN HISTORY for thousands of years. They have done so for varying reasons and with different understandings of how the past should be constructed. The historical-critical discipline of biblical research appears, at least on the surface, to lie within a greater tradition of human inquiry about the past. In the next several chapters, we will begin to trace the "history of history," as it were, leading up to the formation of historical criticism of the Bible. Unfortunately, what is presented in these chapters will not, and indeed cannot, be comprehensive. Many studies have attained such lofty status, and I rely on several of these for my research. But the goal here will be to locate historical criticism within the stream of historical study to understand where it comes from and how it might legitimately function within biblical exegesis.

It should be pertinent before beginning this investigation to define some key terms. In John Van Seters's influential book *In Search of History*, he distinguishes between "historiography" and "history writing." The former is a broad category that encompasses all texts with antiquarian interest. The latter is subsumed under the label of historiography and is defined best by the work of philosopher Johan Huizinga, who defines it as "the intellectual form in which a civilization renders account to itself of its past."[1] We will concern ourselves in this study with both. Van Seters uses this to explain the following five distinct characteristics of history writing: (1) It is a specific form of literary tradition. (2) It considers the reason and significance of past events, rather than merely reporting them. (3) It attempts to explain the historical causes for present circumstances. (4) It is national or corporate in character. (5) And it is a part of the literary tradition of a people and plays a significant role in that people's corporate tradition.[2]

Lester L. Grabbe criticizes Van Seters for misusing Huizinga's definition of history by excluding the genres in his succeeding analysis that Huizinga includes in his.[3] William W. Hallo likewise argues that Van Seters misreads Huizinga in ignoring the phrase "to itself" in his definition. This phrase indicates that historiography is a subjective enterprise and each culture will engage in presenting antiquarian events in its own unique way.[4] Indeed, it appears that Van Seters has taken liberty with Huizinga's definition by adapting it to his own goals for constructing the biblical Deuteronomistic Historian as a historian in the vein of Herodotus and Thucydides (more on this below). In actuality, Huizinga has produced a definition for the literary genre of history that is broader than Van Seters admits.

All this wrangling over the definitions of history within biblical studies makes it clear that, in attempting to write about history, how one defines history is pivotal to one's conclusions. Grabbe writes,

> One may legitimately use a variety of definitions for determining what is "history" or "history-writing" in antiquity. The definition chosen may go a long way toward determining one's conclusions; at least the particular definition used will limit the possible conclusions. However, any definition chosen must not exclude important works from antiquity that have long been considered examples of history-writing, and it certainly must not exclude the work of modern historians.[5]

---

1. Huizinga, "Definition," 1–10. His definition of history appears on p. 9. For Van Seters's engagement with Huizinga's definition, see Van Seters, *In Search*, 1–7.

2. Van Seters, *In Search*, 4–5.

3. Grabbe, "First Real Historians," 158.

4. Hallo, "Biblical History," 6. K. Lawson Younger argues further that Van Seters's definition of history is inadequate for describing history writing in the ancient Near East and Israel, the subject of Van Seters's work. Younger, "Underpinnings," 305–11.

5. Grabbe, "First Real Historians," 179. In this, Grabbe also critiques the work of Diana Edelman, who argues that critical history is a modern phenomenon. For Edelman,

The Place of the Past

For the purposes of this work, we will trace with broad strokes the intellectual study of the past according to Huizinga's definition. We will not attempt to be as narrow in this as is Van Seters, but rather press that, for a very long time before the rise of historical criticism, humans have portrayed the past by different means and for different purposes. So we will examine the approaches to history writing leading up to and including historical criticism.

Ancient Forms of History Writing

Before understanding how researchers have investigated the history of the Bible, it should be helpful to review the interest in history that has gripped ancient Near Eastern and western culture for millennia. History writing predates not only the critical study of the Bible, but, debatably, the people of the Bible themselves. We shall first investigate why ancient peoples were interested in writing history and how they understood the practice of writing history.

There is no small dispute among historians as to who the first historians were. Again, definitions play an important role here. In terms of simple interest in past events, historical writings of various sorts appear among some of humanity's earliest writings. A number of extant texts from the Early Dynastic period onward indicate how scribes reckoned with past events. These include narratives of both historical and mythical figures, king lists, memorial inscriptions, and iconographic descriptions. By the Late Bronze Age (LBA), these genres remain, and do so well into the Iron Age. Perhaps the most significant shift by the LBA in how cultures communicated about their own past came in an increased concern for chronological precision. In previous eras, chronographic numbers served symbolic purposes. The lone exception to this is the Egyptian Early Dynastic period Palermo Stone, which records apparently accurate data for Nile River flood heights and events during the reign of various kings. Curiously, this precision disappears from historical record until the LBA.[6] But by the LBA,

---

modern critical historians are more simplistic in their explanations of truth, do not invent character speeches, do not include the divine as a cause of historical factors, and cover broader subjects than ancient historians. Yet Grabbe contends that the critical spirit among the Greek historians was an important impetus for modern historical writing and certainly revolutionary in the ancient world. For Edelman's article, see Edelman, "Clio's Dilemma," 247–55.

6. Van Seters notes that this makes it difficult to assert that this was the beginning of a true annalistic tradition in Egypt. Van Seters, *In Search*, 131–34. Redford writes

scribes became more concerned to account for past events with numerical particularity. For instance, in Kassite Babylonia, king lists were organized by ordinal years of a king's reign rather than the previous practice of identifying years by major events. And in Egypt, early New Kingdom pharaohs kept records of their deeds with a chronological acuity not seen previously in the ancient world.[7]

Examples of writings with historical interest from the later Iron Age include the prominent Assyrian annals, in which Assyrian kings would proudly display their conquests and political victories to inspire awe in all who could view them. Surely this tradition carried over from similar displays by Early Dynastic kings, Egyptian pharaohs, and Hittite rulers from the Bronze Age. Annals are clearly intended for political propaganda and demonstrations of piety before the gods.[8] Along religious lines, one may also add omen texts of ancient Mesopotamia, which surveyed past events in order to predict the future.[9] Such examples as annals and omens, on the one hand, display a keen interest in understanding events of the past. On the other hand, we cannot read them as antiquarian in the sense of studying the past *for the sake of the past*. Rather, they evince texts in which the past serves a purpose for the present and the future. Although contemporary historians will depend on these texts to some extent, we must recognize the limitations of their original purposes. We may consider such texts as having some antiquarian interest, but certainly not as "history writing" in any critical sense.

The first critical portrayal of history arguably is found in Mesopotamia of the Iron Age in the Mesopotamian Chronicles. Continuing the concern for precise chronology already present in scribal circles (and also seen in the concurrent king lists),[10] these tablets plainly portray political events of Babylonia and Assyria, including for the first time among extant texts, admissions of defeat of the author's own kingdom.[11] An excerpt from our largest extant chronicle, ABC 1, notes for instance,

---

concerning the time of Asosi of the 5th dynasty, "for most of the remainder of the Old Kingdom, the ascendancy of the mythical concepts which rationalized kingship and the state effectually dampened an historical attitude toward the past." Redford, *Pharaonic King-Lists*, 136.

7. Holland, "They Are Written," 70–72.
8. Holland, "They Are Written," 75–78.
9. Holland, "They Are Written," 78–80.
10. Holland, "They Are Written," 80–82; Schreiner and Holland, *Silhouettes*, 101–19.
11. Holland, "They Are Written," 82–86.

The Place of the Past

> The first year of Nergal-u-še-zib, the month of Tammuz, the sixteenth day, Nergal-u-še-zib seized Nippur, robbed it, and looted it. The first day of Tishri, the army of Assyria arrived in Uruk. They seized the gods of Uruk and its inhabitants. When the Elamites went and carried off the gods and inhabitants of Uruk, on the seventh day of the month of Tishri, in the district of Nippur, Nergal-u-še-zib did battle against the heart of the army of Assyria. And in battle he was taken prisoner and he was sent to Assyria. The twenty sixth day of the month of Tishri, Nergal-u-še-zib reigned over Babylon.[12]

Mordechai Cogan describes these chronicles accurately in contrast to other ancient Near Eastern forms of historiography:

> The most prominent characteristic of the Babylonian Chronicles, which distinguishes them from other chronographic texts, such as king lists and the eponym chronicles, is the recital of discrete, unrelated events arranged according to the years of the king's reign. These accounts are concise; they lack polemics and express neither praise nor disparagement, traits that suggest their non-royal genesis.[13]

Herbert Butterfield considers texts like these from Mesopotamia as the "first interpretations" of history.[14] Indeed, they appear as self-conscious reflections of past events, thus conforming in some sense to Huizinga's definition. In the events these early historians select, we witness bias in choosing to portray some events as having an impact on the authors' present. What they lack, however, is an overtly critical or evaluative attitude towards the events.

For this reason, Van Seters argues the Deuteronomistic Historian (Dtr), the author of Joshua, Judges, Samuel, and Kings in the Hebrew Bible, represents the first example of this more comprehensive style of historiography. Although there were many attempts to portray past events accurately in ancient civilizations, no culture was able to produce the type of literature Dtr's work contains. Alongside precise historical data, lists of palace inventory, dry recountings of battles and building projects, among other banal data, Dtr's evaluations of a king's performance in "YHWH's eyes" permeate

---

12. ABC 1 iii.45–iv.6 found in Grayson, *Assyrian and Babylonian Chronicles*, 79–83.

13. Cogan, *Raging Torrent*, 7. A similar definition comes from Van der Spek, who defines them as "terse, often paratactic . . . , [with] a primary interest in dating." Van der Spek, "Berossus," 277.

14. Butterfield, *Origins of History*, 35. Curiously, Momigliano ignores Mesopotamia altogether in his treatment on the history of history in Momigliano, *Classical Foundations*.

1–2 Kings. Dtr's work is intellectual in its creative use of inherited sources and portrays a wide-ranging national history that had not been evident prior to him.[15]

Dtr's work slightly precedes that of Herodotus, although the two share much in common. This includes the melding of various sources within a chronological framework to achieve a specific purpose.[16] Thus, for Van Seters, Dtr was the first to produce a genre of literature conforming to Huizinga's definition as well as the parameters Van Seters himself sets out in the introduction.

Baruch Halpern critiques Van Seters, not based on his conclusion of Dtr as the first historian, but on his understanding of historiography. While for Van Seters Dtr was a creative historian operating in the exilic period with his "uniform style and outlook,"[17] Halpern finds Israel's closest history-writing analogues in the pre-exilic period and is willing to recognize the Bible's literature as heterogeneous and compositionally complex.[18] The bulk of Halpern's book is dedicated to understanding the compositional background of numerous biblical passages in order to demonstrate this point. Grabbe correctly notes the unfortunate omission on Halpern's part of not offering a definition of history, but that he does appear to view "history-writing" as interchangeable with "historiography."[19]

Grabbe further pushes Van Seters's definition of history writing by examining the concept of criticism in historical judgments. Although Dtr is reflective on past events, a constitutive feature of what Van Seters considers history writing, Dtr's criticisms are theological, not historical, in nature.[20] The later biblical writings of 1 and 2 Maccabees also betray similar

15. Van Seters, *In Search*, 354–62.
16. Van Seters, *In Search*, 357–59.
17. Van Seters, *In Search*, 359.
18. See especially his critiques of Noth and Van Seters in Halpern, *First Historians*, 29–32. Similarly, in a 1990 article, A. R. Millard demonstrates contra unnamed (presumably "minimalist" opponents) the comparability between Samuel-Kings and extant Aramean inscriptions. Thus, Millard contends for Samuel-Kings as a "compilation drawn from contemporary records, not a largely theological fabrication to establish a particular theology." See Millard, "Israelite and Aramean History," 170.
19. Grabbe, "First Real Historians," 159.
20. Grabbe, "First Real Historians," 175. To this I also note a work predating Van Seters's, that of Giovanni Garbini. Garbini downplays the role of the Bible as a historical source due to its character as a religious book. He writes, "The Old Testament has set out a sacred history of universal value, but it is not very reliable as evidence of a secular history of the kind that the Hebrew people experienced." See Garbini, *History and Ideology*,

historical traits as that of the Deuteronomistic History. They also contain detailed chronologies, evince the use of sources, and assign causality to divine means for didactic value.[21] It is only with the Greeks that an evaluative spirit towards historical sources first appears, so from this perspective of history writing, they were the first historians.[22] Arnoldo Momigliano adds that it is with the Greeks that we find a critical attitude toward distinguishing "facts and fancies," thus counting their contribution to historical study unique.[23] So it is to these classical historians that we now shift our attention.

History Writing in the Greco-Roman World

As far as contemporary historians can tell, history writing in ancient Greece has its origins with the fifth-century scholars Hellanicus of Lesbos and Hecataeus of Miletus. The term "history" itself originates from the Greek word for "investigation," although it has come to mean a particular kind of investigation.[24] In investigating the past, Hellanicus developed a chronological system from myths and genealogies.[25] Hecataeus constructed a significant work of geography at once dependent upon Homer but seeking to find out information for himself. Hecataeus thus introduced the concept of *autopsy*, the principle of discovering information for oneself as opposed to hearsay.[26] He is famously quoted, "I write down what I consider to be true,

---

18. Although in my estimation Grabbe adds more weight to the historical witness of the text than Garbini, the latter represents a more recent stream of interpreters who emphasize the religious nature of these texts over the historical.

21. Attridge, "Historiography," 171–84.

22. Grabbe, "First Real Historians," 179–80. Grabbe follows this particular definition of historiography as having a critical spirit from Thomas L. Thompson, although he discerns that Thompson has confused the terms "historiography" and "history writing." Thompson distinguishes between "historians" with a critical spirit and "antiquarians" who simply keep track of past events. For Thompson's article, see Thompson, "Historiography," especially 209. In the debate about the "first historians," however, I find authors tend to move the target of defining "history" in order to defend one group as "first." Is it simply attempting to portray past events accurately? Is it a critical attitude towards the events? Is it a critical attitude toward the sources? History writing appears to me to have been a gradual process of thinking and rethinking the practice of studying the past. Finding an origin or "first" historian is futile.

23. Momigliano, *Classical Foundations*, 30.

24. See Young, *Biblical Exegesis*, 79.

25. Grabbe, *History of the Jews*, 2:11.

26. Grabbe, *History of the Jews*, 2:11; Butterfield, *Origins of History*, 134. Sterling demonstrates how Hecataeus's work on geography was seminal to later people groups

for the things that the poets tell us are in my opinion full of contradictions and worthy to be laughed out of court."[27]

Although little of the works of these early historians remains to us, the title of the "Father of History" is attributed to one for whom we have extensive historical writings from ancient Greece, Herodotus (ca. 484–25). Influenced by Hecataeus, Herodotus became critical of many of the former's conclusions after checking them himself. Herodotus roamed across the known world, compiling oral histories about the past and blending them together into a coherent story. He was no documentary historian, but a world traveler and collector of traditions, skillfully able to narrate a meaningful past through an interweaving of various sources.[28]

Herodotus' critical approach is evident in his meta-comments, strung alongside his narration of history. For example, writing about the Persians, he remarks,

> Cyrus had subjugated this Astyages, then, Cyrus' own mother's father, for the reason which I shall presently disclose. Having this reason to quarrel with Cyrus, Croesus sent to ask the oracles if he should march against the Persians; and when a deceptive answer came he thought it to be favorable to him, and so led his army into the Persian territory. When he came to the river Halys, he transported his army across it—by the bridges which were there then, as I maintain; but the general belief of the Greeks is that Thales of Miletus got the army across. The story is that, as Croesus did not know how his army could pass the river (as the aforesaid bridges did not yet exist then), Thales, who was in the encampment, made the river, which flowed on the left of the army, also flow on the right, in the following way. Starting from a point on the river upstream from the camp, he dug a deep semi-circular trench, so that the stream, turned from its ancient course, would flow in the trench to the rear of the camp and, passing it, would issue into its former bed, with the result that as soon as the river was thus divided into two, both channels could be forded. Some even say that the ancient channel dried up altogether. But I do not believe this; for in that case, how did they pass the river when they were returning?[29]

---

using historiography to defend their status in the Greco-Roman world. Sterling, *Shaping the Past*, 17–18.

27. Butterfield, *Origins of History*, 134.
28. Momigliano, "Place of Herodotus," 3.
29. *Her. Hist.*, 1.75.

Thus, we see in this instance that Herodotus adds his own beliefs about the event based on his knowledge of the location and rational logic. Often with such comments, Herodotus appeals to a broad historical coherence in concert with other sources and adds his evaluation of the historical events from these other authors.[30] Such editorializing about historical sources was a novel contribution to the historical enterprise. Unfortunately, though, Herodotus never left us a reflection of his historiographical method.[31]

Herodotus's approach, however he may have defined it, was deemed insufficient for many ancient critics. Plutarch, for example, called Herodotus the "father of lies" for his treatment of Plutarch's own people, the Boeotians, in the Persian War.[32] Thucydides, most notably, sought to refine Herodotus's method in investigating the past. He believed that historians should only deal with events that occurred in their own lifetime.[33] This provides more accurate (*akribeia*) judgments on the part of the historian. It is in this concern for historical reliability that Thucydides stands apart from Herodotus and attempts to improve upon whatever methods the latter may have used.

Thucydides's method is found in the introduction to his *The Peloponnesian War*. He contends that history should contain the following features: (1) This historian should not rely on every detail of tradition; (2) He should not rely on the evidence of poets; (3) He should not rely on those whose goal it is to catch the attention of the public; (4) He must rely on those whose authority can be checked; (5) He must rely on evidence; (6) He must not rely on general impressions; (7) He must check the facts; (8) and, though eyewitness reports are crucial, one must judge them with discretion.[34] Not only does Thucydides provide these criteria as a guardrail against poorly written history, but also against rhetoric and myth.[35]

Although admittedly drier than Herodotus's approach to history writing, Thucydides more rigorously commits himself to historical accuracy through a critical eye toward bias and reliance upon facts. These facts were only seldom documentary, not found in Athenian archives, and were

---

30. For this I am indebted to a conversation with Kevin Burr.
31. Momigliano, "Place of Herodotus," 3.
32. He wrote a lengthy essay on Herodotus's errors entitled *De Herodoti malignitate*.
33. Momigliano, "Place of Herodotus," 3–4.
34. *Hist. Pel.* 1.20–22. See also the summary in Grabbe, *History of the Jews*, 2:13.
35. On Thucydides and the relation to myth, see Kelley, "Mythistory," 6.

Historical Thinking in Antiquity Through the Medieval Period

primarily oral in nature.[36] Thus we do not have clear evidence of dependence upon archival history of the rudimentary sort that seems evident in Mesopotamia and Israel,[37] let alone with the insistence we find in modern history writing.

But the extreme concern for accuracy in Thucydides mitigates against accusations of history writing as a branch of rhetoric, the most common educational field in the Greco-Roman world.[38] One could certainly and rightly accuse Herodotus of bias, but to do so for Thucydides would require a strong challenge from this historian. At the least, we witness in his introduction an awareness of factual reporting. Contemporary philosophers would surely push him on such an objective stance, but Thucydides is obviously keen to set aside any assumptions about the past.

The charge of historians operating rhetorically may persist for some historians after Thucydides, who utilized previous interpretations more than reliance upon facts and were not as self-aware in their historical methodologies.[39] One exception, though, is the second-century BCE Greek historian Polybius. Writing in Rome in defense of his own people, he sets forth several rules as a groundwork for writing history. First, he believes the historian cannot show favoritism, even towards one's friends and country. To do so would mean that "History is stripped of her truth" such that "all that is left is but an idle tale."[40] This sort of objectivity is extended to speeches, in which the historian must portray them accurately rather than put words in the mouths of historical actors and do the hard work of historical investigation rather than rely on others' interpretations.[41]

Polybius explicitly argues that historians should find causes (*aitia*) for historical events, not simply present the evidence. Although we see this concern in other historians, Polybius outwardly views the historian's task as discovering the rationale behind historical events.[42] In the introduction to his *Histories*, he writes,

---

36. Fox, "Thucydides and Documentary History," 11–29; Momigliano, "Place of Herodotus," 8.
37. Holland, "Form and Function," 559–70.
38. Grabbe, *History of the Jews*, 2:17–18.
39. Grabbe, *History of the Jews*, 2:15–16; Momigliano, "Place of Herodotus," 4.
40. *Hist.* 1.14. See also Grabbe, *History of the Jews*, 2:14.
41. Grabbe, *History of the Jews*, 2:15.
42. Grabbe, *History of the Jews*, 2:15.

The Place of the Past

> Can any one be so indifferent or idle as not to care to know by what means, and under what kind of polity, almost the whole inhabited world was conquered and brought under the dominion of the single city of Rome, and that too within a period of not quite fifty-three years? Or who again can be so completely absorbed in other subjects of contemplation or study, as to think any of them superior in importance to the accurate understanding of an event for which the past affords no precedent.[43]

Thus we see a rather audacious aspiration in Polybius's work. He wishes to explain how his world got to be in the state he and his contemporaries find it.

He even searches for causation in micro-level events, such as wars and political machinations. In the introduction to Book 3 of the *Histories*, he writes,

> First I shall indicate the causes of the Punic or Hannibalian war: and shall have to describe how the Carthaginians entered Italy; broke up the Roman power there; made the Romans tremble for their safety and the very soil of their country; and contrary to all calculation acquired a good prospect of surprising Rome itself.
>
> I shall next try to make it clear how in the same period Philip of Macedon, after finishing his war with the Aetolians, and subsequently settling the affairs of Greece, entered upon a design of forming an offensive and defensive alliance with Carthage.
>
> Then I shall tell how Antiochus and Ptolemy Philopator first quarrelled and finally went to war with each other for the possession of Coele-Syria.
>
> Next how the Rhodians and Prusias went to war with the Byzantines, and compelled them to desist from exacting dues from ships sailing into the Pontus.
>
> At this point I shall pause in my narrative to introduce a disquisition upon the Roman Constitution, in which I shall show that its peculiar character contributed largely to their success, not only in reducing all Italy to their authority, and in acquiring a supremacy over the Iberians and Gauls besides, but also at last, after their conquest of Carthage, to their conceiving the idea of universal dominion.[44]

The repetition of "how" (*pos*) underscores the fact that Polybius is not simply undertaking a bare recounting of facts. Instead, he is searching for

43. *Hist.* 1.1.
44. *Hist.* 3.2.

Historical Thinking in Antiquity Through the Medieval Period

deeper present meaning in the past, a task that separates a historian from an antiquarian, and one of the qualifiers Van Seters lists for the true writing of history.

Polybius found a sympathetic successor in Josephus, a Jew who had likewise come under the thumb of the Roman Empire and sought to produce an apology for the acts of his people against the Romans in war.[45] Of his extant works, Josephus composes a history of his people in *Antiquities of the Jews*, an account of the Jewish War against Rome in his *The Wars of the Jews*, and a defense of Jews against Greeks who doubted his previous claims in *Against Apion*.

Josephus, like Thucydides and Polybius before him, strives to present the most accurate portrayal of the past available to him, mostly through oracular "witnesses." In the preface to *Antiquities*, he appeals to the tradition of Greco-Roman historiography that his history "will appear to all the Greeks worthy of their study."[46] In contrast to those who show off their rhetorical skills, Josephus seeks to produce facts for the good of posterity.[47] In *Wars*, he tries to eschew bias to "prosecute the actions of both parties with accuracy."[48] In his later defense of the Jews, Josephus speaks against "voluntary falsehood" by verifying his history through witnesses.[49]

Despite his own claims to the contrary, historians have revealed the bias of Josephus's accounts.[50] Nevertheless, he clearly stands within the stream of Greco-Roman history writing initiated and explained by luminaries such as Hellanicus, Hecataeus, Herodotus, Thucydides, and Polybius. From a modern perspective, these represent the most rigorous attempts to write history separated from "myth." They attempt an understanding of the facts of the past, try to avoid rhetorical bias, and search for causes for present events. Throughout the book, we will examine critiques of this kind of "objective" history, but these historians remain paragons of the aims of historical writing to the present day.

---

45. Attridge, "Josephus," 185.
46. *Ant.* Preface 2.5.
47. *Ant.* Preface 1.1–4.
48. *J.W.* Preface 4.9.
49. *Ag. Ap.* Preface 1.4–5. Sterling finds Josephus's works as exemplars of what Sterling calls "apologetic historiography." See especially pp. 17–21, 29–30, 36, 43–60 in Sterling, *Shaping the Past*.
50. Grabbe, *History of the Jews*, 2:73–74; Attridge, "Josephus," 185.

The Concern for History in Early Christianity

The concern for accurate history in the vein of these early Greco-Roman historians lapses into the background with the launching of the Christian movement. It is not that accurate history was unimportant, but that, for the early Christians, history had reached its apogee in Jesus of Nazareth. Explaining who Jesus was (or is) as the messiah of the "Old Testament" and the Son of God became urgently paramount for early Christian interpreters. The writing of history did not fade, but it certainly became deemphasized as the early church strove to defend and deepen its understanding of Jesus.

We begin in the New Testament itself, in which traditions about Jesus and the early church are passed down in the Gospels and Acts. The Gospels are generally accepted by scholars to serve as laudatory biographies of Jesus in the vein of other Greco-Roman praises of leading historical figures. The Gospels, however, do not contain a concern for strict chronology and they conflict on certain events (such as, did Jesus eat when tempted in the wilderness or not? When did he turn over the table of the money changers in the temple, early in his ministry or late? How many days was he in the tomb?). Craig S. Keener has recently argued that Greco-Roman biographies of the first century tended to contain less concern for chronology and are less historically precise than some later *encomia*, but certainly preserve a more "historiographic direction" than earlier biographies and strive to depend on sources and eyewitness accounts close to the historical figure they portray. Although they do not serve as strict histories in the sense of Thucydides and primarily serve as moral instruction and for praise of their subject, biographies of this era serve some useful historical purposes.[51] Keeping the *telos* of the Gospels in mind is significant for us to retain perspective on history (at least in the way we do in the contemporary West) as a secondary goal of the early witnesses about Jesus. But Keener's analysis suggests that there is much more that is historically reliable in these accounts if we read and understand them in their first-century context—and they are especially more reliable than many critical studies of the historical Jesus (discussed below) suggest.

---

51. Keener, *Christobiography*. Summaries of his argument can be found on pp. 25–26 and 498–99. For the importance of Luke's view of the historicity of the resurrection, see Rae, *History and Hermeneutics*, 83–84. Sterling contends that Luke-Acts is less biography than "apologetic historiography" comprising an early history of the people called Christians, of which Jesus is the founder. See especially pp. 61–85 in Sterling, *Shaping the Past*.

Of the Gospel writers, Luke is the most forthright in his attempt to write a reliable biography. The famous introduction to his Gospel begins,

> Since many have undertaken to set down an orderly account of the events that have been fulfilled among us, just as they were handed on to us by those who from the beginning were eyewitnesses and servants of the world, I too decided, after investigating everything carefully from the very first, to write an orderly account for you, most excellent Theophilus, so that you may know the truth concerning the things about which you have been instructed. (Luke 1:1–4 NRSV)

Although Luke confesses he was not an eyewitness (*autoptai*) to the events, we can see his careful investigation (*pareklouthekati*) relies upon those who were. His own *autopsy* of the events then depends upon the most direct eyewitnesses. Luke thus follows the historiographical convention of his day by achieving a critical, or at least self-aware, understanding of his sources to compose a biography he finds reliable.[52]

Luke's second volume, Acts of the Apostles, is less explicit in his historical methodology. Yet, given that its preface and other features throughout the work clearly connect to the Gospel, we can assume he continues with the same procedure in mind. If the Gospel serves as a laudatory biography of Jesus, Acts serves as a historiographical "succession narrative." As the book connects Jesus to the early Jerusalem apostles and the coming of the Holy Spirit at Pentecost, Luke portrays the continuing mission of Jesus in the Greco-Roman world and with a common Greco-Roman genre. It carries much of the same language, themes, and literary patterns of succession narratives so that the apostles "rule . . . within and under the reign of Christ."[53] Viewing the Gospels and Acts in its Greco-Roman context, we can see these texts portraying something of historical value in their world. Again, we must be cautious in viewing these accounts as strict reports, given the inconsistencies and chronological uncertainties, but they are written with an attempt to portray something of the realities of the characters and events they describe.

After the New Testament period, Christian scholars gave most immediate attention to christological readings of the Old Testament. The focus

---

52. See also Keener, *Christobiography*, 226–29. The larger section on Luke as a historian in context appears in pp. 221–39.

53. Talbert, *Reading Acts*, xxi. See the larger section on this Greco-Roman genre on pp. xix–xxvii.

The Place of the Past

for interpretation became understanding the Scriptures as illuminating the centrality and significance of Christ. According to Keith D. Stanglin, having a christological center in exegesis allowed for "a variety of exegetical practices" without much attention to method.[54] A primary exemplar of these early readings is Irenaeus of Lyons (ca. 130–202). Irenaeus believed in a reciprocal relationship between Scripture and faith. Scripture was in some sense, for Irenaeus, clear enough on its own. Difficult passages could be interpreted in light of the clearer ones to enable a coherent meaning within the text, a principle known as the *analogia scripturae*, the "analogy of Scripture." But in order to prevent readings of the text from serving purposes outside of the orthodox faith, the church incorporated the *regula fidae*, the "rule of faith."[55] This served as a guardrail to ensure an exegete would draw meanings from Scripture that conformed to the apostolic teachings of the church. At times, Irenaeus would employ an early Christian attempt at *typos*, or "typology," to read Christ as a figure of the Old Testament, a method consistent with Scripture itself in its proclamation of Christ as the fulfillment of the prophets or as the consummation of, for example, prefigured baptism in Noah (1 Pet 3:18–21).[56] We thus sense a distinction in this early stage between the "letter" and the "spirit" of the text, already present in Greco-Roman readings of texts and Jewish interpretation.[57] But any exegetical method at this point takes a backseat to a defense of Christ within the Scriptures for the benefit of the church.

Historical study of the New Testament itself appears primarily in discovering the authorship of the documents contained in the New Testament. In the struggle to establish which texts would become canonical for the church, the question of authorship—especially for texts without attribution within them—became significant for investigations of the New Testament. Figures such as Origen of Alexandria, Dionysius of Alexandria, and even as late as Jerome, attempted to establish the authorship of the would-be canonical texts. They did not always consider these texts authentic to the popularly attributed author, even if they would consider the writings

---

54. Stanglin, *Letter and Spirit*, 22.

55. On the rule as used against heresies, see Reventlow, *History of Biblical Interpretation*, 1:172–73. Matthew T. Bell investigates the definition of the rule and its relation to Scripture, finding this relationship a "dynamic spiral" in which the rule serves as a guide to Scripture's meaning, not a determinant of it. Bell, *Ruled Reading*, 29–54.

56. Stanglin, *Letter and Spirit*, 29–36. Francis Young notes that typology was not neatly separable from "allegory at this stage." Young, *Biblical Exegesis*, 292.

57. Stanglin, *Letter and Spirit*, 41–42.

"apostolic" in the sense of carrying on the apostolic tradition.[58] Origen (ca. 184–253) attributes the Epistle to the Hebrews, for instance, to another author than Paul:

> But as for myself, if I were to state my own opinion, I should say that the thoughts are the apostle's, but that the style and composition belong to one who called to mind the apostle's teaching and, as it were, paraphrases what his master said.[59]

Eusebius (260–339), for instance, writes several times about the attribution of the Gospel according to Matthew to the tax-collector appearing in the Gospel, information he learned from Papias of Hierapolis, a second-generation Christian.[60]

It is these latter two early Christian scholars who might be considered the most historically oriented of our extant witnesses. Origen has been widely mischaracterized for his usage of allegory in interpreting the biblical text,[61] and he is often overlooked as a progenitor of historical-critical practices—although he is far from a contemporary historical critic. For example, Frances M. Young describes Origen as "professionalizing" the study of Scripture in the manner of Greco-Roman schools, utilizing similar reading techniques, but with the Bible as its basis.[62] As we will see later on, similar criticisms are made today of contemporary historical criticism. Among Origen's methods for reading the Bible includes the already-prevalent lens of allegory, to be sure. His appropriation of Platonic readings of the Bible yielded interpretations that appealed to the deeper sense of moral and mystical approaches as his methodical treatise, *De Principii*, suggests.[63]

However, Origen's work also includes other elements that would become standard features of later historical criticism. In line with much classical education of his day, Origen was concerned, for one, to establish the best text for the scholar to use. After all, interpreters cannot rightly argue for their point if they do so on the basis of a poor text. His *Hexapla*, which

---

58. Kümmel, *New Testament*, 13–19.

59. Excerpted from Kümmel, *New Testament*, 15.

60. Cf. *Hist. eccl.* 3.24; 3.39; 5.8. In the Reformation, Martin Luther revived these debates and used them to marginalize Hebrews, James, Jude, and Revelation. Kümmel, *New Testament*, 23–26.

61. See, for example, criticisms against him in his own time. Stanglin, *Letter and Spirit*, 48–49.

62. Young, *Biblical Exegesis*, 292. See also Stanglin, *Letter and Spirit*, 62.

63. Stanglin, *Letter and Spirit*, 53–55.

comes down to us incomplete, contained parallel columns of the biblical text in the best-known versions of his day, including the Hebrew text, with his own diacritical markings. His extant commentaries also demonstrate text-critical issues.[64] Clearly, Origen was concerned to build his arguments on a solid textual footing.

Further, he was aware of contradictions, not only in textual versions, but within the biblical text itself. This is, as we will see, a common sticking point for modern biblical criticism, and one that has launched many a modern historical-critical approach. As for Origen, Young offers the example of how the church father handles the contradiction between versions of Matthew 16:20. One version reads that Jesus "charged" his disciples; another reads that he "commanded" them. To boot, Mark's version of the story favors the former and Luke's version includes both terms. While this is a problem on the literal level, the big-picture issue for Origen is the identity of Christ.[65] To read a text as pointing to Christ is the "correct" reading of Scripture, the "doctrinal and moral edification" of the text.[66] So the resolution to contradictions for Origen is not to engage in further search behind the text, but to point its *telos* in the church.

Origen was also concerned with *historia*, or what we might now describe as the explanation of the text's historical background. This could include learned excurses on objects mentioned in a biblical text, such as the pearls mentioned in Matthew 10:7–10, or clarifications of difficult words, such as the *kepphos* in Proverbs 7:22.[67] He was also not bothered by biblical events that he thought were clearly fictitious, such as the creation story of Genesis 1:

> What intelligent person can believe that there was a first day, then a second and third day, evening, and morning, without the sun, the moon, and the stars; and the first day ... even without a sky? Who is foolish enough to believe that, like a human farmer, God planted a garden to the east in Eden and created in it a visible, physical tree of life from which anyone tasting its fruit with bodily teeth would receive life; and that one would have a part in good and evil by eating the fruit picked from the appropriate tree? When God is depicted walking in the garden in the evening and Adam hiding

---

64. Young, *Biblical Exegesis*, 82–84.

65. Young, *Biblical Exegesis*, 83–84. See also Young, "Alexandrian and Antiochene Exegesis," 1:338–41.

66. Stanglin, *Letter and Spirit*, 59–60.

67. Young, *Biblical Exegesis*, 86–87.

behind the tree, I think no one will doubt that these details point figuratively to some mysteries be means of a historical narrative which seems to have happened, but not in a bodily sense.[68]

As Origen obviously had not met a contemporary fundamentalist, he seems unshaken by unlikely historical events and assumes his readers would be as well. The "bodily" sense of history clearly has some concern for Origen, and he understands it within the canons of his day. But it is also true that, for Origen, the literal sense of Scripture is subservient to deeper meanings pertaining to the centrality of Christ and the life of the church. As R. R. Reno writes, "Getting the facts right was clearly important for Origen. But the goal of exegesis is interpretation, not description."[69]

Eusebius was a follower of Origen's teachings and inheritor of his library at Caesarea. Aside from his arguments on the authorship of the Gospels, he mentions historical issues in the Gospels, such as conflicting chronologies and genealogies, as well as the history of apostolic figures, many of whom were authors of biblical texts.[70] He is concerned for issues of geography in the biblical text as well as text-critical issues.[71] He is perhaps best known, however, for his *Church History*. This chronicle of the church from the days of Christ into the fourth century exhibits a penchant for historical understanding. Unlike historiographies of the church prior to him, Eusebius recounted the history of the church in order, with a concern for chronology. In so doing, he cites almost 250 passages from other authors, half of which are only extant in Eusebius's writings.[72] This work of Eusebius represents a watershed moment, not only for our understanding of the early church, but in history writing. Although the point was less antiquarian than apologetic, his reliance upon source material to undergird his defense is remarkable.[73]

68. *Princ.* 4.3.2.

69. Reno, *End*, 66. Reventlow points out the various ways that Origen reads on different levels, but the literal level is "milk" for those who are newer to Christian understandings of Scripture. Reventlow, *History of Biblical Interpretation*, 1:183, 194. His larger section on Origen is found from pp. 174–99.

70. Cf. *Hist. eccl.* 1.7; 3.1; 3.24.

71. Young, *Biblical Exegesis*, 295.

72. Chestnut, "Eusebius," 2:675.

73. Young, *Biblical Exegesis*, 79–80. Young also notes some ways in which Eusebius differed from Origen. This includes the understanding of the literal sense to include prophecy of Christ, as this serves a function of its genre. Further, Eusebius is concerned more with God's providential oversight of the world rather than the individual soul. Young, *Biblical Exegesis*, 121–22, 129, 295. New Testament scholar Kevin Burr has pointed out to me that modern historians of Greco-Roman antiquity remark how Cicero, Plutarch, Suetonius, and others were no less "apologetic" than the Evangelists.

Gregory E. Sterling writes that Eusebius "can lay claim to stand at the head of a distinct historiographical tradition" that had its origins in apologetic Jewish sources such as Josephus and continued through Luke-Acts and later, lesser-known historiographies in the early Christian tradition.[74]

For as much as these two figures utilized and adapted *historia* as part of their Greco-Roman education, interpreters of the "Alexandrian" school were opposed by those from the so-called "Antiochene" school. Scholars of the late fourth and early fifth centuries such as Diodore of Tarsus (d. 390), Theodore of Mopsuestia (ca. 350–428), and John Chrysostom (ca. 347–407) serve as paragons of the alternative to Origen and the Alexandrians. In their theological debates, the Antiochenes stressed the human side of Christ more than that of Christ as the divine Logos, as we see in the writings of their Alexandrian counterparts. Similarly, in exegesis, the Antiochenes emphasized the literal, or human, sense of the biblical text.[75] This includes more attention to the genre, words, narrative, and historical background of a biblical text. For example, Theodore engages in frequent textual criticism of corrupted passages in the Septuagint, makes in-depth comments on grammatical issues, and considers both genre and historical backgrounds of the Psalms.[76] By no means do Theodore's, or other Antiochenes', exegesis exclude higher, theoretical meanings of texts. Neither do they include a full-fledged historical methodology as we have come to know it in the modern period.[77] But the emphasis on the literal sense is that one must establish what the text and its author present to the reader first before jumping too quickly to theological truths.[78] A methodological comment from Diodore proves instructive:

> We shall treat of [the text] historically and literally and not stand in the way of a spiritual and more elevated insight. The historical sense, in fact, is not in opposition to the more elevated sense; on the contrary, it proves to be the basis and foundation of the more elevated meanings. One thing alone is to be guarded against, however, never to let the discernment process be seen as an overthrow

---

74. Quote from Sterling, *Shaping the Past*, 15. His section on Eusebius appears on pp. 13–17.

75. Stanglin, *Letter and Spirit*, 64.

76. Reventlow, *History of Biblical Interpretation*, 2:7–9.

77. Young notes Theodore used a biblical chronology to understand the context of the prophets, something that would be nonsensical to a modern historical critic. Young, *Biblical Exegesis*, 206–7.

78. Stanglin, *Letter and Spirit*, 63–66.

of the underlying sense, since this would no longer be discernment but allegory; what is arrived at in defiance of the content is not discernment but allegory. The apostle, in fact, ever overturned the historical sense by introducing discernment despite calling discernment allegory.[79]

Diodore is evidently not keen on allegory and argues that Paul does not use it in the way other exegetes of Diodore's day (such as the Alexandrians) might. The key, however, is to fully understand a passage in its literal sense before theorizing. The Antiochenes preserve an understanding of the biblical author's intention and purpose, creating a more unified vision of what each author wished to convey. This stands against more "atomizing" approaches of other patristic and rabbinic exegetes.[80] The Antiochenes witness an early Christian attempt to stabilize certain basic, or "literal," understandings of the text as a foundation for doing theology.[81] This includes literary concerns, but also fundamental historical issues, such as establishing a historical background to the text.

It seems that these early church scholars view historical understanding as part, however small we may consider it from our contemporary perspective, of the process of interpreting the Bible. The final point of Scripture centers around Christ and is for the benefit of the church, but there is an acknowledgement that some (and not all) of the events, characters, authors, and scribes of Scripture are situated within human history. There is certainly no outright condemnation of historical interpretation, and it is evident historical understanding plays a role in biblical interpretation in this early stage. We might rightly describe historical understanding of the Bible as a matter of emphasis. Historical questions of the ancient era are not all of the type we would ask today, even though we see some similar concerns. Historical understanding stood in the service of the more urgent interests of theology. Young writes, "The difference between ancient and modern exegesis lies in the massive shift in what is found to be problematical. We have had problems about historical coherence; they had problems about doctrinal coherence."[82] Or, in the words of John Barton, historical insight

---

79. Excerpted from Stanglin, *Letter and Spirit*, 65.

80. See Barton, *Nature*, 132–33; Young, *Biblical Exegesis*, 176.

81. For more on *Historia* as it was utilized in Antioch as, in one sense, opposed to Alexandria but, in another sense, preparing the reader for theological conclusions, see Young, "Alexandrian and Antiochene Exegesis," 1:341–47.

82. Young, *Biblical Exegesis*, 207.

"was often neutralized, and its insights ignored or discouraged, because of a commitment to the religious authority of the biblical text."[83]

Jewish Exegesis

As antiquity shifts into the medieval period, historical concerns behind the biblical text are suppressed further. Although one could not call early Christian interpreters of the biblical texts "historical critics" in our contemporary sense, we have at least witnessed a smattering of concern for authentic biblical authorship, textual criticism, and the historicity of some biblical events. Nevertheless, the authority of the biblical text is either defended or assumed among such scholars. In the Middle Ages, paganism fades and the Abrahamic faiths take hold in the West and Near East. The sacred texts of Judaism, Christianity, and Islam become central to scholarship, and interpretation of these texts serves to deepen the faith of the faithful or defend one faith against the others. What good might historical criticism of the Bible have served in this period?

In all three faith traditions, Greco-Roman strategies of textual interpretations served as tools to elucidate sacred texts. Platonic modes of interpretation dominated in Judaism and Christianity while Aristotelean thought, lost in the West, had permeated early Islamic interpretation of the Qur'an. Seldom did historical concerns of a scholar like Thucydides assist the faithful in deepening or defending the faith. But, as we will see, some traces of historical thought and attempts to get behind the biblical text appear in the Middle Ages.

In antiquity, Judaism was faced with a crisis of recontextualization of the Torah. With no temple, the legal texts so central to Jewish faith had to be reinterpreted in the Diaspora. The rise of rabbinic Judaism in this period evinces widespread commentary on the legal texts through *halakhic* exposition and *aggadic* folkloric midrash. The emphases in these early rabbinic texts are the centrality of Torah and chosenness of Israel against Christians and Muslims. Within such boundaries a wide array of interpretations are possible, but the crux of the interpretation still lies on the normative value of the authoritative text without much concern for historical issues.[84]

But in the later medieval period, important shifts in rabbinic exegesis lead to additional perspectives on the biblical text. In the Islamic world,

---

83. Barton, *Nature*, 132.

84. For a summary of midrash in antiquity and the early medieval period, see Bakhos, "Jewish Midrashic Interpretation," 2:113–40.

the Jewish Gaonic academies in Babylonia produce the first translation of the Bible into Arabic and witness to a concern for the meanings of words within the text, much as the Septuagint translators centuries before had done. Saadia ben Joseph (882–942) remains the most well known of these *geonim* for his work in translation and commentary. Saadia notably was concerned that a fundamental step of commentary should be to fix the meanings of biblical words that were widely known to readers.[85] In Spain, also against the backdrop of Muslim hegemony, a bevy of scholars in the early medieval period likewise produced important linguistic works, such as comprehensive grammars and dictionaries to establish the foundational meaning of the biblical text before explication.[86]

The pinnacle of the Spanish school is Rabbi Abraham Ibn Ezra (1089–1164). He rejected midrash, except in cases of *Halakah* and preferred philological and grammatical exegesis in his commentaries. He writes, "I will search out diligently the grammatical meaning of every word, to the best of my ability, and according to this, I will interpret."[87] An example of such is that he chastises early rabbinic interpreters for reading Esau's kiss of Jacob in Genesis 33:4 as an intention to bite Jacob to death. For Ibn Ezra, such liberties with the text were not allowable if taking linguistic and semantic scholarship seriously. Further, Ibn Ezra openly suggested that portions of the Torah were not Mosaic, and he welcomed a previous suggestion that chapters 40–66 of Isaiah come from an exilic prophet, ideas that would become foundational ideas for biblical critics in the nineteenth century.[88] He clearly presages a rationalistic impulse towards reading the sacred Scripture that was unique and influential for later generations.

Ibn Ezra was adapting a technique already at work in the Northern French school of rabbinic exegesis at the hand of his older contemporary Rashi (1040–1105). This approach, known as *peshat*, seeks to interpret the text according to its literary and linguistic context instead of with ongoing, traditional midrash. Rashi did not forsake midrash and often contributed his

---

85. Harris, "Medieval Jewish Biblical Exegesis," 2:141–43.

86. Harris, "Medieval Jewish Biblical Exegesis," 2:143–44.

87. Quoted in Harris, "Medieval Jewish Biblical Exegesis," 2:152. See also Reventlow, *History of Biblical Interpretation*, 2:236–37.

88. Harris, "Medieval Jewish Biblical Exegesis," 2:152–54; Reventlow, *History of Biblical Interpretation*, 2:244.

own opinions to the traditional readings, but added *peshuto* as novel grammatical and literary supplement to the sacred stream of interpretation.[89]

But the work of Rashi's grandson, Rabbi Samuel ben Meir, or "Rashbam" (1080–1160), reveals the most full-fledged attempt at *peshat* from this school. Like his grandfather, Rashbam commented on the rarely touched biblical texts outside of Torah with contextual exegesis, yet he radically persisted with *peshat* in his Torah commentaries. A methodological note in his commentary on Exodus 21 is suggestive: "I have come to explain the contextual meaning of Scripture. And I will explain the statutes and laws according to common sense [literally 'the way of the world']. And I will do this even though the rabbinic understanding of the laws is the essence."[90] Thus Rashbam honors the earlier midrashic exegesis as a higher form of understanding the law, but is committed to read the text in a "secular" (for lack of a better term) manner, systematizing the distinction identified by his grandfather.[91] Robert A. Harris offers the example of Rashbam's interpretation of the use of *teffilen* in prayer (Exod 13:9; Deut 6:8). Here, Rashbam interprets the use of *teffilen* metaphorically rather than as a literal commandment, although he probably practiced the literal use of *teffilen* himself.[92]

Finally, another rabbi of importance here is the Spanish scholar Rabbi Moses ben Nahman, also known as Ramban or Nahmanides (1194–1270). Ramban sought to blend together the methods of *peshat* and midrash, ultimately pursuing what later generations of rabbis would deem a "fourfold exegesis," utilizing *peshat*, *remez* (typological exegesis that views early biblical figures as types of later ones), *derash* (midrashim of the rabbis), and *sod* (mystical interpretation).[93] This distinction would become foundational for generations of later rabbis who would adapt this scheme into threefold approaches or other divisions of viewing the text. A sample from his commentary on Genesis 2:5 is illustrative:

> In the opinion of our Rabbis in Bereshith Rabbah, [every herb of the field created] on the third day [did not come forth above the ground but] they remained just below the surface of the earth, and on the sixth day they grew after He caused rain to fall on them. In

---

89. Harris, "Medieval Jewish Biblical Exegesis," 2:144–47.

90. b. Sota 16a, translation and excerpt from Harris, "Medieval Jewish Biblical Exegesis," 2:148.

91. Reventlow, *History of Biblical Interpretation*, 2:233.

92. Harris, "Medieval Jewish Biblical Exegesis," 2:148–49.

93. Harris, "Medieval Jewish Biblical Exegesis," 2:156–59.

my opinion, in accordance with the plain meaning of Scripture [*hapeshat*], on the third day the earth did bring forth the grass and the fruit trees in their full-grown stature and quality as He commanded concerning them. And now Scripture tells that there was no one to plan and sow them for future purposes, and the earth would not produce until a mist would come up from it and water it, and man was formed who would work it—to seed, to plan, and to guard." This is the meaning of the *shrub of the field . . . had not yet grown*. It does not say "the shrub of the ground" for only a place which is cultivated is called "field," as in "*Which thou has sown in the field* [Exod 23:16] and *We will not pass through field of through Vineyard* [Num 20:17]."[94]

Ramban's exegesis here demonstrates a mature version of *peshat*, in which he recognizes the authority of the earlier rabbis, but he also avails himself of the lexical tools and reason of his day to comment upon the sacred text.

We see that Ramban and other scholars utilizing *peshat* assume the historical narrative and solve difficult problems of interpretation using other parts of Scripture (see the *analogia scriptura* in Christian circles of antiquity above). They also do not undermine the tradition, and in many places defer to it. This is why Jon D. Levenson writes,

> A plain-sense exegete (pasthan) like Rabbi Samuel ben Meir ("Rashbam") could be uncompromising both in his pursuit of the plain sense and in his allegiance to halakah . . . , which often bases itself on the biblical text in a way that contradicts peshat. He is paralleled by those Christian exegetes who recognized a "historical sense" to the Old Testament without relinquishing a Christocentric interpretation of it. In both the Jewish and the Christian cases, the unity of the overall religion was maintained, and even though it was not seen as operative in all forms of exegesis. There could be concentric circles of context, but the smallest circle, the plain sense, finally yielded to the largest one, the whole tradition, however constituted.[95]

At the same time, the use of the plain sense by scholars such as Ibn Ezra and Rashbam indicates a desire to understand the biblical text on its own terms in addition to its traditional meanings. Although later historical criticism of the Bible would seek to completely set these traditional understandings

---

94. Ramban, *Commentary on Torah*.
95. Levenson, *Hebrew Bible*, 2.

aside and add to the kinds of inquiries behind the text, such readings of the biblical text are remarkable in the history of interpretation.

Medieval Christian Interpretation

Ramban's use of a fourfold interpretation of Scripture was already at play in Christian circles centuries before this vaunted rabbinic interpreter. Anticipated by the spiritual readings of Origen and others who distinguished these higher meanings from a plain or literal sense,[96] medieval interpreters unfolded these discrete approaches to the text in myriad ways.

Augustine of Hippo (354–430) continues the patristic tradition and lays out several principles for biblical interpretation in his *De Doctrina Christiana*. The *telos* of Scripture is love of God and neighbor. In fact, if one were to read Scripture for this purpose "even though he does not happen on the precise meaning which the author whom he reads intended to express in that place, his error is not pernicious, and he is wholly clear from the charge of deception."[97] Thus, Augustine views the literal sense as a means to a moral and religious end. What is more important than grasping the precise translation of a word is the impact Scripture has on the life of the believer. Mary A. Mayeski writes of Augustine's impact: "medieval exegetes were unanimous in their conviction that the extended sense (however they may have subdivided it) was the superior meaning, and determining it was the exegete's primary task."[98]

Moreover, Augustine appeals to the *analogia scriptura* and the *regula fidae* in the case of difficult interpretations when our own study fails to make sense of the passage. "Accordingly if," he writes, "when attention is given to the passage, it shall appear to be uncertain in what way it ought to be pronounced, let the reader consult the rule of faith (*regula fidae*) which he has gathered from the plainer passages of Scripture, and from the authority of the Church."[99] So Augustine would not have us jump to

---

96. I do not here, as others might, distinguish between the "plain" and "literal" sense, as they appear synonymous among the ancients, despite our modern worldview that might distinguish between "literal" scientific reading of a text like a creation story and an ancient "literal" reading that would attend more to the intended genre of a creation story.

97. *Doctr. chr.* I.36.40.

98. Mayeski, "Early Medieval Exegesis," 2:93. See also Reventlow, *History of Biblical Interpretation*, 2:86; Norris, "Augustine," 1:397.

99. *Doctr. chr.* 3.2.2.

certain interpretations of the Bible, but first do our own study, and resolve difficulties with the principles long laid by patristic interpreters to accord a reading with plainer passages of Scripture and church doctrine. In one place in his *City of God*, Augustine notably appeals to the *analogia scriptura* as a way of understanding the author's intention, a hot-button issue among contemporary interpreters. After looking to the plainer parts of an author's passage, Augustine believes we will "either arrive at the meaning intended by whoever wrote the passage, or failing this, the examination of a profoundly obscure passage will lead to the statement of a number of other truths."[100] For Augustine, then, while author's intention is discernible in many cases, it is not the only true understanding of a passage. As Stanglin writes of Augustine, "*a* true interpretation is not necessarily the *only* true meaning."[101] But neither can we take whatever meaning we wish, as the meaning we draw must concern love and belief.[102] This is possible because the literal nature of the text serves higher ends of Christian love, which remain the most significant guardrails for interpretation of the text.

Augustine's aspiration to the higher senses of Scripture and his outright appeals to others to follow suit are followed in the medieval period by interpreters using what would come to be known as the "Quadriga." Developed most explicitly by John Cassian (ca. 360–435) and utilized throughout the medieval period, this mode of interpretation begins with the literal, or "historical," sense that appeals to the visible and knowable parts of a text. Beyond this are the "spiritual senses": the allegorical, or "mystery prefigured in history," the anagogical, which prefigures a heavenly reality, and the tropological, or moral, sense.[103] In a popular example, Cassian refers to the historical sense of Jerusalem as the city of the Jews. In the allegorical sense, Jerusalem is the church. Anagogically, Jerusalem serves as the heavenly city. Tropologically, Jerusalem is the human soul.[104]

For some modern readers, these spiritual senses may take too many liberties with the text. But, building on Augustine, we can see how these senses exist to fulfill the purposes of Scripture for the church, to love God and neighbor.

---

100. *Civ.* 11.19.

101. Stanglin, *Letter and Spirit*, 89. For Stanglin's entire treatment of Augustine, which I have found helpful here, see pp. 81–92.

102. Norris, "Augustine," 2:397–99.

103. Stanglin, *Letter and Spirit*, 93.

104. See Stanglin, *Letter and Spirit*, 93; Ocker, "Scholastic Interpretation," 2:263.

For our purposes, however, most significant is the "historical" sense, identical to what we have elsewhere called the "literal" or "plain" sense. At this juncture, it is not helpful to consider the concept of "historical" identical to the "investigation" of Thucydides or a modern sense of "how it actually happened." As Mayeski notes, "for medieval exegetes, history is always salvation history, divinely initiated and providentially guided with an eternal *telos* . . . in heaven."[105] Rather, the historical sense refers to the literal and linguistic context of the biblical text.[106] Stanglin's comment on this point proves instructive:

> To the early church father the Greek word *historia*, borrowed by Latin, denoted more than historicity or historical reliability, although it could include that idea as well. It referred primarily to the narrative and its straightforward interpretation. It is the letter (*littera*), the description of "what happened." This level concerns what the text actually reports. The literal sense also takes into consideration a document's genre and figures of speech, and thus does not intend to interpret figures of speech "literally." In this case, the "literal," straightforward interpretation of a figure is figurative.[107]

This concept of taking the narrative of a text for granted requires attending to what Hans Frei referred to as the "history-like" shape of the text (see chapter 4). As Stanglin notes, this is not naïve assumption of historical facts, but takes into account literary factors such as genre and figurative speech. To do this is to study the Bible with the tools and in the manner known to scholars of this period for the more urgent purpose of Christian love.

This "historical" sense was deepened during later scholastic interpretation of the Bible. Dependent upon the non-mathematical core of medieval education, monks of the medieval period began to apply the techniques of grammar, rhetoric, and dialectic (known as the *trivium*) to the biblical text, which stands apart as the most significant of all the texts.[108] The result was an emphasis on the literal level of the text that became necessary before the interpreter springs to higher truths. Written commentary on elements of

---

105. Mayeski, "Early Medieval Exegesis," 2:93.

106. Or, Mayeski, "the historical meaning focuses on the events narrated." Mayeski, "Early Medieval Exegesis," 2:92. See also Reventlow, *History of Biblical Interpretation*, 2:165.

107. Stanglin, *Letter and Spirit*, 97.

108. Ocker, "Scholastic Interpretation," 2:263–64; Reventlow, *History of Biblical Interpretation*, 2:163–64.

the biblical text appeared as glosses affixed to the biblical text itself, with the so-called "Ordinary Gloss" the most widely used.[109]

The twelfth-century Victorenes, such as Hugh (ca. 1096–1174), Richard (d. 1173), and Andrew (d. 1175), taught that, "to achieve spiritual knowledge of a thing indicated by the text of the Scripture was to move from word to thing to the divine."[110] This prevents the interpreter from moving too quickly to spiritual truths and meditating firstly on the literal meanings of the text. Hugh, in particular, stresses the importance of establishing the "historical" and philological meaning of a text before applying philosophical concepts, even describing those who make the theoretical move too quickly as "asses." Moreover, he argues this plain sense of the Old Testament text must be established using the Hebrew version, rather than the Septuagint, as Jerome had also preferred in his translation of the Vulgate.[111] Still the theological payoff remains with Hugh and the Victorenes, but they take care in first establishing the literal basis of the text in order to draw sound theological judgments.

Using the tools of the glosses and their emphasis on the literal sense, scholastic interpreters developed a deeper understanding of genres and authorial intention than had been employed before. Thomas Aquinas (1225–74) was attentive to parabolic language as part of the plain sense so long as it was intended by the author.[112] Nicholas of Lyra (ca. 1270–ca. 1349), who was heavily influenced by Aquinas, referred to the "double literal" sense of prophetic passages that spoke both to their own day and to future events fulfilled in Christ.[113] This technique was useful in dialogue with Jews about messianic prophecies, as was his knowledge of Hebrew to establish the plain meaning of the text. The literal meaning of the text became so important that he writes, "I intend with God's help to insist on the literal sense and occasionally insert a few, brief mystical explanations, that is, seldom."[114] Heinrich Graf Reventlow argues that Nicholas's exegesis had "epoch-making effects" in his insistence on reading Scripture with the

---

109. Ocker, "Scholastic Interpretation," 2:259–62.

110. Ocker, "Scholastic Interpretation," 2:264.

111. Reventlow, *History of Biblical Interpretation*, 2:164–70.

112. Ocker, "Scholastic Interpretation," 2:267; Stanglin, *Letter and Spirit*, 104; Reventlow, *History of Biblical Interpretation*, 2:196.

113. Ocker, "Scholastic Interpretation," 2:267; Stanglin, *Letter and Spirit*, 106–7.

114. Quoted from his *Postilla* in Reventlow, *History of Biblical Interpretation*, 2:252. Reventlow's summary of Nicholas's interpretational approach can be found from pp. 248–59.

literal sense in comparison to his predecessors.[115] Nevertheless, we have seen that his readings fall within a larger tradition that witnesses to an ever-increasing significance of the literal sense.

Yet for scholastic readings, the spiritual senses still remain higher than this newly elevated literal sense. In the end, the Bible is a theological book.[116] The literal sense in this period, as Stanglin writes, "provides another limit to spiritual interpretation. The necessary relationship of the literal sense to the spiritual sense is a recurring theme throughout the patristic and medieval eras. The literal sense is understood to be the foundation of the literal."[117] So while a deeper understanding of the literal sense appears in scholasticism and tensions even begin to rise against them and those who excessively "allegorize," the goal of its usage is clear: the literal, or "historical," sense serves the spiritual purposes of the church, theology and morality.

Historical thinking in antiquity through the Middle Ages is, on the one hand, subservient to other issues. Thinking about history was a tool to serve the rhetorical ends of ancient Greeks and the theological ends of rabbis and Christian scholars. In places where the forerunners to historical criticism appear, it is usually in the service of establishing a plain, or literal, meaning to prepare one's understanding for theological reasoning. On the other hand, we do see some impulse for scholars to engage in historical research, including in ways we might consider part of historical criticism today. Textual criticism was widely practiced in antiquity and the medieval period as part of the educational curriculum. Similarly, the scholarly ethos of the ancient and medieval worlds dictated close attention to philological issues using the texts available to them in their day. Early Christian and medieval Jewish scholars engaged in theorizing about the authenticity of traditional attributions to biblical authors. Neither is historical thinking toward the biblical text outwardly denied. Instead, it appears from scholars like Hugh of Saint Victor that there were some who considered philological and proto-historical questions of this age burdensome en route to attaining the higher

---

115. Reventlow, *History of Biblical Interpretation*, 2:258–59.

116. Ocker writes, "In late medieval Scholasticism, a particular view of biblical textuality evolved. It was believed to be physically manifest in the Bible's literary organization, which reflected the religious purpose of Scripture to document the history of salvation. Theories of verbal signification and of the divine inspiration of writers and readers reinforced textuality, encouraging a decidedly theological orientation to the meaning of biblical literature, rather than a philological or historical focus." Ocker, "Scholastic Interpretation," 2:270.

117. Stanglin, *Letter and Spirit*, 110.

truths of Scripture. But, as we will see, momentum will continue to build for those who find these kinds of questions essential to proper exegesis.

3

Sprouts of Historical Criticism in the Renaissance Through the Enlightenment

WE HAVE THUS FAR seen that historical thinking, at least as we would define it in contemporary times, has been subservient to larger issues, such as rhetoric and theology. Nevertheless, seeds of historical thinking were planted by thinkers such as Herodotus, Thucydides, and Polybius. As the western world became Christian, historical thought was applied to the Bible and within the church at large by Origen and Eusebius. But these historical concerns were not quite the same as we might today place under the rubric of historical criticism. Moreover, historical thinking, especially in reference to the Bible, went dormant throughout the medieval period. Some exceptions, such as those found among Jewish scholars of the medieval age, appear. And there is much concern to establish the "plain" or "literal" sense of the text through the use of philology and some surface-level knowledge of historical concerns in order for exegetes to engage the text in theological conversation. Yet it is clear that we are miles from contemporary historical criticism at this point.

We continue the "history of historical criticism" at a point of no small debate among biblical critics today. The nature of the debate is the origin of historical criticism as we know it. Most often, we read that historical

Sprouts of Historical Criticism in the Renaissance Through the Enlightenment

criticism has its roots in the Enlightenment,[1] an era which we will discuss in short order. With its radical epistemological skepticism and nurturing of modern, "scientific" history, it is a prime candidate to which we can point for historical criticism's origins. However, some scholars are more apt to find historical criticism's origins in the sixteenth-century Reformation.[2] Given the Reformers' slogan of *sola scriptura*, mistrust of Roman Catholic ecclesiastical authority, and consequent focus of the interpreter's reading of the biblical text, this period stands as an intriguing option as well. But we also must not ignore the impulses towards historical thinking in the era preceding the Reformation and Enlightenment, the Renaissance.

Antiquarianism and the Renaissance

Any historical impulses from the medieval period gather steam in the next era of western history, the Renaissance. As scholasticism began to decline by the fourteenth and fifteenth centuries, scholars increasingly took interest in classical texts and languages, focusing knowledge away from the monastery and toward the world. Renaissance education involved study of texts from the classical period as a focus on the human subject. In a sense, this involved a rebellion against the previous millennium with its hyperfocus on theology and interests of the church, but it nevertheless maintained its Christian belief and incorporated "gothic," medieval elements into its art and education.[3]

The "humanist" focus of the Renaissance would not include the radical shift away from God as the source of knowledge, but it did both consider attention to the human subject more than previous eras, and it took up the title "humanities" for its education because of its broader focus on

---

1. Levenson, *Hebrew Bible*, 117–18; Nissinen, "Reflections," 29; Keck, "Historical Critical Method," 116; Linnemann, *Historical Criticism*, 28–29; Brueggemann, *Theology*, 13–14; Perdue, *Collapse*, 113–14; Braaten and Jenson, "Introduction," x; Yeago, "New Testament," 162. It should be noted that Yeago also finds some strands of humanistic, Reformation, and Pietistic thought in contemporary historical criticism. For a review of this perspective, see Barton, *Nature*, 118–21.

2. Collins, *Bible After Babel*, 4. Barton, "Historical-Critical Approaches," 16; Barton, *Nature*, 118–23; Stuhlmacher, *Historical Criticism*, 36–37; Krentz, *Historical-Critical Method*, 73–76.

3. Cf. Gonzalez, *Story of Christianity*, 1:365–68; Placher, *History of Christian Theology*, 175–77.

The Place of the Past

the classical texts (in contrast with the medieval emphasis on "divinity").[4] This focal shift is known for its humanist rallying cry "*ad fontes*," or "to the sources." A significant part of returning to the sources was establishing the correct versions of classical and medieval texts. Renaissance humanists such as Petrarch (1304–74) and Lorenzo Valla (1407–57) diligently exposed forgeries in regnal documents, with Valla most notably discovering falsehoods in the *Donation of Constantine* and the Apostle's Creed.[5] Valla also compiled different versions of Greek and Latin manuscripts of the Bible and was known to question traditional authorship of the book of Job.[6] Valla explicitly challenged the ability of medieval philosophers to deal with real life and thus what it means to be human.[7] Keith D. Stanglin thus describes Valla as "encouraging a little healthy skepticism about this received, written tradition."[8] In response to the ivory-tower view of medieval philosophers, Valla contends from the perspective of his rejuvenated classical learning that, "The discourse of historians exhibits more substance, more practical knowledge, more political wisdom . . . , more customs, and more learning of every sort than the precepts of any philosophers. Thus we show that historians have been superior to philosophers."[9]

Valla's humanistic successor, and perhaps the most well-known humanist, was Erasmus of Rotterdam (1466–1536). He produced the first publicly available Greek New Testament. This was as an eclectic text of his own educated research in determining the best text from the best available manuscripts, along with a new Latin translation. Erasmus also wrote commentary on the New Testament, preferring to keep with the "historical sense" as a means to establish a basis for spiritual readings. Erasmus seems to find theological and even allegorical readings most important, but the literal sense is still necessary.[10] In addition to his work on the New

---

4. Cf. Gonzalez, *Story of Christianity*, 1:366.

5. Gonzalez notes that Valla's ideas were apparently not bothersome to the Pope, for whom he worked. Gonzalez argues that Valla's thoughts only circulated among academic elites, and it would take time for skeptical approaches to tradition to become popular. Gonzalez, *Story of Christianity*, 1:368. See also Reventlow, *History of Biblical Interpretation*, 3:13–14.

6. Hayes, "History," 12; Stanglin, *Letter and Spirit*, 14–15; Rummel, "Renaissance Humanists," 2:289–90.

7. Hayes, "History," 12.

8. Stanglin, *Letter and Spirit*, 115.

9. Quoted from Hayes, "History," 12.

10. Stanglin, *Letter and Spirit*, 117–22; Rummel, "Renaissance Humanists," 2:291–93; Reventlow, *History of Biblical Interpretation*, 3:54–60.

Testament text, Erasmus authored several works on patristic writings. In a biography of Jerome, Erasmus continues Valla's skepticism toward tradition by noting that legendary traditions of the saints can be contaminated and that we ought to prefer Jerome's own perspective on historical events.[11] Erasmus thus demonstrates a tinge of historical-critical consciousness toward these non-biblical, but still authoritative, figures.

Such an eye toward historical accuracy became possible in the Renaissance as scholars began to grow more conscious of their distinctions from past eras. John H. Hayes recognizes the paintings of Giotto that depict Pilate in antique Roman dress and Petrarch's portrayals of pre-Constantinian Rome in a nostalgic manner as demonstrating an awareness that there is a "historical relativity to all things."[12] Moreover, antiquarian interest in collecting ancient coins and inscriptions, as well as concerns for reconstructing ruins and geography to illuminate the past, characterize an increased consciousness of early modern historical research.[13]

Part of the "practical knowledge" emphasized in the Renaissance was a return to understanding the words of a text more closely. As the Renaissance progressed, knowledge of Greek and Hebrew waxed, to the point of the foundation of lectureships and colleges intended to teach classical languages by the beginning of the sixteenth century.[14] New editions and translations of the Bible, in addition to Erasmus's, appeared in rapid succession in this era, with a focus on the many versions of the Bible in its many extant languages.[15] The *Complutensian Polyglot* was a new edition of the Bible compiled and translated by a team of humanist scholars beginning in the early sixteenth century that included the Old Testament in Greek, Hebrew, and Latin. Later editions included Greek and Latin of the New Testament and even lexical and grammatical aids.[16] One of the lead editors for this project, Nebrija (c. 1444–1522), contended that biblical study, at least in its textual and literary approaches, required philological, instead of theological, training. This was important to establish the correct text

---

11. Hayes, "History," 11.
12. Hayes, "History," 9.
13. Hayes, "History," 9–10.
14. Rummel, "Renaissance Humanists," 2:282.
15. For an excellent treatment of this, see Rummel, "Renaissance Humanists," 2:282–93.
16. Rummel, "Renaissance Humanists," 2:283.

and speech of the text in order to fix a correct meaning.[17] Interestingly, we see presaged here in this earlier stage the contemporary struggle between biblical scholars and theologians.[18] But in its own time, the revolutionary attitude of the Renaissance humanists with its hyper-focus on issues of language, grammar, and text stood in such contrast to medieval exegesis and the esoteric world of the explanatory gloss that Hayes calls these "two different worlds of thought."[19]

Clearly, Renaissance humanism shifted the attention of the academic study of the Bible. In attempting to search behind the background of given traditions, languages, and texts, the humanists explicitly (although not with much clear methodology)[20] sought to bring study of classical texts, and sometimes the Bible itself, from the dark monastic chamber into "practical," everyday light. Humanistic approaches become, as Erika Rummel contends, "key factors in subsequent methodologies."[21] Yet, we have also seen that these approaches are not *de novo*, unique ways of viewing classical texts. The Renaissance in part saw itself returning to a classical vision of education, of which history is a part. And we have already seen earlier concerns for historical accuracy, or at least musings thereon, with Ibn Ezra, and the establishment of a correct biblical text as early as Origen. So the Renaissance cannot be said to articulate new questions per se. But the kind of questions humanists ask are given greater emphasis than we have seen in the earlier Christian period. Still the humanists retain a stable belief in theological orthodoxy. In the succeeding eras, however, we will witness a drastic change in the intensity of historical study and even reach the point at which history becomes the chief end rather than a means for biblical study.

---

17. Rummel, "Renaissance Humanists," 2:285.

18. Rummel writes, "The humanistic enterprise also met with strong resistance from professional theologians who were determined to safeguard their exclusive right to deal with sacred texts." Rummel, "Renaissance Humanists," 2:281. This is eerily similar to contemporary debates, which I discuss throughout this work, between theologians and biblical scholars.

19. Hayes, "History," 12.

20. See Rummel's argument that humanist approaches to philology and textual criticism were not "fully developed." Rummel, "Renaissance Humanists," 2:293.

21. Rummel, "Renaissance Humanists," 2:294.

Historical Criticism in the Reformation

The life of the father of the Reformation, Martin Luther (1483–1546), dovetails with the late Renaissance. His work and those of his associates, such as Philip Melanchthon (1497–1560), are in many ways a product of it. They were known to utilize the tools of Renaissance education, such as rhetoric, grammar, and geography to study the biblical text. And neither were they averse to more spiritual readings upon close examination of the text at its literal levels. However they went about it, they are most known for the theological conclusions they drew from the text, conclusions that clashed with the prevailing stances (particularly on justification) of the Roman Catholic Church.[22]

The movement Luther launched triggered a new era in Western history on its own. By rejecting the authority of the Roman Catholic Church, Luther inaugurated a radical break in what came before. We have seen that Renaissance, and even some medieval, interpreters could question historical aspects of Scripture, but the prevailing faith-claims of the day stood as a bedrock that readings of the text could not undermine. In splitting from the Roman Catholic Church, Luther cracked fissures in that foundation, locating final authority away from ecclesiastical power and towards the Bible itself.

Underscoring the old concerns for the unity of Scripture, the Reformers held to the "perspicuity" of the Bible, in which the analogy of Scripture takes on such force that there is little room for overt tradition in interpretation. From a later confessional Protestant perspective, the Westminster Confession of Faith contends,

> All things in Scripture are not alike plain in themselves, nor alike clear unto all; yet those things which are necessary to be known, believed, and observed for salvation, are so clearly propounded, and opened in some place of Scripture or other, that not only the learned, but the unlearned, in a due sense of the ordinary means, may attain unto a sufficient understanding of them.[23]

Luther and the Reformers who followed in his footsteps retained a Renaissance approach to the biblical text by focusing heavily on the literal

---

22. We will examine Luther's approach below. For Melanchthon, see Wengert, "Philip Melanchthon," 2:319–40; Reventlow, *History of Biblical Interpretation*, 3:87–94.

23. *Westminster Confession*, I.7 For a discussion of perspicuity, see Stanglin, *Letter and Spirit*, 125–32.

sense of the text before moving to any theologizing. Luther asserted, "The Holy Spirit is the plainest writer and speaker in heaven and earth, and therefore His words cannot have more than one, and that the very simplest, sense, which we call the literal, ordinary, natural sense."[24] Early on for Luther, this involved conscious adherence to the Quadriga. But, as time progressed, Luther collapsed the meanings into one, with the grammatical and historical readings functioning in contemporaneous interplay with the spiritual senses.[25] As Mark D. Thompson writes of Luther, "Letter and spirit were not so much two levels of meaning as two elements in a dynamic, which can be traced throughout the OT and the NT."[26]

Although this shift reveals a deepened emphasis on the plain sense from Renaissance humanism, and although Luther was much more willing to abandon the interpretations of Scripture foisted upon the church by the hierarchy, his readings are not presuppositionless. The entirety of Scripture ultimately existed to appeal to Christ, and Scripture was to be read and interpreted in the Spirit for the church.[27] Despite Luther's skepticism toward the church's dogma of his day, he was confident that Scripture should be the source for constructing church dogma and that it was supportive of right doctrine. This confidence was surely taken for granted, and we do not see in his work a mistrust in the Bible for teaching the church about God, as we will find in later periods.

This *telos* of Scripture for the church continues in the work of John Calvin (1509–64), the Reformer most often associated with a "Reformation reading" of the Bible. He continues the Reformation insistence on the

---

24. Quoted from Hayes, "History," 13. See also Reventlow, *History of Biblical Interpretation*, 3:86–87.

25. Stanglin, *Letter and Spirit*, 122–25; Thompson, "Martin Luther," 2:306–10.

26. Thompson, "Martin Luther," 2:309.

27. Thompson, "Martin Luther," 2:304–6, 310–12. See also statements in Gonzalez, *Story of Christianity*, 1:30. Frei, *Eclipse of Biblical Narrative*, 40; Yeago, "New Testament," 152. Stanglin notes that it is not that Luther neglects the church fathers, but it is rather a matter of which ones he utilizes for his purposes. Stanglin, *Letter and Spirit*, 125. Reno argues that early Protestant statements do not presume a suspicion of theology, but rather find "accordance" between the Bible and what the church teaches. As opposed to the Roman Catholics of Luther's day, the difference is in the starting point, the Bible or church teaching. Reno, *End*, 12. In contrast to Luther's view here, we must also note the Anabaptist reformers, who taught that the Luthers, Melanchthons, and Calvins of the mainstream Reformation were not paying enough attention to the plain sense, particularly in matters of ecclesiology and ethics. For them, Scripture constituted a more self-contained unity that risks a certain literalism for many contemporary readers. See Murray, "Anabaptist Reformers," 2:403–27.

primacy of Scripture for theological matters and supports this notion with voluminous commentaries and reflections on the role of Scripture. In the commentaries, he reads the text closely and with grammatical acuity as one might expect from one trained in law (which he was). His commentary witnesses to a "simplicity" or "brevity" which he outwardly champions, often leading him to overlook matters of doctrine in interpretation. Readings with this concision and omission testify to a further merger of letter and spirit.[28] But this emphasis of reading the text at a literal level, even with a disdain for certain kinds of allegorical readings, was not unique to Calvin, as we have already seen. Nevertheless, he is notably prodigious in his output of producing examples and clarifying this perspective.[29]

For our purposes, an interesting facet of Calvin's interpretation is his emphasis, within the focus on the literal sense of the text, on understanding the "author's intention" (*mens scriptoris*). Calvin believed that literal exegesis should illuminate, not every jot and tittle of grammar, but the "design of the speaker."[30] This design includes the theological takeaways of the passage intended by the original author, leaving little room for the multiplicity of meanings that had dominated theretofore.[31] This includes a resistance to applying the so-called "protoevanglium" of Genesis 3:15 directly to Christ, simply noting that the passage serves as a presage of enmity between humans and serpents.[32] Instead of the kinds of readings that had dominated the church through the Middle Ages, this restrained mode of exegesis demonstrates the emerging rule of the literal sense of the text and that exegetes are becoming more reticent than ever to jump to theological meanings from the biblical text before first establishing its plainer meanings.

Still, we have already seen that the intention of the author is prevalent as far back as Augustine. Calvin's exposition certainly serves as a revival of that interest in concert with the increased focus on the plain sense of the text in tandem with Renaissance exegetical interests. But, as Stanglin writes, "Calvin's exegetical practice may reflect the long transition between medieval and modern critical exegesis, but in nearly every respect, he is

---

28. Stanglin, *Letter and Spirit*, 132–33. See also Pitkin, "John Calvin," 2:352–53.

29. Pitkin, "John Calvin," 2:346–49; Reventlow, *History of Biblical Interpretation*, 3:131.

30. Quoted in Stanglin, *Letter and Spirit*, 133.

31. Pitkin, "John Calvin," 2:354.

32. Stanglin, *Letter and Spirit*, 133–34.

closer to medieval than to modern critical exegesis, and he should be interpreted in the former context.[33]

Further, we must keep in mind that, though the plain sense of Scripture is flourishing in this period, it is still for the benefit of the church. Neither does literal and grammatical exegesis command the historical rigor it would in the succeeding centuries, as Calvin mostly takes the historical world of the Bible for granted. Barabara Pitkin writes,

> For Calvin, the literal-historical sense was not the bare, grammatical sense; nor did it refer to the history behind the text in the way it often does in modern historical criticism. Rather, it included both the "history" or the events that the author narrated and the spiritual or moral lessons that the writer sought to inculcate—lessons, moreover, applicable both to those in the author's original setting and to later generations of the faithful.[34]

The Lutheran theologian Matthias Flacius Illyricus (1520–75), who produced one of our earliest handbooks on exegesis, stands as a classic representative of the Reformation program. On the one hand, he contends that exegetes should decide whether a biblical text "deals with narrative or history, a piece of teaching or instruction, a text offering consolation or an accusation, the description of something, or a speech or something similar."[35] This should come from close study of the text's words, sentences, the spirit of the author (including God), and the application for the life of the believer.[36] Thus, the reader should attend to the author's intended genre and all that presupposes in the vein of classical Renaissance scholarship. On the other hand, the humanistic tool of generic study should be paired with an assent to the faith and a belief that Scripture cannot contradict itself.[37] He writes that "nowhere is there a real contradiction in Scripture." If there is, the fault lies in us as interpreters, not the Scripture itself.[38] Scripture interprets Scripture, and the *analogia Scriptura* still provides guidance

---

33. Stanglin, *Letter and Spirit*, 139. See also Reventlow, *History of Biblical Interpretation*, 3:127–28.

34. Pitkin, "John Calvin," 2:356. See also Stanglin, *Letter and Spirit*, 137–38; Reventlow, *History of Biblical Interpretation*, 3:127–28.

35. Barton, *Nature*, 128.

36. Kümmel, *New Testament*, 29.

37. Hayes, "History," 14.

38. Kümmel, *New Testament*, 30. For more on Flacius' hermeneutics, see Reventlow, *History of Biblical Interpretation*, 4:7–13.

to the faithful. These twin emphases within Illyricus's work underscores Stuhlmacher's assessment of the Reformation view of the Bible that "the hermeneutical circle encompassing Scripture and the church's consciousness of faith is thus preserved intact. But what is decidedly new is the distribution of weight within this circle and thus the theological evaluation of the process of interpretation itself."[39]

Calvin's insistence upon finding the author's meaning in Scripture continues with a second generation of Reformers known as the "Remonstrants." These theologians, represented by names such as Simon Episcopus (1583–1643) and Étienne de Courcelles (1586–1659), belonged to the Dutch Arminian branch of Reformed thought and are known in theological circles for their teachings against Calvinist orthodoxy's views on predestination. But they continue, and even further, Calvin's humanist exegetical enterprise. In contrast to many other Reformers, and influenced by contemporary Italian unitarians such as Faustus Socinus (1539–1604),[40] they stress that human reason can be utilized to reveal Scripture's perspicuity. Moreover, those with the greatest reason, academics, are in the best position to analyze the all-important plain sense to determine the meaning of the text. Doctrines that derive from the text are in the domain of preachers.[41] Courcelles writes,

> The interpretation of Scripture is of two kinds. For the one interpretation merely and simply describes its true sense; but the other interpretation, in addition, elicits some doctrines from this sense, which doctrines it applies to the use of the hearers and readers. For the most part, professors in the schools are occupied with the former interpretation, but preachers employ the latter in the church and for the people.[42]

Stanglin contends that this view marks the earliest split between dogmatic and biblical theology.[43] Such division will be formalized under Gabler, as

39. Stuhlmacher, *Historical Criticism*, 32.

40. Stanglin, *Letter and Spirit*, 158; Hayes, "History," 16.

41. Stanglin, *Letter and Spirit*, 156–60.

42. Quoted from Stanglin, *Letter and Spirit*, 153. He cites this from *Institutio* 1.14.9 in *Opera*, 31.

43. Stanglin, *Letter and Spirit*, 160. The professionalization of history, particularly in the Bible, has drawn critique in Moore and Sherwood, *Invention*. They view the professionalization of the historical-critical scholar as a product of the Enlightenment that is, in some sense, a self-fulfilling prophecy of creating and attempting to solve unsolvable problems. See especially pp. xii–xiii and 80–81. Also see McGrath, "Reclaiming Our

we will soon see. Yet it is also pertinent to note that, as significant as such a shift is, the Remonstrants apply reason for the purpose of perspicuity. That is, reason is employed to see the Bible as a unified whole.[44] Certainly this assumes a doctrinal confession of the nature of the Bible, however it may be implied.

So the historians of biblical interpretation surveyed here are not confident that biblical exegesis has yet reached the realm of modern historical criticism. The Reformers retain a trust in the Bible as the Word of God, in addition to its unity. They continue historical inquiry in the same mode as the Renaissance, including concerns of grammar and geography, although these interests lack the resources and depth of the later modern period. And Calvin, the paragon of Reformation exegesis, revives and refines a previous interest in authorial intention. The Reformers both use exegetical methods that are not unique to them and they have not questioned the role of the Bible as the church's Scripture. The Bible's ultimate purpose still lies in its use for the theology and life of the faith community.

Yet, those who locate historical criticism's origins in the Reformation press one further point. Describing the view to which he is sympathetic, John Baron writes, "biblical criticism is a true child of the Reformers, because it enables readers to make up their own minds about the meaning of Scripture, rather than accepting existing readings on authority."[45] Granted, this authority still includes theological conceptions and faith claims that were likely assumed and implicit. The worldview of the Reformation in Europe may have been shifting away from Catholicism, but it was still Christian. Nevertheless, we may accept the claim that the Reformation engendered a liberation of the Bible from institutional authorities, claiming a reading for oneself (however affected one's own reading may be by other preconceptions). Hayes writes about the Reformation that "theological positions were capable of absorbing modernity while claiming to be founded upon true antiquity. This permitted significant shifts on the questions of authority and revelation, which made biblical criticism not only possible but sometimes desirable."[46] This freedom *from* biblical interpretation in the

---

Roots," 63–64. Assmann notes that the split between history and memory owes itself to the professionalization of history. Assmann, "Transformations," 59.

44. Stanglin, *Letter and Spirit*, 159.
45. Barton, *Nature*, 121. He clarifies his sympathies to this view here through p. 123.
46. Hayes, "History," 16.

Roman Catholic Church opened up myriad questions in the succeeding era on what biblical interpretation was freed *for*.

Historical Criticism in the Enlightenment

If the Remonstrants were viewed with suspicion by their contemporaries for incorporating too much reason into the interpretation of Scripture, we could at the same time allow that they did so for the service of the church. The same could not be said for the contemporary progenitors of the Enlightenment, British attorney Francis Bacon (1561–1626) and French mathematician René Descartes (1596–1650). Bacon sought to construct knowledge using "a more perfect use of human reason" than the Aristotelian logic prominent in his day.[47] Focusing on the self as the knower without recourse to traditional knowledge, Bacon devised what we now know as the scientific method. Descartes explicitly rejected received knowledge with his statement of skepticism: "The first rule was never to accept nothing for true which I did not clearly know to be such; that is to say, carefully to avoid precipitancy and prejudice, and to comprise nothing more in my judgment than what was presented to my mind so clearly and distinctly as to exclude all ground of doubt."[48] And thus the Bible would follow as one of many objects of study subjected no longer to tradition but to *human reason alone*. Michael C. Legaspi writes,

> At a fundamental level, Enlightenment involved the development of ways to understand and reappropriate traditional culture and, thus, to situate oneself anew with respect to this traditional culture and its accompanying social and political forms. That confessional Christianity and the Bible formed essential aspects of the old order of things in this arrangement is clear.[49]

Benedict (Baruch) de Spinoza (1632–77) emerged as one of Descartes's interlocutors on the nature of reality, but he bought into the skeptical program that sought to use reason to free knowledge from traditional bounds. In his *Theological-Political Treatise*, he supported using "scientific" reason to understand the biblical text. This was not only an affront to the church, but it was a means of liberation. From now on, we had the tools

---

47. Durant and Durant, *Story of Civilization VII*, 172–76.
48. Descartes, *Discourse on Method*, 15.
49. Legaspi, "Enlightenment," 3:74.

through human-centered research to make sense of the Bible. Moreover, Spinoza insisted that using these tools recovered the true sense of Scripture rather than hiding it behind a veil of tradition.[50] Spinoza's insights on Scripture were limited in contrast to modern historical criticism, but earth-shattering for their time. Notably, he promoted views that the prophets were not inspired,[51] that Moses was not the author of the Pentateuch, and that it was not even written in his lifetime.[52] However, we have seen that Spinoza was not the first to doubt the traditionally attributed authors of biblical books.[53] Yet when we tie this pessimism into a more comprehensive mistrust of ecclesial tradition, the stakes for biblical interpretation are raised. Reventlow reveals the trenchant power of Spinoza's exaltation of reason when applied to the Scriptures,

> The worldview that presupposed the Bible, the church, and believing humans were authoritative and binding in their requirements, both before and after, was forfeited. Since this worldview was explained as bound to the past, it no longer stood in the way of modern, natural scientific bodies of knowledge.[54]

Frenchman Richard Simon (1638–1712) further applied human reason to understanding the Scriptures, also with a sympathetic eye to its value, but from a Roman Catholic perspective. Using the tools of Hebrew philology, textual criticism, and literary insights, Simon sought to undermine the extant Protestant view of inspiration to argue that every stage of composition and transmission in the Old Testament was spiritually inspired; not just the initial writing.[55] In so doing, Simon introduced the term "criticism" to describe his approach, a term still applied today, not only to historical criticism but to all rigorous study of the Bible. Despite his earnest attempt to merge the literary techniques of his day with a Catholic

---

50. Stanglin, *Letter and Spirit*, 160–64; Krentz, *Historical-Critical Method*, 14–15. See also Rae, *History and Hermeneutics*, 7–9; Frampton, "Spinoza and His Influence," 3:126–30.

51. Legaspi, "Enlightenment," 3:78; Frampton, "Spinoza," 3:135; Reventlow, *History of Biblical Interpretation*, 4:95–97.

52. Stanglin, *Letter and Spirit*, 161.

53. Aside from those we have mentioned, we have not had occasion yet to mention Hugo Grotius, an older contemporary of Spinoza who expressed doubts about biblical authorship. Reventlow, *History of Biblical Interpretation*, 3:219–20.

54. Reventlow, *History of Biblical Interpretation*, 4:97.

55. Hayes, "History," 20; Stuhlmacher, *Historical Criticism*, 56; Barton, *Nature*, 125–26; Legaspi, "Enlightenment," 3:79–80.

understanding of Scripture, Simon's work was condemned by the Congregation of the Index in 1683.[56] Only in more recent years on the other side of historical criticism's initial wave would Simon be appreciated for blending criticism and tradition.[57]

Nevertheless, Simon's enterprise continued in fellow Frenchman Jean Astruc (1684–1766) and German Bernhard Witter (1683–1715). These noted several signals indicating the multi-layered nature of the Old Testament, including the use of different names for God, linguistic and stylistic vicissitudes across texts, contradictions, duplications, and other features of the text still utilized today by contemporary historical critics.[58] Germans Johann Salomo Semler (1725–91) and Johann David Michaelis (1717–91) were also inspired by Simon's text-critical and rational approaches to the Bible and considered the implications of treating the Bible as a secular text. Semler attempted to distinguish between the "Holy Scripture," which contained the simple biblical writings, from "the Word of God" found within them. This enabled Semler to study the books of the Bible from a historical, rather than dogmatic, perspective.[59] In so doing, his writings evince sporadic concerns with the formation of the canon, which he finds was split between Jewish-Christian and gentile-Christian traditions.

Semler's writings are not systematic, though, and it appears that Michaelis picked up where he left off. Michaelis added critical observations on the canonicity of New Testament writings and religio-historical understandings of New Testament concepts. He also spent more time dealing with the Old Testament and reckoning with cultural and philosophical issues than did Semler. Nevertheless, his study has apologetic tendencies, as he demonstrates the trustworthiness of the New Testament texts, even if they are not all divinely inspired.[60]

56. Hayes, "History," 20.

57. Stuhlmacher, *Historical Criticism*, 56. Reventlow writes, "According to present understanding, one is astonished that Simon experienced the degree of persecution that he did." Reventlow, *History of Biblical Interpretation*, 4:88.

58. Hayes, "History," 24–25.

59. Reventlow shows that the historical readings of the Bible for Semler are "secular," whereas the Bible's moral understandings are religious, and thus of a different nature. Reventlow, *History of Biblical* Interpretation, 4:189. Krentz notes that some view Semler as the "Father of historical-critical theology." Krentz, *Historical-Critical Method*, 18–19.

60. Kümmel, *New Testament*, 62–73. Krentz contends that the connection between authority and apostolicity still "burdens" scholarship today. Krentz, *Historical-Critical Method*, 20. See also Legaspi, "Enlightenment," 3:82–84; Baird, "Historical Criticism," 3:100–101.

The Place of the Past

Johann Gottfried Eichorn (1752–1827) followed the same course with the Old Testament, critically examining its canon and inspiration. He believed that scholars should investigate the worldview to which biblical authors were bound, particularly in their views of God. It is important for us to study the mythical lens through which they saw divinity at work in the world, even though that lens might appear primitive to us today. This led him to join Michaelis in setting "the pattern still in use today"[61] in separating the ancient worldview from our own to understand what theological purposes the text might have originally served. Eichorn is credited with introducing the term "higher criticism," thus formalizing this form of exegesis that had become *en vogue*.[62] W. G. Kümmel perceptively writes concerning the New Testament, though it may also apply to the view of the Old Testament in this period:

> All this introduces a fateful and perverse factor into the situation. At the very moment that the New Testament texts are recognized as historical entities that must be subjected to rigorous historical investigation, this historical investigation is declared to be the criterion by which the inspiration of the New Testament writings is established.[63]

Far less committed to traditional confessions and the authority of Scripture, another Frenchman, Voltaire (1694–1778), popularized criticism of the Bible through open critique of the church's claims about it. After building on the knowledge collected over the previous century's boom in literary criticism, antiquarian collections of artifacts, a burgeoning professionalization of history,[64] not to mention the crumbling of popular trust in orthodoxy, Voltaire was able to claim that divine authorship of the Bible was a farce. To argue that God wrote the Bible is to make "of God a bad geographer, a bad chronologist, a bad physicist; it makes him no better than a naturalist."[65] For such a well-known figure to pair this overt disparagement of divine authorship (and the historical claims of the Bible itself)

---

61. Krentz, *Historical-Critical Method*, 20. Also see the summaries in Hayes, "History," 25; Legaspi, "Enlightenment," 3:84; Baird, "Historical Criticism," 3:101; Reventlow, *History of Biblical Interpretation*, 4:211–29.

62. Brettler and Arakaky, "Historical-Critical," 207.

63. Kümmel, *New Testament*, 73.

64. For a summary of these developments in the seventeenth century, see Legaspi, "Enlightenment," 3:82–85; Hayes, "History," 16–17.

65. Quoted from Hayes, "History," 23.

Sprouts of Historical Criticism in the Renaissance Through the Enlightenment

with his own speculative and radical deism left an impression on biblical scholarship and also popularized skeptical and unorthodox claims for the literati outside of the academy. Hayes writes about biblical scholarship after the deists: "It would never again be easy to present Israelite and Judean history by simply retelling and amplifying biblical narratives."[66]

In Germany, the philosopher Gotthold Ephraim Lessing (1729–81) published fragments from the skeptical unitarian Hermann Samuel Reimarus (1694–1768) questioning how the Israelites could have traversed the Red Sea with 600,000 Hebrew men, not to mention the women, children, and animals accompanying them.[67] This is one of many examples Lessing uses to expose the "ugly, broad ditch" between the miraculous claims of the Bible (and thus the church) and the canons of historicity newly emerging in Europe during this time, which we will soon address.[68] Lessing himself turns the critique of historicity to the New Testament. When Paul claims in 1 Corinthians 2:4 that Christians have "proof of the Spirit and of power," Origen had read the "proof of Spirit" as the fulfilled prophecies and the "power" as miracles. But Lessing inferred that Origen cannot claim this historically, since he was not present to witness them. Instead, Lessing views the claims for the miraculous as human interpretations of certain events.[69] Stuhlmacher sees Lessing's claims as emblematic of the new Enlightenment rationality and the liberation it grants interpreters of the Bible. He writes,

> Fastening upon texts of the past an uninhibited, rational fashion thus serves the dual purpose of setting free and initiating a new communication with the truth. It sets free from the pressure and compulsion of clerical tradition, still undisputed in value but now felt to inhibit freedom, and initiates a genuine communication with the truth, since according to the Enlightenment view, reason is manifest in the thought of single historical individuals and in the forward progress of history as a whole.[70]

Lessing clearly anticipates the flood of questions, still attendant in historical criticism today, about the historicity of events in the Bible. This

---

66. Hayes, "History," 24.

67. Hayes, "History," 23; Rae, *History and Hermeneutics*, 9–14.

68. Stanglin, *Letter and Spirit*, 165. A contemporary expression of the dilemma caused by the "ugly, broad ditch" is seen in Jenson, "Hermeneutics," 103.

69. Stanglin, *Letter and Spirit*, 164.

70. Stuhlmacher, *Historical Criticism*, 40. For more on Lessing, see Krentz, *Historical-Critical Method*, 17; Reventlow, *History of Biblical Interpretation*, 4:165–75.

The Place of the Past

is in addition to the already-present investigations of the literary development of the biblical text, intense linguistic study of the Bible in its original languages, and debates on authorship, all hallmarks of historical criticism today. What the Enlightenment clearly ushers in to these enhanced critical inquiries of the Bible is a growing mistrust of traditional claims about the Bible supported by independent rational study. It will prove difficult for biblical studies to change course after this moment in history, severing study of the Bible from the faithful community that produced it and opening up its claims to a broader and more suspicious audience.

During this period, even the Bible drifts away from the center of the church's teaching. The Renaissance and Protestant focus on the Bible as the source for faith-claims and the Enlightenment exaltation of human reason meet in a 1787 lecture by the German professor Johann Philipp Gabler (1753–1826) entitled "An Oration on the Proper Distinction Between Biblical and Dogmatic Theology and the Specific Objectives of Each." Gabler contends for the division of biblical theology and dogmatic theology based on what the "holy writers felt about divine matters" in the former and "what each theologian philosophises rationally about divine things" in the latter.[71] The approach is for the scholar to first discern the "pure and unmixed"[72] theology with its "unambiguous words"[73] by understanding the ancient context,[74] including rigorous study in its native languages.[75] From there, the dogmatic theologian can then apply "the harmony of divine dogmatics and the principles of human reason."[76] The order of exegetical operation strikingly reverses the medieval approach to the Bible as a support for theology. And, most importantly, it has set the tone for academic study of the Bible. From this point on, humanistic study of the biblical text takes on a life of its own, with its own assumptions and fields of inquiry. No longer does the study of the Bible have to be tied to particular faith-claims, but one can appeal rather to the light of human reason. Seminaries, state universities, publishers, and so on have adopted this delineation that mostly still stands

---

71. Gabler, "Oration," 501.

72. Gabler, "Oration," 505.

73. Gabler, "Oration," 506.

74. Ollenburger refers to this as a kernel-and-husk approach. Ollenburger, "Old Testament Theology," 4.

75. Note the importance of a historically contextual reading in Ollenburger, "Old Testament Theology," 502, 504.

76. Gabler, "Oration," 506.

Sprouts of Historical Criticism in the Renaissance Through the Enlightenment

today. It must be noted that Gabler intended for study of the Bible to lead to dogmatic theology, and he could not have foreseen the implications of the strict separation between them we experience today. Regardless, his address illuminates the blending of several principles that emerged since the transition from the medieval period: the primacy of Scripture characteristic of the Reformation, grammatical-historical study characteristic of the Renaissance, and the clarification of Scripture using human reason before it is applied to the church.[77]

An Enlightenment Revival of Historical Thinking

By the dawn of the nineteenth century, historical inquiry into the Bible was becoming commonplace. Advances in philology enabled deeper study of the biblical text in its original languages. Growing knowledge of the world led to new questions about biblical geography and the ancient context. Scholars had already resumed asking questions from the ancient period about authorship of biblical books, the veracity of certain events, and began to investigate the fragmented nature of the origins of the biblical texts. And we have seen that study of the Bible was increasingly becoming the domain of scholars rather than the church.

In this period, several critical histories of ancient Israel appeared, utilizing a growing knowledge of the ancient world, but primarily reading the literature of the Bible from a rational lens.[78] Heinrich Ewald (1803–75) produced the most famous of these histories and did so in "the knowledge of what really happened—not what was only related and handed down by tradition, but what was actual fact."[79] The "facts" Ewald utilized were meager by comparison to today's standards. His primary objective was to extract from Bible's literary tradition whatever was clouded by memory and to retain what was historical. But he also had recourse to the growing knowledge of the ancient world that was slowly emerging from the nascent

---

77. For critiques of the impact of Gabler's address, see Brueggemann, *Theology*, 13–14; Prickett, *Words*, 25; Perdue, *Collapse*, 13–14.

78. Hayes, "History," 17, 21, 27–34.

79. Cited from Hayes, "History," 32. Reventlow notes that Ewald was more conservative than some of his contemporaries, though. For him, the Bible is the single source of truth, and we must master its material to understand it better. Reventlow, *History of Biblical Interpretation*, 4:303.

The Place of the Past

discipline of archaeology, as antiquarian interests had grown over the past several hundred years.

The professionalization of biblical study in its grammatical-historical mode received a boost in the nineteenth century with the parallel growth and self-reflection of the historical discipline in total. Theodor Mommsen (1817–1903), for instance, produced a pioneering work on the ancient Romans using exacting detail to understand the available artifacts and produce a narrative from such realia.[80] He thus blended together the interests of antiquarians, who collected artifacts, with those of historians, who had heretofore mostly dealt with literary appraisals of history.[81] His precise work with primary sources and ability to narrate a history from those sources marks a period in which historians viewed themselves as doing distinct work from other academicians. Because of this Mommsen quipped that historians are "not trained but born" due to the of the tacit nature of weaving facts into historical narrative.[82]

Professionalization of the historical discipline, however, was aided by the work of historian Leopold von Ranke (1795–1886). Often cited by today's biblical scholars as a progenitor (and sometimes bogeyman) of historical writing in the Enlightenment vein, Ranke was a man of devout Lutheran faith, yet worked not as a historian of the Bible but of his native Germany. Ranke's methodology, which in many ways was not novel, was promulgated far and wide across many continents and disciplines. Ranke's technical approach to history involved a close dive into sources, favoring the witness that was closest to the studied event.[83] From the data drawn in these "primary" sources, the historian must venture into "art" by recreating historical subject matter.[84] The result is that the historian should understand history "*wie es eigentlich gewesen.*" We might translate this as "how it *actually* was"; however, Georg Iggers has made the case that a better translation is "how it *essentially* was."[85] The idea is that the historian should,

---

80. For brief summaries of Mommsen's work, see Evans, *Defense*, 19–20; Collingwood, *Idea*, 127; Walsh, *Philosophy of History*, 183.

81. Hayes, "History," 17.

82. Evans, *Defense*, 54–55.

83. Braw, "Vision as Revision," 49; Evans, *Defense*, 16–17; Clark, *History, Theory, Text*, 10.

84. Iggers, "Introduction," xxvii.

85. Iggers, "Introduction," xxiii–xiv.

Sprouts of Historical Criticism in the Renaissance Through the Enlightenment

thorough the study of primary sources, be able to comprehend the spirit of a bygone event.[86]

Ranke's approach influenced generations of historians after him, with many misinterpreting his aims, especially in the English-speaking world.[87] Part of this misperception has been to view Ranke as a historical positivist, construing historical facts found in primary sources to be empirically true without recourse to hypothesis, a claim that later interpreters have debunked.[88] Peter Burke, in fact, contends Ranke did not introduce much new into historical study, as the phrase *wie es eigentlich gewesen* preceded him and the insistence on the use of source material stretches back to the sixteenth century, if not earlier.[89] But what stands out about Ranke's program is that it both veers away from Romantic views of history in the eighteenth century and the professionalization and technical character of the task of history that had not yet existed.[90] In many ways, Ranke saw his work as reviving that of Thucydides, with a self-conscious approach to understanding events of the past in a way that had been lost since the great Greek historian.[91]

We should not overstate Ranke's direct importance upon historical study of the Bible. Again, this was not his field of expertise. So in some sense Ranke only formalizes the impulses that were already existent in biblical studies of his day. What Ranke, in tandem with the lesser-cited Mommsen, brought to the table for all historians, including historians of the Bible, was a rigorous and professional approach of utilizing the available sources to make sense of the past. As the sources continued to grow

---

86. This connection between fact and spirit in Ranke is underscored in Braw, "Vision," 46–47. Harvey, taking the more traditional translation of Ranke's phrase, sees the objectivity more about seeing the past in a way that does not necessarily accord with the historian's own preconceived notions. Harvey, *Historian and Believer*, 183.

87. Clark, *History, Theory, Text*, 13; Iggers, "Introduction," xi–xii; Iggers, "Image of Ranke," 17–40.

88. For a characterization of Ranke's misperception, see Nissinen, "Reflections," 41. For a correction of this view, see Braw, "Vision," 48. Also, David Hackett Fischer locates the positivistic "Baconian Fallacy" to Ranke's contemporary Foustel de Coulanges. Fischer, *Historians' Fallacies*, 6.

89. Burke, "Ranke the Reactionary," 36–37.

90. Burke, "Ranke the Reactionary," 37; Iggers, "Introduction," xix; Mark Day, *Philosophy of History*, 5–9.

91. On Ranke's penchant for Thucydides, see Iggers, "Introduction," xvi–xvii; Kelley, "Mythistory," 6; Burke, "Ranke the Reactionary," 42; Braw, "Vision," 53–54.

through archaeology, this put stress on biblical scholars to make reasoned connections to the biblical material they studied.

In the next generation, Enlightenment optimism toward understanding events of the biblical past reaches its peak in the work of Ernst Troeltsch (1865-1923). Trained not as a historian but as a theologian, Troeltsch saw historical criticism as the greatest tool of theology, because it "enables theology with all of its religious experience to share in a universal historical progress and in its own way even to help give it shape."[92] Troeltsch's project thus intends to marry theology and history under the umbrella of human reason in an unapologetically positivistic fashion.

For Troeltsch, historical criticism involves the following three key principles: criticism, analogy, and correlation. Criticism describes our understanding of the past beginning with skepticism, and any positive assertions about its events must appear as matters of degree and open to revision. Analogy asserts that we can only make these judgments if we understand that our own present experiences are not wholly dissimilar from those of historical actors. Finally, correlation privileges causation preceding the historical event and consequences of the event because historical events do not occur in a vacuum.[93] He contends,

> There is no need for us to demonstrate that this approach constitutes the foundation of all principles of historical explanation. The historian's craft combines the art of intuiting the original import of the sources with the discovery of correlative and mutually determinative changes. The historian's ultimate problems arise from the attempt to understand the nature and basis of the whole historical context and to arrive at value judgments regarding various forms.[94]

Troeltsch's system frees the historian to see the world rationally and in a manner that privileges the consistent human experience. There is, for example, no reason to believe in miracles as reported in the Bible. They exist outside of the realm of cause and effect, are thereby not historical, and should be regarded as useless for modern religious experience.[95] Har-

---

92. Stuhlmacher, *Historical Criticism*, 46.

93. Troeltsch, *Religion in History*, 13-14. See summaries in Harvey, *Historian and Believer*, 14-15; Stuhlmacher, *Historical Criticism*, 44-46; Collins, *Bible After Babel*, 5-6; Barton, *Nature*, 46; Krentz, *Historical-Critical Method*, 55-59; Rae, *History and Hermeneutics*, 16-17; McKnight, *Post-Modern*, 46-47.

94. Troeltsch, *Religion in History*, 13-14.

95. For Troeltsch's comments on the special pleading of dogmatic theology with regard to miracles, see Troeltsch, *Religion in History*, 22-23. See also Barton, *Nature*, 46-48.

Sprouts of Historical Criticism in the Renaissance Through the Enlightenment

vey summarizes Troeltsch's view thusly: "Troeltsch himself believed that these principles were incompatible with traditional Christian belief and, therefore, that anyone who based his historical inquiries upon them should necessarily arrive at results which an orthodox Christian would consider negative and skeptical."[96] Troeltsch's approach clearly opens the door for skeptical readings of the Bible's historical claims and places a high bar for the historian in claiming what is true. The benefit is a theology that is liberated from viewing the Bible's historical claims as essential.

Troeltsch's legacy is mixed. On the one hand, support still exists for his insistence on stringent historical claims for those who read the Bible for matters of faith. Harvey notes that Troeltsch's criticisms of orthodox faith and history "still haunt us"[97] because historians of faith wind up falling prey to fallacies such as special pleading, denying distinction between fact and significance, and ignoring the "field-encompassing" nature of perspectives on history.[98] Iggers sympathetically contends that Troeltsch sought to deal with the threat of relativism in historical judgments.[99] Contemporary biblical scholar John Collins has even produced a thorough defense of contemporary historical criticism from a Troeltschian perspective.[100]

But, on the other hand, many contemporary historians of the Bible are convinced that Troeltsch has gone too far in his positivism.[101] Instead, Stuhlmacher and others would contend that history is much messier, with, for instance, complex causality involved in it and diverse perspectives needed to make sense of it.[102] Barton critiques Troeltsch as a poor secular historian given that he arrives at his historical axioms from the perspective of a theologian and has picked only the more positivistic aspects of

---

96. Harvey, *Historian and Believer*, 15.

97. Harvey, *Historian and Believer*, 17. Krentz echoes this in Krentz, *Historical-Critical Method*, 55.

98. Harvey addresses these particular issues in Harvey, *Historian and Believer*, 204–45.

99. Iggers, "Image," 34–35.

100. Collins, *Bible After Babel*. Support for Troeltsch is found on pp. 5–6. Legaspi contends that Collins picks and chooses the parts of Troeltsch he prefers. Legaspi, "Historical Criticism," 5–7. For another contemporary appropriation of Troeltsch's principle of analogy, see Miller, "Reading the Bible Historically," 357–58. For a contemporary appropriation of correlation within biblical studies, see Deist, "Contingency, Continuity and Integrity," 373–90.

101. Among the critiques mentioned here, see also hints in Perdue, *Collapse*, 19–20n2; Levenson, *Hebrew Bible*, 122–23; Long, "Historiography," 155.

102. Stuhlmacher, *Historical Criticism*, 45–46.

historiography.[103] Although Barton's critique of Troeltsch may contain an *ad hominem* flavor, he is correct that Troeltsch's work is siloed within biblical theology, and it has not been influential in historiography more generally. Krentz, while acknowledging Troeltsch's impact on historical study of miracles within biblical theology and dimensions of his historical theory still at work among historians, demonstrates that these principles have been modified and that contemporary understandings of the mutability of natural laws has affected the way history is written.[104] Indeed, we will see in our penultimate chapter that this is the case.

This brief survey of historical theory after the Enlightenment has shown that, from the mid-nineteenth century on, it is difficult for biblical scholars to avoid questions of history. Not only has the Renaissance already promoted many of the tools of historical study of the Bible, but the Reformation and Enlightenment have slowly created academic space free from ecclesial control over its interpretation, freeing historians of this age to ply their trade on the sacred book. These historians are increasingly professional. And as this profession develops, it becomes self-conscious of its aims and begins to read the Bible with a critical eye, supposedly without recourse to theological truths. This superstructure of secular historical practice with its centrality of human reason, as opposed to church dogma, imposed upon the Bible marks the arrival of full-fledged historical criticism.

We began this chapter by posing the question of where historical criticism came from. Did it originate in the Reformation or the Enlightenment? If anything, it is obvious that historical criticism did not replace previous methods in one fell swoop. Rather, it emerged gradually in fits and starts. Undercurrents of historical criticism, such as text criticism, questions surrounding biblical authorship, and historical veracity appeared in antiquity and the Middle Ages, though historical questions about the Bible clearly do not dominate exegetical discourse. After this period of relative dormancy, we began this chapter by noting the shoots of historical thinking that emerged during the period of the Renaissance. This era was characterized by a renewed interest in recovering the best available texts in textual criticism, linguistic study in classical languages, and even some antiquarian concerns. All of this was done to bring study of any text, and only provisionally the Bible, to the hands of the more practical "historians" and away from the more abstract "philosophers" (to use Valla's terms). In study of

---

103. Barton, *Nature*, 47.
104. Krentz, *Historical-Critical Method*, 55–61.

the Bible this sought to do as all interest in the historical or plain sense had done to this point, namely establish a sound basis for spiritual readings. We can thus point to the Renaissance as the point in which more systematic study of historical facets such as language and geography take on a more systematic tone. The Reformation began to undo any moorings the text had from church authority, even if it later meant in the Enlightenment that the text could be studied apart from any confession at all. Still the Bible belonged to the church (that is the universal church, if not the ecclesial hierarchy) at this point. The Reformation also witnesses to a diminishment of spiritual senses of the text, as scholars pressed the humanist agenda in finding theological meaning embedded in the author's intended meaning. It is in the Enlightenment, however, that we see a superstructure of skepticism introduced onto the text, such that historical skepticism could be primary even to a committed Christian or Jew. In our next chapter, we will see the full fruits of biblical study unhitched from dogmatic concerns.

4

The Normalization of Historical Criticism

BY THE LATE NINETEENTH century, historical criticism had become nearly synonymous with biblical criticism itself.[1] Given the dominance of historical criticism in the study of the Bible in this period, it will be necessary at this point to provide less a chronological overview of historical criticism than an examination of the notable ways in which historical criticism manifested itself over the next hundred years. Up to the middle of the twentieth century, historical criticism became the norm by which biblical criticism thrived. With historical criticism becoming the figural air that biblical critics began to breathe, subfields of historical criticism arose and became refined. Of the major aspects of historical criticism in this period, we will review the disciplines that become the most fully developed by the middle of the twentieth century: archaeology, comparison, textual criticism, source criticism, redaction criticism, form criticism, the quest for the historical Jesus, and the approach that seeks to integrate these into the life of faith, the Biblical Theology Movement.

---

1. For the merging of "biblical criticism" with "historical criticism," see Barton, *Nature*, 1–3.

Archaeology

New horizons opened to western academics slowly throughout the Middle Ages. The Crusades enabled Europeans to rediscover Aristotle, contributing to the emergence of scholasticism. Exploration and colonialism pried open new worlds in some instances and renewed old connections between East and West. During the Renaissance, antiquarians collected and studied artifacts assembled from these strange lands. In the nineteenth century, Napoleon's incursion into Egypt led to the discovery of the Rosetta Stone (later deciphered by Champollion), and British colonial interests in the Near East promoted Sir Henry Rawlinson's (1810-95) efforts to copy and decode the Behistun Inscription. We have already mentioned the geographic concerns of biblical interpreters, which were further bolstered by Charles Robinson's (1794-1863) visits to Palestine and the establishment of the Palestine Exploration Fund to further investigate biblical lands. Charles Warren's (1840-1927) PEF mission and the discovery of "Warren's Shaft" in Jerusalem constituted a boost for early biblical archaeology.[2]

In addition, archaeology of biblical lands in general had already been well under way with discoveries from Mesopotamia (with the most notable being Austen Henry Layard's (1817-94) excavations beginning in 1845 at Ashurbanipal's palace), and it received an extraordinary boost in popularity from the 1922 discovery of Tutankhamun's tomb by Howard Carter (1874-1939). In 1872, British Museum Assyriologist George Smith (1840-76) gave a famous lecture in which he described his encounter with cuneiform tablets he was piecing together, fragments that revealed a flood story similar to that found in Genesis 6-9. Smith's discovery of the Mesopotamian flood story (we now know from its Sumerian Atrahasis version and the Utnapishtim version in the Epic of Gilgamesh) launched a new era of comparison, in which biblical texts were set alongside ancient Near Eastern texts.[3] Friedrich Delitzsch, assessing these myriad newly encountered texts, gave an address in 1902 entitled "Babel and Bible," in which he asserted the intellectual and moral inferiority of the Hebrew Scriptures.[4] Controversial in its time (not to mention today), Delitzsch's popular lecture ignited a firestorm of comparative studies between the Bible and ancient

---

2. For a helpful introduction, see Cline, *Biblical Archaeology*, 13-16.

3. Smith, "Chaldean Account," 213-34. See also Schreiner and Holland, *Silhouettes*, 1-2.

4. Arnold and Weisberg, "Centennial Review," 441-57.

Near Eastern literature. Especially as new texts emerged from across the world, even outside of the Near East, every segment of the Hebrew Bible, especially creation narratives, legal material, poetry, and prophecy, became fair game for comparison to outside texts.

Rapidly, archaeological knowledge of the biblical world spread through the efforts of British and French archaeologists (often with nationalistic competition as a backdrop) such as George Adam Smith (1856–1942, not to be confused with the George Smith mentioned above) and Charles Clermont-Ganneau (1846–1923). Ganneau's discovery of the Moabite Stone and Siloam Inscription, in particular, have been massively influential to this day. But in the early period of archaeology, methods for digging were still crude. Gottlieb Schumacher's (1857–1925) excavations at Megiddo, for instance, uncovered a stele of Pharaoh Shishak/Shoshenq in the dig garbage dump, rather than *in situ*. However, techniques improved with the introduction of stratigraphy to biblical archaeology by Sir William Matthew Flinders Petrie (1857–1925), who also was the first to create a standard pottery typology and was the discoverer of the Merneptah Stele.[5]

Contemporary archaeology owes much to the pioneering work of several archaeologists of the postwar period (especially the establishment of the modern nation of Israel in 1948). Polymath archaeologist William Foxwell Albright (1891–1971) refined Petrie's pottery typology and constructed a chronology still in use by archaeologists today. He produced an array of publications in a variety of subfields and helped found the influential American Schools of Oriental research. Dame Kathleen Kenyon (1906–78) incorporated a meticulous method of digging, now known as the "Kenyon-Wheeler method," from her work in European archaeology into biblical archaeology. Her excavations at Jericho during the 1950s, in which she discovered that Jericho's wall was long destroyed by the time the Israelites would have arrived, were shocking to the archeological community once comfortable with confirming biblical events through the efforts of the spade.[6]

The 1944 discovery of the ancient settlement of Qumran and its cache of over fifteen thousand scroll fragments, known as the Dead Sea Scrolls (DSS), have altered the course of both Old and New Testament studies. As for the latter, for which archaeology does not often have occasion to come across significant finds dealing directly with the biblical text, the

---

5. Cline, *Biblical Archaeology*, 16–25.
6. Cline, *Biblical Archaeology*, 30–42.

DSS illuminated the Jewish background of the first century. Presumed to have been a settlement of Essenes, historians have finally uncovered here a deeper understanding of this sect mentioned in Josephus's works but not in the Bible. New Testament scholars have been interested to find that many concepts in the DSS, and even near direct quotations, approximate the teachings of the early church.[7]

Although much smaller in proportion to the number of texts dealing with the Essene community, segments of every Old Testament book, with the exception of Esther, have appeared in digs at Qumran. These fragments represent our oldest witnesses to the texts of the Hebrew Bible, antedating the Greek of Codex Vaticanus by approximately four hundred years and the Hebrew of the Aleppo Codex by approximately a thousand years. It also includes forerunners (known as *Vorlage*) of the Hebrew Masoretic Text, the Samaritan Pentateuch, and Greek Septuagint. From the collections here, textual critics have had a solid basis from which to argue over developments of the textual traditions of the Hebrew Bible.[8]

Textual Criticism

We have already seen that textual criticism of the Bible has been a preoccupation of scholars from Origen, to Erasmus, to Richard Simon, and beyond. Textual criticism, sometimes known as "lower criticism," receives the least controversy from critics of historical criticism due to the antiquity of its practice, the necessity of establishing the correct text for addressing literary and theological questions, and the facts that *realia* such as hard copy, verifiable texts produce. But this does not mean debate is absent in textual criticism. In the Old Testament, for instance, the variety of textual traditions, such as the discrepancy between the Masoretic and Septuagint (which is shorter by almost a third and with rearranged chapters) versions of Jeremiah,[9] lead to disagreements over the trajectory of these traditions and the aims of OT textual criticism.[10] New Testament textual criticism,

---

7. The literature on the DSS is enormous. For the sake of brevity, I suggest Dimant, "Qumran Sectarian Literature," 483–550; Murphy, *Early Judaism*, 167–212.

8. For the texts of the Hebrew Bible discovered at Qumran, see the excellent overview in Tov, *Textual Criticism*, 100–117.

9. Wolters, "Text," 20–21.

10. See Wolters, "Text," 28–37; Tov, *Textual Criticism*, 155–97. Sanders notes that the increasing knowledge of textual differences paved the way for Enlightenment-era critics such as Simon and Astruc. Sanders, "Textual Criticism," 3:228.

by comparison, contains fewer textual traditions from texts written over a shorter period of time, allowing a higher degree of confidence in the critic's ability to uncover the original texts of each book.[11]

Higher Criticism

While the foregoing areas of historical criticism deal with the history of the biblical text in light of external evidence, "higher criticism" involves a more conjectural search for the text's history based on deductions and inferences from the text itself. Mainly this task falls under the rubrics of *source criticism*, the idea that literary sources lie behind the canonical form of the Bible. In New Testament studies, this has meant reckoning with the work of German scholars such as Johann Jakob Griesbach (1745–1812), Christian Gottlob Wilke (1786–1854), Christian Hermann Weisse (1801–66), and Heinrich Julius Holtzmann (1832–1910). Griesbach, a student of Strauss, worked diligently with the manuscript traditions of the Gospels and, from this work, produced a "synopsis" of the Gospels of Matthew, Mark, and Luke. He promoted what would become an eponymous theory that Mark is an abridgement of the other two, and it is therefore difficult to conclude that Mark was in any way divinely inspired.[12] Wilke, on the other hand, contended after close study that the presence of almost all of Mark within Matthew and Luke, as well as the arrangement of this material, suggests instead that Mark was first (what has come to be known as "Markan priority") and the other two Gospels were dependent upon it.[13] Weisse and Holtzmann

---

11. Jongkind notes, "By the end of the nineteenth century, hardly any scholar still accepted the *Textus Receptus* but instead used a critical text constructed on the basis of the oldest known authorities." Jongkind, "Text and Lexicography," 3:276. Kümmel notes that Karl Lachmann was the first to attempt to find the oldest and most reliable text of the New Testament, though he did not have the manuscript evidence at hand that we do today. Kümmel, *New Testament*, 146–47. For a survey of issues involved in New Testament text criticism in the Enlightenment, see Kümmel, *New Testament*, 40–50. As for the differences in Old and New Testament textual criticism, compare the introduction to the 27th edition of the Nestle-Aland New Testament, which contends that this text is not definitive, but is "a stimulus to further efforts toward defining and verifying *the* text of the New Testament" (p. 45, emphasis mine) to Tov's statement that OT textual criticism "aims neither at the compositions written by the biblical authors, nor at previous oral stages, if such existed, but only at that stage (those stages) of the composition(s) which is (are) attested in the textual evidence." Tov, *Textual Criticism*, 288.

12. Kümmel, *New Testament*, 74–75.

13. Kümmel, *New Testament*, 146–48. Kümmel notes that Lachmann had also come to a similar conclusion.

went further by positing that, not only was Mark a source, but that the discourses shared between Matthew and Luke must have a common source (now known as "Q").[14] Kümmel avers that Holtzmann's analysis was so thorough that "the study of Jesus henceforth could not again dispense" with his method of argumentation and analysis.[15]

In Old Testament studies, no name stands out more than that of Julius Wellhausen (1844-1918). Inspired by Ewald, Wellhausen sought to be first and foremost a historian of the biblical text, utilizing linguistic and literary skill to draw conclusions about the history of Israel. By the time he produced his famous *Prolegomena to the History of Israel* in 1878, the concept of many sources lying behind the canonical text had become commonplace. Not only had the pioneering works of Frenchmen Simon and Astruc become influential, but W. M. L. De Wette's (1780-1849) identification of a "D source" behind Deuteronomy[16] and Karl Heinrich Graf's (1815-69) intuition that the priestly material (which Wellhausen identified as "P") was the latest strand of the Pentateuch[17] had influenced Wellhausen to investigate these issues further. The result was the *Prolegomena*, in which Wellhausen formalized the order of the J and E sources (so called because of the German translation of the names for God appearing in each, "Jahweh" in J and "Elohim" in E) as the earliest layers of the text, followed by the D source and finally P.[18] Although Wellhausen stood in a long line of Old Testament scholars identifying these sources and their respective orders,[19] his work stands out in its clarity and sharpness of insight.[20] Wellhausen's thesis

---

14. Kümmel, *New Testament*, 148-52.

15. Kümmel, *New Testament*, 151.

16. Rogerson, "Wilhelm De Wette," 3:237-38; Reventlow, *History of Biblical Interpretation*, 4:235-36. Brettler and Arakaky have recently attributed the popularization of the term "historical-critical" to De Wette, although introduced into Old Testament scholarship by G. L. Bauer. Brettler and Arakaky, "Historical-Critical," 208-11.

17. On Graf's "scholarly eclecticism" and interaction with the perceived sources of the Pentateuch, see Arnold and Schreiner, "Graf and Wellhausen," 3:254-56.

18. Although the entirety of the *Prolegomena* deals with this issue, a convenient summary is found in the introduction, Wellhausen, *Prolegomena*, 1-13. See also Arnold and Schreiner, "Graf and Wellhausen," 3:257-58.

19. See his acknowledgement of those upon whose work he was building in Wellhausen, *Prolegomena*, 10-12. See also Reventlow, *History of Biblical Interpretation*, 4:315.

20. Clements, *One Hundred Years*, 7-12; Rentdorff, "Paradigm," 51-53; Hayes, "History," 34-37. To Wellhausen's own theory, we must add another similar standard literary-historical theory in Bernhard Duhm's argument of three layers of Isaiah. Rentdorff, "Paradigm," 53-54; Reventlow, *History of Biblical Interpretation*, 4:326-34.

was challenged many times, but had become so standard in Old Testament studies that Gordon J. Wenham writes, "Since it was first advocated, there had been some powerful challenges to the documentary hypothesis, but by 1970 these had been forgotten, and everyone who wanted to be thought a serious Old Testament scholar had to believe in J, E, D, and P and in the dates assigned to them by the consensus."[21]

A parallel approach to the history behind the biblical text is found in *form criticism*. This approach holds to the idea that oral traditions underlie the present text, only later to have been written down. Such a concept has its origins in the work of Johann Gottfried Herder (1744–1803), who identified discrete forms of literature that had oral backgrounds.[22] Until Wilke, the oral traditions behind the Gospels had been assumed to account for the discrepancies between them. Form criticism had thereafter primarily been of use for determining the oral backgrounds of stories about Jesus and Jesus' own teachings.[23]

But it is in the study of the Old Testament that we find the pervasive use of form criticism. This is because of the assumed dearth of literacy in ancient Israel and parallels with other "primitive" cultures. The main promoter of form criticism in the study of the Old Testament was Hermann Gunkel (1862–1932), whose work applied form criticism to many parts of the Old Testament. Regarding the "legends" of Genesis, he finds it more about religion than history and asserts that "the overall style of the accounts, in particular . . . can only be understood on the presumption of their oral transmission."[24] In the prophetic works, he used his method to discern prophetic utterances behind the writings of the text itself.[25] And his insights on the Psalms, developed further by Sigmund Mowinckel, suggested that the diligent scholar could identify literary types in the writings.[26] Moreover, a scholar could not only discern genre but also an original

---

21. Wenham, "Pondering the Pentateuch," 116.

22. Kümmel, *New Testament*, 79–82.

23. Hayes and Holladay, *Biblical Exegesis*, 109–11.

24. Gunkel, *Genesis*, viii; Martin Noth (1902–68) also proposed an oral "G" source (for the German *Grundlage*) behind the J and E strands of the Pentateuch. See Wenham, "Pondering," 117–18.

25. Clements, *One Hundred Years*, 57–63.

26. Gunkel, "Fundamental Problems," 57–69. For Mowinckel's seminal work, see Mowinckel, *Psalms*.

Sitz im Leben, a prototypical cultic "situation in life" in which the original utterance appeared.[27]

Both source and form criticism converge in the discipline of *redaction criticism*. This method seeks to uncover the witnesses behind the final form of the text using insights from source and form criticism. But it acknowledges that these sources, whether literary or oral, have been incorporated into a larger literary context containing a multiplicity of sources. The goal, then, is to understand why the author (or "redactor") has placed these sources together and for what purpose. As Lawson G. Stone has described it, redaction criticism has the twin aims of identifying "diversity in origin" of sources on the one hand and a "unity of conception" on the other.[28] Within the New Testament, this means understanding that the evangelists used a variety of sources, but for a specific purpose or emphasis in communicating the details of Jesus' life. This is obvious, for instance, in John's acknowledgement that he is aware of other events in Jesus' life but has composed his gospel "so that you may come to believe" (John 20:31).

In the Old Testament, in which the term "redaction criticism" has come under greater scrutiny, the landmark work is Martin Noth's study of the "Deuteronomistic Historian."[29] Noth connected the histories of Deuteronomy through Second Kings to an exilic-era redactor who sought to explain why YHWH's people had experienced a collapse of their kingdoms. Noth sought to identify the sources behind this history, some of which are explicitly mentioned in the text, but also argued that the editorial comments of the redactor unified these sources to explain a comprehensive history. Although Noth's thesis has undergone severe criticism, it remains one with which contemporary redaction historians must engage before constructing further appraisals.[30] And his approach of looking backwards from the final form of the text to construe a purpose for bringing together disparate materials has undoubtedly changed the way this material is viewed.

---

27. For a helpful introduction to form criticism in the Old Testament, see Tucker, *Form Criticism*. For more on Gunkel's work and legacy, see Reventlow, *History of Biblical Interpretation*, 4:337–58.

28. Stone, "Redaction Criticism," 85–86.

29. Noth, *Deuteronomistic History*; originally published in German in *Überlieferungsgeschichtliche Studien*, 4–110.

30. For a review of scholarship on the Deuteronomistic Historian, see Römer, *So-Called Deuteronomistic History*, 13–43.

The Place of the Past

The Quest for the Historical Jesus

So far, we have discussed what John H. Hayes and Carl R. Holladay call the "history *of* the text." What remains is what they deem the "history *in* the text."[31] In the New Testament, the watershed moment for determining the historicity of the events of the life of Jesus is David Friedrich Strauss's (1808–74) *The Life of Jesus Critically Examined*. Strauss undertook a rational, historical investigation of the events narrated in the Gospels by understanding the mythical and messianic elements within them. His goal was to "restore the dogmatic significance" in the reality of Jesus, taking seriously the historical particularities of one man for the sake of all humanity. He writes that the "absolute sense of Christology . . . is annexed to the person and history of one individual" and that this "is a necessary result of the historical form which Christianity has taken."[32] Strauss further understood the stories of Jesus' life more as recordings of the significance of the events, particularly in their relationship to the Old Testament, than as actual historical events. For instance, the Spirit descending upon Jesus and God's voice speaking from heaven (Luke 3:22) did not actually happen, but something did occur that was construed by the evangelists as such. Strauss's attempt at a historical view of the New Testament was revolutionary, to be sure, but lacked a systematic treatment of Jesus' life as well as understanding of the dynamics of the newfound source criticism.[33]

Strauss's teacher, Ferdinand Christian Baur (1792–1860), however, investigated these sources thoroughly. His approach was not to be influenced by any dogmatic understandings, but only as a "purely historical" undertaking because of the need for a historical basis to religious claims.[34] He began by systematically explaining debates within the early church between the Hebrews and Hellenists (noted by previous commentators), contending that Acts and the epistles reveal debate and doctrinal growth within the early church. With a segmenting and dynamic view of the early church, he later sought to take a thoroughly historical view to the Gospels. He discounted the historical witness of the Gospel According to John and

---

31. Hayes and Holladay, *Biblical Exegesis*, 56–58; italics added.

32. Quoted from Keuss, "David Friedrich Strauss," 3:201.

33. Kümmel, *New Testament*, 120–27; Powell, *Jesus*, 15; Rae, *History and Hermeneutics*, 15; Jodock, "Biblical Interpretation," 177–78; Keuss, "David Friedrich Strauss," 3:196–202; Dunn, "Quest," 3:304; Reventlow, *History of Biblical Interpretation*, 4:250–52.

34. Jodock, "Biblical Interpretation," 3:181.

found Matthew's Gospel to be the most reliable. Yet, even in this Gospel, when Jesus declares he will return soon, Baur's rationalistic impulse pushes him to argue that a historical Jesus could not have said such a thing.[35]

These historical arguments presaged the study now known as the "quest for the historical Jesus." In the early period of this study, a predominant concern became whether Jesus himself preached that he was an eschatological prophet. The defining study came in Albert Schweitzer's (1875–1965) *A Sketch of the Life of Jesus*. Schweitzer determined, through a thorough study of the Last Supper and an acceptance of Matthew's general historicity, that Jesus in fact believed himself, after a series of misunderstandings, to be the Messiah. Schweizer found this in what he determined to be the earliest stratum of the Gospel witnesses and consistent with views of Jewish apocalypticism. Only later did any Hellenistic influence dominate the interpretation of Jesus. Schweitzer's study was welcomed by conservative scholarship, though challenged by the so-called "history of religions" school, which attempted to view early Christianity as consistent with historical development found in other religions and thus not strange and unique.[36]

Schweizer's study engendered a pause in historical Jesus scholarship. He noted that historical Jesus scholars had been trying to construct a Jesus of their own liking and with relevance for their own age. His own attempt was to see Jesus, not as relevant for us, but in history. However, Schweizer contended that the Christ of history is not the same as the Christ of faith.[37] "The truth is," Schweizer writes, "it is not Jesus as historically known, but as spiritually risen with [people], who is significant for our time and can help it."[38] Thus, Schweizer creates the well-known delineation between the "Jesus of history" and the "Christ of faith."

For a time, it became difficult for one to point to Jesus' relevance for us today as a historical figure. Rudolf Bultmann (1884–1976), in response to the little we could say about Jesus historically, promoted an existential view of Jesus, arguing that Jesus' resurrection was a psychological event in the minds of his followers, as opposed to a historically verifiable event. What was important about Jesus for theology, and thus for us today, was

---

35. Kümmel, *New Testament*, 127–43. See also Baird, "Historical Criticism," 3:102–4; Reventlow, *History of Biblical Interpretation*, 4:277–85; Jodock, "Biblical Interpretation," 3:174–84.

36. Kümmel, *New Testament*, 235–44; Powell, *Jesus*, 16–19.

37. Powell, *Jesus*, 16–19.

38. Quoted from Powell, *Jesus*, 19.

not the historicity of what he did, but that he existed.[39] The neo-orthodox view, represented most prominently by Karl Barth (1886–1968), saw questions of historicity as unanswerable in the face of the nature of transcendent revelation.[40] But such views were countered by a historical insistence found in the so-called "second quest" for the historical Jesus initiated by Ernst Käsemann (1906–98). Käsemann contended that the life of Jesus, including his miracles and resurrection, are confessionally found within history, so it is incumbent upon historians (especially faithful ones) to determine the actuality of this history. He writes, "we cannot help being struck by the fact that the Gospels alone present the tidings of the Christ within the framework of the story of the earthly life of Jesus."[41] Because of this, Jesus' earthly life is critical to understand, especially for the faithful who confess a consistent Jesus from his earthly teachings to his resurrection. If the church only speaks of Jesus in theology and not history, "we should be either failing to grasp the nature of the primitive Christian concern with the identity between the exalted and humiliated Lord; or else we should be emptying that concern of any real content, as did the docestists."[42] Käsemann stood on the other side of the horrors of Naziism, noting that Jesus could be, and had been, used to any purpose we wish. If we are to situate Jesus within history, we are limited in the significance we can draw from his life. But, given the advances in archaeology and historiography by the middle of the twentieth century, perhaps we could say more about him than we were able to in the time of Schweizer. For the next few decades, these "new questers" attempted just that, producing myriad works on the historical Jesus, from cataloging the facts of his life about which we can be certain to establishing the likelihood of his authentic sayings.[43]

The study of the historical Jesus reached such a fever pitch by the 1980s that New Testament scholar Robert Funk (1926–2005) convened hundreds of scholars for the controversial "Jesus Seminar." The seminar occurred over several years involving three phases with a revolving roster of biblical scholars to assess the state of studies on the historicity of Jesus. The first phase involved judging the historicity of Jesus's teachings; the second

---

39. Powell, *Jesus*, 18; Rae, *History and Hermeneutics*, 24–28; Harvey, *Historian and Believer*, 164–68.

40. Rae, *History and Hermeneutics*, 28–30; Harvey, *Historian and Believer*, 153–59.

41. Käsemann, "Problem," 21.

42. Käsemann, "Problem," 46.

43. Powell, *Jesus*, 19–22; Rae, *History and Hermeneutics*, 30–33.

dealt with the veracity of basic claims about Jesus' life; and the third outlined individual scholarly perspectives on who Jesus was. The seminar was widely reported in the media, applauded by some, and scoffed at by orthodox and conservative New Testament scholars.[44] Regardless of one's view of the outcomes of the Seminar, it was evident that a historical understanding of Jesus had become the most significant question on the intersection of history and the Bible by the late twentieth century.

Biblical Theology Movement

Although the twentieth century marks some skepticism, especially in the New Testament program, the results of historical criticism more positively impacted studies on the Old Testament. Advances in archaeology had prompted confidence in the faith claims of the Bible. In the postwar U.S., this led to the so-called "Biblical Theology Movement." Archaeologists like Albright, G. Ernest Wright (1909–74), and John Bright (1908–95) married the spade and the text to demonstrate a continuity between Israel's past and confessions of faith that met its fulfillment in Christianity. The most well-known example of this school of thought is Bright's *History of Israel*, in which he concludes that the Old Testament is a history that witnesses to Israel's faith, and this "salvation history" (*Heilsgeschichte*) has a "destination" in "Christ as his gospel."[45] Similarly, G. Ernest Wright describes his theology of the Old Testament as

> theology of recital or proclamation of the acts of God, together with the inferences drawn therefrom. These acts are themselves interpretations of historical events, or projections from known events to past and future, all described within the conceptual frame of one people in a certain historical continuum.

Thus, the Old Testament is for Wright a repository of faith claims based on events in human history. History then is "the chief medium of revelation" in Israel in contrast to an emphasis on God's revelation in mere speech.[46] Wright and the other adherents to the Biblical Theology Movement in the English-speaking world countered the mythical interpretations of the Bible

---

44. Powell, *Jesus*, 65–81; Rae, *History and Hermeneutics*, 21–23. For further assessment and criticism of the New Quest, see Harvey, *Historian and Believer*, 164–203.

45. Bright, *History of Israel*, 458–64. Quote from p. 464.

46. Bright, *History of Israel*, 12–13.

The Place of the Past

with Israel's claims, now backed up by the work of the archaeologist, that God operated in human history.

Concurrently in Germany, Walter Eichrodt (1890–1978) and Gerhard von Rad (1901–71) produced dense Old Testament theologies merging cutting-edge historical and linguistic knowledge with confessional theology. Eichrodt's *Theology of the Old Testament*[47] viewed the events and confessions of the people of Israel through the lens of covenant. This viewpoint unifies Israel's history in a way that was lacking in earlier studies, attempting to trace the development of Israel's confession over time. But history remains at the forefront. And this history assists the Christian in discovering how the Old Testament serves Christian doctrine. Eichrodt contends that "OT theology presupposes the history of Israel. Nevertheless, in so far as the spiritual history of Israel has brought about a drastic remodelling of many religious ideas, the right way to make allowance for this is *to have the historical principle operating side by side with the systematic in a complementary role.*"[48]

Von Rad also sees a natural connection between the Old Testament and history. "History becomes word and word becomes history," he writes.[49] The history von Rad is concerned with, in particular, is the tradition of confessions about God's acts. "When the Old Testament is allowed to speak for itself, in the end it always confronts us with an event, an act of God either past or future."[50] Thus von Rad is not concerned with tracing a theme throughout the Old Testament, as Eichrodt is, but rather with a confession of what God has done in his *Heilsgeschichte*. Neither is von Rad necessarily interested in reconstructing historical events as Bright does. Instead, von Rad is concerned with how Israel expressed its faith in various ways, confessions originating in original "little creeds" such as Deuteronomy 6:20–25.[51]

---

47. Eichrodt, *Theology I*; Eichrodt, *Theology II*.

48. Eichrodt, *Theology*, 1:25–35. Quote from p. 32. See also Brueggemann, *Theology*, 27–31, 38–42.

49. Rad, *Old Testament Theology*, 2:358.

50. Rad, *Old Testament Theology*, 2:368.

51. Rad, *Old Testament Theology*, 1:121–28. For a connection to Gunkel's ideas of orality, see Rentdorff, "Paradigm," 55–60. Wright mentions the same passage with the note that "a belief so ancient and so entrenched will admit of no explanation save that Israel actually escaped from Egypt to the accompaniment of events so stupendous that they were impressed forever on her memory." Bright, *History*, 122. This claim surely does not satisfy the historian because it is a special case of question begging. For a summary of von Rad, see Perdue, *Collapse*, 45–68; Brueggemann, *Theology*, 31–42.

Will It Always Be This Way?

These Old Testament theologians demonstrate, if nothing else, that historical criticism had become part and parcel of biblical exegesis by the middle twentieth century. If one was to study the Bible, one had to be aware of disciplines that looked *behind* the text's construction and portrayal of events. As we have seen, this was not a straightforwardly secular exercise, but had massive import in theology. The rise of historical criticism meant that the text was no longer considered so authoritative as to be beyond question. Instead, the Bible became subject to myriad investigations concerning its veracity and origins. For some, this has been a welcome freeing of the text from ecclesial power. For others, historical criticism undermines the power the faithful had found within the text itself. Regardless, historical criticism, by the middle of the twentieth century, seemed here to stay.

Still, with historical criticism becoming the dominant mode of exegeting the text, biblical scholars had missed the proverbial forest for the trees. On the one hand, they had unlocked exciting new studies on the most significant collections of books in the western world. They had given voice to scribes, redactors, and historical actors whose voices had been lost. They were even able to challenge the hegemony of ecclesiastical authorities who had held sway over the text for almost two millennia. But, on the other hand, their enthusiasm had relegated some of the most vital issues, those that had made the Bible as significant as it had become. Ronald E. Clements points this out in his assessment of historical criticism's dominance over the field of biblical studies:

> Once the goal of a critical historical approach to the literature of the Old Testament has been embraced it becomes a leaven which transforms everything. No part of the literature can be left unexamined, and everything becomes subject to review. That this has resulted in the emergence of a picture of the origins of the literature, and the course of Israelite-Jewish history in which it was produced, which differs greatly from that which had previously been upheld by Jewish and Christian tradition is incontrovertible. It was inevitable that this should have proved disconcerting to the faith of many, and it is not unreasonable to claim that at first many in the Christian church felt that such a critical attitude could be tolerated more readily in respect of the Old Testament than the New. This, if it were true of some, was a misplaced attitude of complacency, for the rigours of historical and literary criticism do not, and cannot,

cease at the last page of the Old Testament. Nevertheless such a historical-critical approach is not an end in itself, but merely a means by which some further end can be achieved. To know when the Old Testament literature arose, what were its sources, and what light it brings to bear upon the history of the people from whom it emerged, are simply preliminary tasks towards understanding the life and religion of these people themselves. In many ways this fact was lost sight of by many of the leading scholars of the late nineteenth century who saw the historical enterprise very much as constituting the primary goal. History was elevated to become the queen of the Old Testament sciences. Such scholars shared a conviction that historical truth was of a purer and nobler kind than the truths about the Bible which theologians had previously canvassed. It was more or less assumed to be the fullest meaning of scripture.[52]

In the final analysis, historical criticism became so appealing that it was the norm for biblical criticism for the period spanning the mid-nineteenth to mid-twentieth centuries. By the end of this period historical criticism had become so speculative and overused in the eyes of many that it had fallen victim to the same fervor that brought the downfall of allegorical exegesis during the Reformation. In the following chapter, we will discuss how historical criticism was challenged. We will see that its critics come both from inside religious institutions and from without. Historical criticism failed to give full voice to the synagogue's and the church's requirements of Scripture. Furthermore, the obsession with historical issues met resistance in twentieth-century analyses of the purposes and limitations of *any* written text, not simply the Bible. Following a study of these critiques, we will see how historical criticism has arisen from these challenges scarred but still alive and well, and, more importantly, claiming that it still has value.

---

52. Clements, *One Hundred Years*, 143–44.

5

The Critique of Historical Criticism

THUS FAR WE HAVE presented the rise and dominance of historical criticism over the field of biblical studies. Yet, historical criticism's hegemony began to wane after the middle of the twentieth century. Currents present in many disciplines, including literature, philosophy, and history, began to infiltrate biblical studies and undermine historical criticism's influence. In this chapter, we will investigate the counterclaims of these disciplines against traditional historical inquiry and how they ultimately seeped into biblical studies and, most especially, biblical theology. Moreover, we will see that many who accept the normative claims of the Bible for theology have found the results of historical criticism insufficient for the life of the synagogue and church. The payoff from Lessing's "broad, ugly ditch" came to be recognized among many interpreters as they asked whether historical questions were relevant to the life of faith at all.

Literature

Perhaps the most logical place to begin our investigation of the challenges against historical criticism is not with history per se, but with literature. After all, for the scholar, the Bible is first words on a page that only then provide a window to the past.[1] And easily the most prominent movement

---

1. Barton, "Historical Criticism," 5–8.

in literary criticism of the twentieth century was a move *away* from viewing any literature as an artifact to be historically dissected, and *toward* its status as a literary thing of itself.

The twentieth-century scholarly movement of New Criticism, also known as "formalism," stands apart as a means of investigating literature as literature. Among the most notable contributors to this school is the great poet T. S. Eliot, but its most prominent systematic theory is laid out in the famous essay on "The Intentional Fallacy" by W. K. Wimsatt Jr. and Monroe C. Beardsley.[2] We have seen that assumptions about the priority of authorial intention in the interpretation of biblical texts goes back to the ancient period and was vigorously promoted by John Calvin. But the "intentional fallacy" as put forth by Wimsatt and Beardsley upended this long-held view for many literary critics, having a significant impact on biblical scholarship. Wimsatt and Beardsley contend that "the design or intention of the author is neither available nor desirable as a standard for judging the success of a work of literary art."[3] The reasons for such a strong judgment on the intention of a literary work is that such authorial intention is rarely, if ever, available, that a poem (the main focus of their criticism) gains its meaning from a *speaker* rather than the author behind it, and that an author may not be able to clearly inscribe intention as such into a text. Thus, the critic's understanding of the author becomes, at best, a secondary consideration to the art on the page.[4]

Continental philosophers, a group to which we will soon turn, have tightened the proverbial screws on authorial intention. The philosopher and literary critic Roland Barthes sees New Critics as only "consolidating" the author, and he went so far as to claim the "death of the author." The author has died, not in the sense that a text never had a writer (for this, he uses the term "scriptor"), but in denying that the key to a text lies in understanding the creator beyond a text.[5] He writes, "As soon as a fact is *narrated* no longer with a view to acting directly on reality but intransitively, that is to say, finally outside of any function other than that of the very practice of the symbol itself, this disconnection occurs, the voice loses its origin, the author enters into his own death, writing begins."[6] The author then is the

---

2. Wimsatt and Beardsley, "Intentional Fallacy," 1–18.
3. Wimsatt and Beardsley, "Intentional Fallacy," 1.
4. See also Longman, "Literary Approaches," 105–7.
5. Barthes's essay "The Death of the Author" is found in *Image–Music–Text*, 142–48.
6. Barthes, *Image–Music–Text*, 142.

"past of his own book... on a single line divided into a *before* and an *after*."[7] But the result is that the reader of the text is then born from the death of the author,[8] freeing the text to be understood apart from its burdensome past.

Michel Foucault similarly views the decline of the author as a liberative act for the reader. "There seems to be an important dividing line," he writes, "between those who believe that they can still locate today's discontinuities in the historico-transcendental tradition of the nineteenth century and those who try to free themselves once and for all from that tradition."[9] Falling on the latter side of this divide, Foucault understands authorship as a "discursive construct" with a "very particular mode of being."[10] Authorship has, for Foucault, a history in legal responsibility, particular to a certain moment in western culture. The marking of authorship as a construct is seen in "specific and complex operations" and has a dubious connection to a real individual given the arbitrariness of the self and naming.[11] Foucault ends his essay with a pointed and simple question: "What difference does it make who is speaking?"[12] It seems that the persona behind the text is a distraction to real textual understanding.

If these critics are correct, the proclamation of the death of the author is a game-changer for biblical studies. Especially given that exegetes, even long before modernity, had attributed intention to an author, how might exegetes be freed to read the Bible if we are not constrained to discovering anonymous authors, their conceptual worldview, and their elusive motives? For some, this is a liberating reading of texts long confined to limited interpretation in the church and synagogue authorities. For others, the prospect of an utterly free biblical text is frightening.[13]

Similarly, the phenomenon of "reader-response" theories has focused on the interplay between the text and its consumer or recipient. Here, the critic looks less to what one can find forensically behind a text instead to what the text does to its readers. Stanley Fish, for instance, contends that

---

7. Barthes, *Image–Music–Text*, 145.
8. Barthes, *Image–Music–Text*, 148.
9. Foucault, "What Is an Author?," 209.
10. Foucault, "What Is an Author?," 209.
11. Foucault, "What Is an Author?," 211–16.
12. Foucault, "What Is an Author?," 222.
13. For a deep dive into the death of the author and its implications in biblical studies, see Vanhoozer, *Is There a Meaning?*, 43–97.

"interpretation is the only game in town,"[14] a proposition possible because facts about texts lead us into inexhaustible argument that "emerge only in the context of some point of view."[15] Such a point of view becomes the dominant mode of studying what a text means, as it is more tangible than some ethereal, bygone author. A natural line of investigation here is to study the impact of texts on individual readers or groups of readers into a "history" of reception—a history about what the text has done to its readers as opposed to a history of the text as artifact.[16]

Edgar V. McKnight has applied this theory specifically to biblical readings and found that, in order for the unity of the text to be maintained and the sacredness of Scripture discovered, the reader must recognize and respond to a relationship with the biblical text. Just as the triune God is revealed in a relationship, so the sacred truth of the Bible is revealed in a relationship with the text.[17] He contends,

> The biblical text shares the inability of the literary text to present fully what it represents. The Bible as Word cannot be identified with the words; yet, there is a relationship. There must never be an easy identification, but there need be no divorce. The experience of the reader and the actualization of biblical texts, then, may be seen in some sense as an experience of ultimacy.[18]

The import of these newer theories for historical criticism of the Bible has been for many, though certainly not all, scholars to place more emphasis on the literary artistry of the text and its reception among both religious and ideological groups than upon an archaeology of the text's construction. As for the former, Robert Alter's works stand out as an attempt to literarily analyze the canonical form of the biblical text. His *The Art of Biblical Narrative* and *The Art of Biblical Poetry* remain as exemplars of literary readings of the biblical text. Although Alter does not find historical readings pointless,

---

14. Fish, *Is There a Text?*, 355.
15. Fish, *Is There a Text?*, 388.
16. Longman, "Literary Approaches," 105–7.
17. McKnight, *Post-Modern*, 263–67. Despite the title, I do not find McKnight's book "postmodern." Although he utilizes many postmodern concepts, he still positively incorporates works by Eco and Hirsch, and he does not run from the unity and stability of the biblical text at many points. However, he notes on p. 14 that he has written this for those who have tired of the then-dominant historical and literary criticisms.
18. McKnight, *Post-Modern*, 265–66.

he finds the final witness of the text a "transhistorical textual community" worthy of study for its own sake.[19]

Stephen Prickett emerges among many others to emphasize that the Bible is a text with a significant reception history that has promulgated more powerful readings than the dominant interpretations of historical criticism. Prickett writes,

> In accepting a particular biblical story—such as, say, that of Elijah on Horeb—as primarily a verbal event, a linguistic happening, one also necessarily accepts it as a "historical" event in the sense that it comes to us with a subsequent critical history. In what it implies about nature and transcendence, for instance, it may well be taken to indicate a decisive and even historic shift in human consciousness that would take centuries (or even millennia) of commentary, midrash, and translation, to be assimilated into the cultural life of the community—in this case, of course, affecting no longer a single linguistic group, but eventually the whole of Judeo-Christendom (considered as a single cultural-linguistic entity).[20]

Thus, the study of the text's history shifts from the history behind the text to the history of what the text has done to others. What becomes most important in a reading of the Bible is how the Bible has been interpreted and appropriated by the synagogue, the church, women, oppressed minorities, and groups of any other religion or ideology. Not only are these readings more accessible than those of the author's original intentions, but they are more palpable for those of us who stand on this side of the biblical text's creation.

One might even argue that the search for an author should not apply to biblical research to begin with. After all, most of the Bible's authors are anonymous. And even when they are not anonymous, serious debate exists as to whether many of the texts were written pseudonymously. Further, the mere fact of pseudonymous writings implies that texts were written by and for certain communities (as opposed to individuals). Given that Jews and Christians of the church catholic still read these texts as addressed to their life and faith, the texts still speak to those communities. So then, shouldn't the meanings of those texts remain on the communities who produced and continue to interpret them? Against authorial intention in the Bible, Sandra Heinen writes,

19. Alter, *Canon and Creativity*, 5.
20. Prickett, *Words*, 34.

> The intentional fallacy, as described by Wimsatt and Beardsley, poses no risk where historical authors and their actual intentions are unidentifiable; and a strong model of authorship, attacked by Barthes and Foucault for its ideological implications, cannot adequately describe the relationship between the Bible and the individuals who contributed to its emergence. Because the Hebrew Bible has no traceable authors but is the result of narratives being handed down over the centuries, which in this process were subjected to repeated revisions, its authorship must be conceptualized as collective and successive rather than individual.[21]

Heinen thus contends that we think of an "author construct," which aids us in considering the fact that the author conveys a particular image about himself, not an objective and dispassionate version of himself, in writing. There is thus an "image of the historical authors who are behind the staging."[22] A plus for readers of faith is that such a reading leaves room for divine inspiration in biblical writing and that the author's control over the text is limited to a certain extent.[23] That is, the restricted authority of a human person over the text creates more space for God to work with the words created by the author and received by the community to which it is addressed. This thus stands as a tantalizing fusion of literary theory and an elusive search for the mystery of divine inspiration in Scripture.

At stake behind these criticisms of the Bible from a literary perspective is the extreme emphasis historical criticism has laid upon authors. In traditional higher criticism, we search both for authors of sources and authors who integrated these sources into the final text. More speculatively, in form criticism, we posit authors *and* speakers who follow conventional literary and spoken forms to produce the utterances we now find in the text.[24] How should biblical scholars then proceed once we have proclaimed the "death" of those who produced, or even spoke, the words of the Bible?

We see, therefore, that literary trends of the twentieth century have impacted the way we interpret the Bible. Literary critics have cast doubt on

---

21. Heinen, "Exegesis Without Authorial Intention," 15.
22. Heinen, "Exegesis Without Authorial Intention," 18.
23. Heinen, "Exegesis Without Authorial Intention," 19–20.

24. This was of acute concern to Jamie Muilenburg in his momentous reframing of historical criticism, which became the genesis of "rhetorical criticism." See Muilenburg, "Form Criticism," 6. For further analysis, see Brueggemann, *Theology*, 53–59. Longman notes Muilenburg as a predecessor to Alter's approach. Longman, "Literary Approaches," 98n3.

the possibility that we can know an author and especially an author's intentions. What has become primary, in turn, is *the text itself* and not the world *behind* that text, which includes the author. Although not all interpreters would go so far as to eliminate the author, literary studies have cast doubt on the author's primacy. This remains a difficult obstacle for historians of the text who wish to study these authors and how they constructed a text.

Postmodernism

Tangential to the literary challenges of authorial intention is the concurrent philosophical movement of postmodernism. As an "anti-foundationalist" approach, postmodernism resists firm definition.[25] It may be best described as a reaction against Enlightenment modernity, with its claims of certainty and objectivity in all realms of knowledge, from language, to history, to science.[26] Postmodernism then takes various approaches to undermine the confidence we have in certain knowledge about what words mean, what actually happened in the past, or whether a dominant interpretation of any text can stake a claim for truth. Such "deconstruction" is not necessarily aimed at finding enjoyment in tearing down the world we thought we knew, but typically intends to liberate our readings of all kinds of texts from being dominated by any singular interpretation. The implications for biblical studies are clear and confrontational, challenging historical criticism's claims to come to some clear understanding of how the Bible was produced and, consequently, how it ought to be interpreted. Aichele, Miscall, and Walsh define a postmodernist approach to the biblical text as characterized by "diversity in both method and content and by an anti-essentialist emphasis that rejects the idea that there is a final account, an assured and

---

25. Adam, *Postmodern*, 5; Bell, *Ruled Reading*, 11.

26. For postmodernism defined as reaction "against," see Collins, *Bible After Babel*, 11–17; Perdue, *Reconstructing*, 239–45; Aichele et al., "Elephant," 397. I choose this more broad definition as opposed to the more atomized one proposed by Ronald Hendel. Hendel distinguishes between the "strong" postmodernism of Foucault and Derrida that radicalize Nietzsche's critiques of rationality and humanism and the "weak" postmodernism that "accepts this critique but also maintains the practical reality of reason and human agency." Hendel, "Mind the Gap," 423. In attempting to be charitable to postmodernists, I find strong postmodernist claims about reality are not as radical as the straw-man arguments against them when pressed by their critics. Further, the concern in this chapter is the effect of postmodernism on historical criticism of literary works, not ontology. Finally we must mention that Derrida and Foucault did not explicitly take up the mantel of postmodernism. Moore, "Watch the Target," 446.

agreed-on interpretation, of some one thing—here the biblical text or any part of it."[27] Thus, the various postmodern approaches challenge the traditional methodologies we have so far described as dominating the field of biblical studies in the nineteenth and twentieth centuries.

Jacques Derrida's deconstruction of language stability comprises a foundational attack on the certainty of all language, biblical language included. Derrida's "post-structuralism" veers against the "structuralist" semiotics of Ferdinand de Saussure, who argued for tight relationships between words (as "signs") and the meanings they entail (the "signified").[28] Derrida contends that signs do not directly correlate to meanings, such that language, in itself, is not stable. The best way to determine a meaning is only by its dissimilarity (Derrida's *differance*) from what it is not.[29] So the best way to understand a biblical word such as *Shalom* is not by using more words to cataphatically ascribe more meaning to it; but only that it is not something else, namely "chaos." Therefore, words do not have some fixed, abstract meaning and all semantics are up for debate, only gaining meaning in apophatic distinction and perhaps "material practices."[30] Summing up Derrida's philosophy is his rallying cry that there is "no world outside the text," also translated as, "there is no outside text."[31] This not to say that the "real world" does not exist; only that our communication about this world is expressed in language, and that this language is inherently elusive.

So, for biblical scholars, whose object of study is a text, postmodernism challenges whether we can speak confidently of a world beyond this text. Even the seemingly infallible criteria of studying the historical context of a biblical text in order to make sense of its claims is under scrutiny.[32] In a system of uncertain verbal meaning, how can historical critics posit an "author"? How can they provide meaningful historical context to a biblical passage? Using Derridean concepts, the postmodern biblical scholar A. K. M. Adam writes,

---

27. Aichele et al., "Elephant," 384.

28. On Saussure, see McKnight, *Post-Modern*; Silva, *Biblical Words*, 35–38.

29. Derrida explores these concepts in many places, but for the sake of brevity, see Derrida, *Of Grammatology*, 6–26.

30. Quote from Jenkins, "Postmodern Reply," 191. See also Perdue, *Reconstructing*, 245–46.

31. Derrida, *Grammatology*, 158.

32. Clark, *History, Theory, Text*, 130–55.

> First, the presence of deconstructive biblicists in the academy and the church will mean abandoning the illusion that there is something behind or within the biblical texts that we might get at by way of sufficient research or the right method. We will have to distance ourselves from most of the metaphors for interpretation that we have woven into our disciplinary identities; no longer will we argue over whether the text is a window through which we look into the past, or a mirror in which we see only our own reflection. We will not try to locate the world behind the text, or the world in the text, or the world in front of the text. We will not talk about extracting meaning from the text. We will explain the title we bear—"exegete"—not from the (misleading) etymology... of a text; instead we will point out that the epithet exegetes . . . as typically applied to a leader or advisor. Where modern critics delve into the text to get something out of it, we will now acknowledge that meaning—to the extent there is such a thing—does not inhere in a text any more than it might inhere in a dream. . . . Meaning is what we make of texts, not an ingredient in the texts.[33]

Such a proposal leaves little-to-no room for the techniques of historical criticism, and purposely so. The dominance of historical criticism, in Adam's view, has tended to control the narrative of meaning without examining its own presuppositions and perspectives.[34] If there is anything to make of what is "behind" the texts, it is only through our own reflection "in front of the text." There is thus no objective past. Such realization should free readers from the domination of traditional historical criticism toward other readings "in front" of them.

Other postmodernists have pressed this liberative dimension, further critiquing traditional views of the past. Jean-François Lyotard notably deconstructed modern "metanarratives," arguing that all knowledge is grounded in mythic narrative requiring faith and is not objective and scientific in nature.[35] Foucault's work on mental illness revealed the way modernist culture has shaped our truths about a seemingly objective narrative toward a solution to certain societal ills.[36] These are only a few of the

33. Adam, *Postmodern*, 32–33.

34. Adam, *Postmodern*, 46–47.

35. Lyotard's most well-known work in English appears in Lyotard, *Postmodern Condition*. I am also indebted to the clarifying work of James K. A. Smith's treatment of Lyotard in Smith, *Who's Afraid of Postmodernism?*, 59–79, and Perdue, *Reconstructing*, 246–47.

36. Foucault, "Madness in Society," 370–76. See also Perdue, *Reconstructing*, 247–48.

noteworthy examples of how postmodernism has attempted to undercut our confidence in truths once proclaimed throughout the Western world. Once more, Adam sums up the postmodern frustration with historical certainties:

> There is no "the past" to be found. Once again, as with "author's intention," so with "the past": when a modern interpreter insists that the historical record of the past makes his interpretation of a text the best, he is always only talking about his own interpretation of that historical record. "The past" changes every time a historian mounts a successful rhetorical campaign to persuade people of one or another account of the past: modern interpreters who claim otherwise mystify the connection between the past they claim to be really true with the past reconstructed in their own work.[37]

We can see the aims of postmodernism struggling against the footings of the dominant academic movements of the Enlightenment and beyond. And the application of these theories to biblical criticism, itself a discipline severely affected by the ideas of modernism, has prompted challenges all biblical scholars must address. Although it is difficult to say that all postmodernists wish to completely do away study of the past *per se*,[38] we are left at the least with the claim of Martti Nissinen that "the challenge of postmodernism has forced historians to interrogate their methods of interpretation and encounter their own subjectivity."[39]

Effects on the General Discipline of History

Much of what we have discussed already in this chapter had a direct and profound impact on the writing of the general study of history. Here we

---

37. Adam, *Postmodern*, 21.

38. Clark mentions that Derrida, for all his concerns about the world of the text, did not deny the usefulness of historical investigation. Rather, he diligently studied historical contexts and precise textual readings to recover "lost heritages." Further, he found deconstruction to be the "most historical of discourses imaginable." Clark, *History, Theory, Text*, 26–27. See also a debate between two historians, one of whom is postmodernist, about whether a postmodernist would deny the reality of the holocaust. Jenkins, "Postmodern Reply," 190; Evans, *Defense*, 159. See also Aichele et al., "Elephant," 400–401. To me, it seems that Ankersmit is correct in his assessment that postmodernism is first and foremost a "theory of writing" and that the concern with history is about the truthfulness of its discourse. Ankersmit, "Reply to Professor Zagorin," 288.

39. Nissinen, "Reflections," 30.

briefly investigate how critiques against the modern approach to history writing affected historical theory more broadly as a means of thinking specifically about historical criticism of the Bible.

First, the postmodern call for authors to recognize their own perspective in communicating knowledge has a clear application in historical writing. For a full explication of this idea within the philosophy of history, no one voice has exerted more influence than that of Hayden White. White's influential *Metahistory* alerted historians to their own perspectives in writing history. For White, our historical explanations are posterior to our own "linguistic protocols,"[40] which give shape to historical interpretations. Historians must then be cognizant of their own present linguistic stances from which they write about the past.[41] The discipline of biblical studies has certainly suffered from a lack of self-awareness, as recent subversive approaches have revealed to us. Truly, historians of any subject often remain blind, not only to their linguistic protocols, but to their entire *Weltanschauung*, which can even dictate evidence the historian chooses to include. And in our present social climate, it might be wise for historians to acknowledge their worldviews in order to assist readers who do not know authors apart from their names on the book cover.[42]

White's call for self-awareness has been picked up by other historians, such as F. R. Ankersmit and Keith D. Jenkins. Ankersmit describes modernist historiography as following "a line of reasoning from his sources and evidence to an historical reality behind the source." By contrast, a postmodernist emphasizes not the past but "other interpretations of the past, for that is what we in fact use evidence for."[43] Similarly, Jenkins pits postmodern history against modernist history, as the latter is "a self-referential,

---

40. White, *Metahistory*, 426. See also Paul Ricouer's incisive analysis of the language use in historical writing that cannot, despite some epistemological breaks, be separated from narrative. Ricouer, *Time and Narrative*, 175–225.

41. Note White's own admission to writing from an "ironic condition" as he understands nineteenth-century European historiography. White, *Metahistory*, 434. Neither is White's observation wholly new, though he is the first (to my knowledge) to expound upon the concept of interpretation in history. For example, Santayana in the early twentieth century; see Santayana, *Life of Reason*, 5:239–40.

42. Day resists such an idea, however. For him, it is part and parcel of writing and reading history to assume that the historian is "not omniscient" and does not hold the only true interpretation. Day, *Philosophy of History*, 179.

43. Ankersmit, "Historiography and Postmodernism," 142–43.

The Place of the Past

problematic expression of 'interests,' an ideological discourse without any 'real' access to the past as such."[44]

For Ankersmit, there are no underlying causes to trace back from the effects, but only effects as primary.[45] And, moreover, these effects are communicated through "opaque" language that leaves history writing as more "art" than science.[46] Jenkins adds that postmodernist historians are not all antirealists, but "they are *all* antirepresentationalists."[47]

Jenkins takes up the Lyotardian approach to metanarratives by referring to history writing as the "creation of 'reality-effects' performatively constituted through various symbolic codes."[48] Another postmodern historian, Nancy Partner, similarly understands such "reality-effects" in the vein of fiction and contends, "The meaning of history depends on the meaning of fiction, not the other way around because fiction is analytically prior."[49] These approaches further stress history writing as more "memory" than something objective,[50] and in so doing point to a focus on memory in contrast to history that we will take up in the next chapter.

In these historians' works, we see the interweaving of postmodern themes, such as the instability of language, the clouding effect of perspective, and the dominance of one particular perspective (i.e., the modernist one) over the way we have told history in the past several hundred years. The effect of postmodernism on history has not been a fringe movement. Rather, one influential textbook on historical theory has absorbed the criticisms of postmodernism on history to argue that it has helped to "revitalize discussion about methods, goals, and even the foundations of knowledge."[51] In the wake of postmodernism's impact on history, it seems historians are no longer privileged in telling a singular true story about the past and that any attempt to speak about past realities must at least be done with fear and trembling.

---

44. Jenkins, *On "What Is History?,"* 9.
45. Ankersmit, "Historiography and Postmodernism," 141–42.
46. Ankersmit, "Historiography and Postmodernism," 143–46.
47. Jenkins, "Postmodern Reply," 185.
48. Jenkins, "Postmodern Reply," 184.
49. Partner, "Historicity," 33.
50. Ankersmit, "Historiography and Postmodernism," 142; Icke, *Lost Historical Cause*, 3.
51. Appleby et al., *Telling the Truth*, 226.

The Critique of Historical Criticism in Biblical Theology

Declining confidence in the results of historical investigation of all texts caused biblical theologians to reexamine the profit of historical criticism for the Bible's claims about God and God's people. On the one hand, much secular historical criticism had attacked the historicity of crucial biblical events and persons, leading theologians to either defend the actuality of such events or diminish the importance of historicity in the Bible.[52] Perhaps no more trenchant accusation has been leveled against historical criticism's application for theology on this front than Jon D. Levenson's when he writes that historical critics "are Christians everywhere except in the classroom and at the writing table, where they are simply honest historians striving for an unbiased view of the past."[53]

Indeed, as we have seen, since the Enlightenment and its turn towards the self as the final arbiter of truth, scholars have brought to light the Bible's disunity, its intersections with pagan religions, and the more "rational" explanations of its miracles. All of these have mitigated against the church's and synagogue's teachings and have led to many a crisis in faith. The conundrum for biblical scholars has clearly been, which worldview is prior? The rational, scientific worldview of the Enlightenment? Or the claims of faith? What if Abraham and Moses did not exist? What if Jesus wasn't really born of a virgin and didn't really rise from the dead? For scholars of faith in the historical-critical vein, this impasse typically leads to one of three choices: fideism, renounce one's faith, or continue to strive for a way to hold these two epistemologies together.

For scholars who wish to find this third way to balance faith and rationality in the study of the Bible, on the other hand, another issue arises. The Biblical Theology Movement's confidence in the reality of God's acts portrayed in Scripture pressed other theologians to consider whether historical deeds of God were the total crux of Scripture at all. Encouraged further by the

---

52. A noteworthy example of the effects of a secular historical criticism on biblical theology is seen in Linnemann, *Historical Criticism*. Linnemann's critiques seem especially pertinent for continental biblical criticism with its more narrowly defined view of historical criticism and not as applicable to American scholarship (see Yarbrough's introduction on pp. 8–9). But the dilemma she faced after her conversion, forced to choose between a scientific view of the text and the worldview of the gospel, is one with which even the most introductory students of the Bible must reckon (see p. 17).

53. Levenson, *Hebrew Bible*, 29.

findings of New Criticism and postmodernism, this latter critique of the Biblical Theology Movement revealed several cracks in the foundation of using historical criticism to uncover what the Bible communicates theologically.

A pivotal essay in critiquing the Biblical Theology Movement was Langdon B. Gilkey's "Cosmology, Ontology, and the Travail of Biblical Language."[54] Gilkey argues that the Biblical Theology Movement was at once a reaction against liberal reviews of general revelation, leading to Biblical Theology's emphases on specific acts of God (for Gilkey, the focus is the exodus), and also the adoption of a liberal causality of understanding those events, thus the efforts of scholars within the Biblical Theology Movement to prove their occurrences.[55] Moreover, the language that scholars of the Biblical Theology Movement use to describe God's acts and speech attribute these verbs to God in an anthropomorphic way inconsistent with confessions of God's otherness.[56] What is needed to construct an intelligible biblical theology, instead, is an acknowledgement of our distance from the religion and worldview of the ancient Israelites balanced alongside an attempt to understand their religion and worldview.[57] Thus Gilkey clearly wants to make room for the intention of the biblical authors. He believes our understanding of their intentions can help us to see how they communicated their religion in contrast to our own theological presuppositions in order to construct a more dynamic biblical theology.

Chief among the voices taking theology of the Bible in a new direction was Brevard Childs. In his *Biblical Theology in Crisis*, Childs chronicles the divisions within the Biblical Theology Movement, challenges in viewing revelation in history, the failure of Biblical Theology to unify such a complex tome through certain themes (like covenant), and the inadequacy of describing a "biblical mentality,"[58] among many other critiques.[59] Childs does not wish to dispense with the descriptive task of biblical studies, but he argues that faith-claims must take center stage in order to construct a

---

54. Gilkey, "Cosmology," 194–205.
55. Gilkey, "Cosmology,", 144–45.
56. Gilkey, "Cosmology," 145, 152–53.
57. Gilkey, "Cosmology," 153–54.
58. This critique of the Biblical Theology Movement is evident in Barr's prominent *Comparative Philology*. Here, Barr dispels the theological force behind the word studies common in the movement, which argued for a unique Hebrew mindset in the ancient Near East.
59. Childs, *Biblical Theology in Crisis*, 13–87.

truly prescriptive theology from the Bible.[60] The normative context of this faith is found in the canon of Scripture. Scripture is the backbone of a faith community, interacting with creedal confessions to construct what one believes in religion. So to earnestly confess what a faith community believes the Bible prescribes for faithful living, the descriptive mode of historical study will not do. Rather, we must acknowledge the faith that verifies the final form of the scriptural witness as authoritative. In Childs's words,

> As a fresh alternative, we would like to defend the thesis that the canon of the Christian church is the most appropriate context from which to do Biblical Theology. What does this mean? First of all, implied in the thesis is the basic Christian confession, shared by all branches of historic Christianity, that the Old and New Testaments together constitute Sacred Scripture for the Christian church. The status of canonicity is not an objectively demonstrable claim, but a statement of Christian belief. In its original sense, canon does not simply perform the formal function of separating the books that are authoritative from others that are not, but is the rule that delineates the area in which the church hears the word of God. The fundamental theological issue at stake is not the extent of the canon, which has remained in some flux within Christianity, but the claim for a normative body of tradition contained in a set of books.[61]

Thus to be a "biblical theology," an author must not overlook the role of faith in what constitutes a normative set of Scriptures. As Childs writes, "The most serious objection is that the real task of doing exegesis as a theological discipline has been lost."[62] Although different religious traditions will vary in which texts their canons include and descriptive scholarship will bicker about the formation of the final text, Childs contends that the final form of the text is the most important for biblical theology because it is this particular form that informs the lives of the faithful. Moreover, Childs recognizes that there are markers of diversity within the final form of the text, but a biblical theology must come to terms with the unity of the "common subject matter that is God's good news.[63]" As Mark G. Brett summarizes Childs's view, the final form "bears witness to the full history

---

60. Childs, *Biblical Theology in Crisis*, 92–93.
61. Childs, *Biblical Theology in Crisis*, 99.
62. Childs, *Biblical Theology in Crisis*, 142.
63. Childs, "Reclaiming," 9–11.

of revelation."[64] In short, a biblical theology must come to the recognition that it is shaped from a certain form of the text, the canon.

An important shift in Childs's work is an emphasis on the context studied. Whereas the Biblical Theology Movement attempted to construct a theology from the backside of a text with historical-critical tools, Childs's canonical "approach"[65] sees *the church* as the most appropriate context for biblical theology, since it is the church that has used the canonical text to construct its theology.[66] Childs's view may appear similar to New Critical and postmodernist approaches that look "in front of" the text, and some similarities in taking seriously the text before the reader are evident. But, unlike postmodern literary theories, Childs believes history is still worth engaging. However, instead of the history of the text, it is the history of its *reception* that takes center stage.[67] He does not construct a clear, step-by-step method of *how* to read the canonical form as his focus is more on *that* the canonical form is most important for doing theology. Nonetheless, he does demonstrate what canonical readings might look like in several places.[68]

Further condemnation of the Biblical Theology Movement comes from both Hans Frei and James Barr, who criticized the movement's reading of historical narratives as more "history" than "narrative." Frei's *Eclipse of Biblical Narrative* notably used the term "history-likeness" to describe the character of biblical narrative, a jarring contrast with accepting these narratives as "history" in the way moderns have understood it.[69] This history-likeness is the "direct interaction of character, descriptively communicative words, social context, and circumstance, whether miraculous or not."[70] For Frei, this story, or world, of the text becomes much more important for the theological meaning of the Bible than the events that may or may not lie behind the story. Indeed, in earlier chapters we have seen that the narrative of the story was often taken for granted before the critical

---

64. Brett, *Biblical Criticism in Crisis?*, 63.

65. See Brett's preference for this term in *Biblical Criticism in Crisis?*, 11–12, although Childs does utilize "method."

66. Childs, *Biblical Theology in Crisis*, 141.

67. See Brett, *Biblical Criticism in Crisis?*, 114–15.

68. For instance, see Part III of Childs, *Biblical Theology in Crisis* (pp. 149–219) and his classic introduction, *Introduction to the Old Testament as Scripture*.

69. Frei, *Eclipse*, 10.

70. Frei, *Eclipse*, 321.

period and sometimes referred to as the "historical sense" of the text. Frei notes that the early church handled both "literal" and "figurative" senses of Scripture relatively easily while assuming this posture towards biblical narrative. This unity came apart centuries later as narratives began to be viewed as historical propositions rather than narrative arcs providing the meaning of the text.[71]

In Barr's "Story and History in Biblical Theology," he concurs with Frei's term of history-likeness, finding the Old Testament to be more "story" than "history." "History" is inadequate to describe the biblical text because several parts adhere more closely to myth and legend than history proper, causation alternates between God and humanity, antiquarian motivations can vary from history (such as in an etiology), and the narratives mostly lack critical evaluation and sources.[72] Further, Barr argues that God's revelation in history appears more "on the basis of confessed history rather than on that of critical history,"[73] thus echoing Gilkey's separation of theology and religion.

Although some differences stand between these early voices critical of the Biblical Theology Movement,[74] they converge on the crucial point that the Biblical Theology Movement's attempts to connect history to theology were impotent. Not only do the adherents of the movement fail to fully appreciate what counts as history, they do not take seriously that the synagogue and church have considered the stories that communicate this history to be more relevant to theology than the events those stories narrate, let alone the history of the composition of the texts narrating that history.

A prominent Jewish critique of historical criticism's role in biblical theology comes from Jon D. Levenson, especially in his *Hebrew Bible, the Old Testament, and Historical Criticism*. Levenson argues that the advent of historical criticism undermined the *literary unity* of sacred texts, disabling

---

71. Frei, *Eclipse*, 12. Put differently, Frei writes on p. 280, "It is not going too far to say that the story is the meaning or, alternatively, that the meaning emerges from the story form, rather than being merely illustrated by it, as would be the case in allegory and in a different way, myth."
This point from Frei is taken up by church historian David C. Steinmetz in "Superiority," 27–38. Steinmetz does not completely discount historical criticism, but argues that in order to be fruitful for theology, it must devise "a hermeneutical theory adequate to the nature of the text which it is interpreting" (p. 38).

72. Barr, "Story and History," 7–8.

73. Barr, "Story and History," 10.

74. See, for example, Brett's discussion of Barr's critique of Childs holding together both the canonical process and a final canon, in Brett, *Biblical Criticism in Crisis?*, 118.

The Place of the Past

fruitful dialogue about texts that are foundational to religious traditions. He contends, "the price of recovering the historical context of sacred books has been the erosion of the largest literary contexts that undergird the traditions that claim to be based upon them."[75] Thus, methods such as source or redaction criticism fragment a text such that it no longer becomes the text we use to communicate about religious faith. At the same time, Levenson contends against New Critical and postmodern devaluations of history as a whole and retains the importance of historical contexts of reading.[76] To devalue history would be to ignore the traditions, evident from medieval Judaism, in reading in the plain sense. But his issue is the radical way historical-critical scholars have dismantled the final form of the text, unable to reconstruct anything meaningful for religious dialogue.[77]

Given that this discussion has primarily centered around the Old Testament (although with clear inferences in New Testament theology), it is necessary to mention some ways in which historical criticism has explicitly affected theological readings of the New Testament. David Yeago, for one, stresses the creedal faith that one brings to the New Testament is prior to critical exegesis.[78] To attempt to derive faith claims from the text, as modern historical critics do,[79] rather than to read the text from the perspective of faith, as the church fathers, Thomas Aquinas, and even Luther have done,[80] is to presuppose another superstructure alien to the text. Yeago contends that the best reading is an intertextual one that supports the "content and unity of biblical teaching."[81]

Regarding the "quest for the historical Jesus," Luke Timothy Johnson has denied the significance of the quest, particularly in the late twentieth century, because of "the perpetuation of the notion that history somehow determines faith, and that for faith to be correct, the historical accounts that gave rise to it have to be verifiable."[82] Moreover, the "pattern and meaning" of Jesus as Messiah is palpable throughout early Christian literature, despite

---

75. Levenson, *Hebrew Bible*, 4. See also McKnight, *Post-Modern*, 177–96.
76. Levenson, *Hebrew Bible*, 110–11.
77. Levenson, *Hebrew Bible*, 2.
78. Yeago, "New Testament," 152–64.
79. In this article, Yeago chooses J. D. G. Dunn's reading of the *homoousion* in Philippians 2:10–11 as his foil.
80. Yeago, "New Testament," 152.
81. Yeago, "New Testament," 162.
82. Johnson, *Real Jesus*, 141.

its diversity in other ways.[83] The only "real Jesus" in the New Testament is a resurrected Jesus of faith, because, "The New Testament writings yield some historical information, but that is not what they do best."[84] Although historical discrepancies arise between the four canonical Gospels, these were not deemed as significant as Jesus' identity and work confessed in the creeds. It is such confessions, as we have already seen with Childs's work on the Old Testament, that should be of the greatest concern for theology. Thus, whether in the Old or New Testament, we see in these examples a scholarly push away from a forensic study of the world behind the text and toward the world of the text itself and the world in front of the text, which the text has shaped, in the synagogue and church.

The most recent monograph challenging historical criticism's readings for theology in both the Old and New Testaments is R. R. Reno's *The End of Interpretation: Reclaiming the Priority of Ecclesial Exegesis*.[85] Reno, who serves as the editor of the unapologetically church-focused *Brazos Theological Commentary on the Bible*, defends his series as "anti-Protestant." By this he means that the church's teachings are prior to empirical, "data-anchored" readings of Scripture.[86] As one reads Reno's work, it is clear that Reno refers here to historical-critical methodologies of biblical interpretation that seek to peer behind the text to find answers to quandaries such as what actually happened, how the text arrived in its final form, and why there are variant readings of biblical texts. Although Reno and the series he founded do not reject historical criticism *per se*, they deny historical criticism's final say in matters of interpretation.[87] Instead, the exegetical approaches that hold the most power display "accordance" between how the Bible is interpreted and what the church teaches.[88] Clearly in the same vein as the critiques of interpreters like Childs and Yeago, Reno understands biblical theology to operate best when it is explicitly theological. And because historical-critical

---

83. Johnson, *Real Jesus*, 141–66.

84. Johnson, *Real Jesus*, 167. Johnson does not rule out historical criticism altogether, but contends for an "experience/interpretation" model that "takes seriously the deeply human character of the writings, the experiences and convictions that generated them, and the cultural and historical symbols they appropriate." Historical criticism does not fully encapsulate the purpose of these sacred texts. See pp. 171–74.

85. Reno, *End*.

86. Reno, *End*, 159. With this claim, Reno assumes the origins of historical criticism to be in the Protestant Reformation, a claim that is hotly debated.

87. Reno, *End*, 158.

88. Reno, *End*, 1–50.

The Place of the Past

methodologies cannot hold their focus on the final form of the text,[89] they cannot speak to what the text is finally about and the community to which it speaks. For this reason, Reno rejects "efforts to 'build bridges' between theology and biblical studies."[90] Rather, biblical scholars concerned with theology must submit to the will of theologians, who know the *telos* of Scripture better than they.[91] In brief, historical-critical approaches to the Bible's theology are not theological enough.[92]

In the wake of such devastating critiques of the Biblical Theology Movement and the confidence of historical criticism to construct faith claims, Leo G. Perdue proclaimed a "collapse" of history within the theological study of the Bible.[93] This collapse is not total, and the criticisms of history have not been without their own flaws,[94] but it represents a shift from the "epistemological rule" of historical criticism.[95] Although Perdue attempts to strike a conciliatory tone between history and theology,[96] others like Johnson

---

89. Reno, *End*, 29.

90. Reno, *End*, 46.

91. Reno, *End*, 157–58, 162–63. I note especially Reno's conversation with the late Jaroslav Pelikan, who quips, "War is too important to leave to the generals" (157). By this, Pelikan claims that biblical scholars "make important contributions. But they are not to be trusted as high priests of exegetical integrity" (158).

92. See where Capetz mentions the critique that historical criticism's most significant issue is the "normative uses to which it is put." Capetz, "Theology," 460.

93. Perdue reads this collapse alongside Childs and Barr, particularly illuminating how Wright struggled to locate salvific events in history, missed the emphasis on salvation in human history found in other ancient Near Eastern cultures, as Albrektson had argued, and overlooked the difficulty of reconstructing Israelite origins. As for von Rad's approach to biblical theology, Perdue criticizes von Rad's overemphasis on Deuteronomy, the thematic unity he finds in the plurality of ancient Israelite traditions, the problem of placing the Sinai tradition late in Israel's history, his blending of wisdom with law, and his neat representation of otherwise scattered promise-fulfillment schemes. Perdue, *Collapse*, 38–41, 64–67. For Albrektson's still-debated hypothesis about divine engagement in human history in other ancient Near Eastern cultures, see Albrektson, *History and the Gods*.

94. For instance, Perdue mentions several critiques of Frei. These include the claim by many scholars that the Bible is not one story but many, that Frei ignored the concept of genre, and that the focus on the canonical text downplays marginalized people groups, among other salient counters. The first of these points is especially relevant for Jewish scholars, many of whom hesitate to engage in biblical theology with Christians who might wish to read the Old Testament through the lens of Christ without examining the various traditions, conversations, and disagreements within it. Perdue, *Collapse*, 261–62.

95. Perdue, *Collapse*, 4.

96. See especially Perdue, *Collapse*, 15, 154, 302. Although he leans on Perdue's work,

Teng Kok Lim are more ready to proclaim the decline of historical criticism's role in theology so that we may concentrate on the more pertinent final literary form of the text.[97] Regardless, the proverbial shots against historical criticism's use in theology have been fired, and there is much curiosity about whether, and if so how, the wounded can get up.

Common Threads of Critique

For the differences that may exist between literary critics, postmodern philosophers, historians, and biblical theologians, we have seen in this chapter a convergence of criticism against traditional modes of history writing. Whether finding some value in historical inquiry or none, whether believing in the presence an author's intention or not, whether contending that the Bible has value for a religious and ethical life or not, many late-twentieth-century academics have identified various issues with a critical examination of the past. This attack has cohered across these disciplines in a couple of ways.

One common critique of historical inquiry is its pretension to be "objective" and "scientific." Noting the swift changes in history writing after the dawn of the Enlightenment, critics will point out that history writing has sought since this period to treat matters of the past as if they were laws of nature waiting to be discovered by an exacting researcher.[98] For example, Prickett writes regarding the origins of modern historical criticism and its impact on theology, "This quest for historical certainty in the eighteenth and nineteenth centuries was in itself partially the result of an earlier failure . . . to give theology the same kind of external certainties as those apparently enjoyed by the natural sciences in the age of Royal Society and of Newton."[99] Thus, historical critics see their data as simple facts that can be mined with the right skills and tools. The ensuing results then provide the new "faith" to which we must submit our assent.

Brueggemann, a student of Muilenburg and adherent to rhetorical criticism, is less willing to retain Perdue's more charitable approach to historical criticism. Brueggemann, *Theology*, 46–49.

97. Lim, "Beginning of an End," 252–71.

98. I.e., Adam, *Postmodern*, 5; Brueggemann, *Theology*, 8–14; Prickett, *Words*, 24–25; Aichele et al., "Elephant," 384.

99. Prickett, *Words*, 25.

The Place of the Past

Many readers of historical works, and especially biblical criticism, will sympathize with such attacks on historical claims. Who among us has not read the works of biblical historians and wondered where they bought their time machines and historical mind-readers? With a cool detachment, some historians confidently reach certain conclusions that otherwise remain under intense debate. Others seamlessly deduce the motivations of historical characters who have been dead for thousands of years. In viewing some historical conclusions that appear off-putting in their hubris and omniscient mood, it is clear to see why many students have been turned off from studying the Bible's past.[100]

From the side of biblical theology, Michael C. Legaspi contends that the historical-critical leap was an academic one with the best intentions. He writes,

> Historical criticism did not develop merely as an intellectual project. Rather, it emerged, with its appeals to reason and a shared human past, as an interpretive framework thought to be capable of uniting humanity, overcoming religious divisions, and advancing an enterprise in which all confessional commitments were treated equally—because all commitments were equally excluded. In this way it merely facilitated the relocation of personal commitment: from belief in the creeds of the Church to belief in the critical canons of the academy.[101]

Nevertheless, as an academic discipline, historical criticism lost its way in terms of its value for the church, thus undercutting its usefulness for biblical theology, as we have seen with the arguments of scholars such as Childs, Yeago, and Reno.

From a literary, historical, and philosophical perspective, however, the objective and scientific origins of historical criticism are equally as damnable. Lyotard and White have been the most prominent of voices among many to point out the ideological foundation of narrative writings, and especially historical ones. The worldview of any writer, with her blind spots, limitations, and prejudices, is inherently inscribed in any written work. How, then, can a literary explanation of the past, no matter how heavily supported by data and evidence, be detached from subjectivity? Moreover, since historical studies of the Bible have mostly been done by individuals

---

100. See, for instance, the "arrogance" Reno finds in the works of biblical critics. Reno, *End*, 1, 162–63.

101. Legaspi, "Historical Criticism," 5.

of similar gender, ethnicity, and socioeconomic backgrounds, doesn't this limit the interpretations one can find in historical judgments and create a consensus that fails to consider other perspectives?

It is true that historical-critical scholarship of the Bible has a difficult road to escape the charge of anachronism. As we will survey in the next chapter, critics have questioned the presuppositions of historical-critical scholars in various areas, from Wellhausen's anti-Semitism leading to his placement of the P source as the latest or to the dominant understanding Paul's use of "grace" with a western lens. The question becomes, can we meaningfully construct any reading of the biblical past that is unencumbered by presuppositions? It seems through the critiques examined here that deconstruction of historical hypotheses, whether total or in part, seems much surer.

Another critique of historical criticism common to many of these approaches is their ignorance of the Bible as, first and foremost, a *text*. The text exists as a world of its own, with its own narrative, message, and locutionary force that exists apart from the world behind it. From Derrida's rallying cry that there is nothing outside the text, to Frei's insistence upon the "history-likeness" of the Bible, to Childs's emphasis of the canonical form, we have seen here a common insistence upon the more epistemologically certain final form. Historical criticism has given us a means to divide the biblical text and posit hypothetical origins giving rise to the text. These are ultimately unknowable. And the centuries of historical-critical study have not provided the consensus promised.[102] But the text's final form gives us a firm foundation from which to argue and is, frankly in the perspective of these views, more important than what lies behind the text.

It is this canonical form that, after all, has been the text used by the worshiping community for millennia and thus bears the religious meaning (the most significant meaning) without recourse to dubious origins and background. In addition, the final form of the biblical text itself has produced enough history in the synagogues, churches, and the Western world in general for meaningful discussions, making glances behind the text seem to be mere a spinning of our academic wheels.

By way of example, we could cite the near-consensus among archaeologists that Jericho was not destroyed by a historical Joshua (if one ever existed).[103] If historical criticism is one's dominant view of the Bible, this

---

102. Keck, "Historical Critical Method," 116.
103. Cf. Cline, *Biblical Archaeology*, 40–42.

provides the prism from which we now must read and understand Joshua 2–6. The biblical story is a "pious fraud"[104] and is thus sapped of its power. Scholars are left to figure out why the text reads the way that it does, and the faithful must recalibrate their expectations of what the Bible delivers for them. But the question the reactionaries against historical criticism in this chapter would ask is, "Why does it matter?" After all, the text is richly constructed, such that literary study alone seems inexhaustible. It also has millennia of interpretation in both the synagogue and the church for us to consider, not to mention the ongoing questions about religiously supported genocide the text seems to create. These are concerns that are immediately more accessible, as they work upon data tangible to everyone and they are more directly pertinent to the religious and political discussions of our day.

As we will see in the following chapters, all of these critiques of historical criticism have affected its various methodologies in numerous ways. Some points have been absorbed and led to adjustments in how historians do their work. Other points are vigorously challenged by historical critics, either as not applicable or as a misunderstanding of how historians operate. At minimum, the critiques of historical criticism have driven more self-awareness on the part of historians. Critical examinations of the past have continued in all areas of study, and especially the Bible. But, aside from criticism of their objects of study, historians have been forced to be more self-critical. Historians of all stripes must contend with their own biases and the literary shape of the narratives with which they work and which they also create in writing about the past. For historians of the Bible, however, an added dimension of these critiques creeps in as they are forced to explain how such study of the past assists us understanding a text that is ultimately religious.

---

104. This phrase originates from a footnote in Wilhelm De Wette's dissertation in reference to the "Book of the Law" discovered in 1 Kings 22 and has become a catchphrase for many researchers of that event. For a summary of De Wette's seminal work on this passage, see Reventlow, *History of Biblical Interpretation*, 4:235.

6

The State of Historical Criticism

WE HAVE JUST REVIEWED the many and severe critiques of the ways in which historical criticism served as the dominant mode of reading the Bible. Whether in the literary realm with New Criticism, in theory with postmodernism, or in theology with recent calls to read the Bible for the church, historical criticism's hegemony over biblical criticism as a whole has been severely called into question.

Despite these challenges, historical criticism trudges on. Archaeologists still dig, lower critics compare and contrast biblical manuscripts in myriad languages, higher critics theorize about the development of the text in ways not evident by the extant manuscripts, and so on. Journals, annual meetings, religious studies departments, seminaries, and publishers continue to promote research on traditional historical questions even in the face of the many challenges against it.

Neither can we aver that historical criticism continues as it always has. The various methodologies subsumed under its heading no longer dictate the agenda of biblical criticism in the way they did in the early and middle twentieth century. Literary, postmodern, and ecclesial-theological readings of the Bible have intermingled with the cadre of historical-critical research in the numerous avenues in which biblical research is available. As noted in the introduction, practitioners of such final-form readings and those of historical criticism do not often converse with one another, however much we may see their research combined under the larger rubric of biblical criticism.

The Place of the Past

Here, we will see how it is that historical criticism has weathered the storm of the critiques. Historical critics still justify their existence, and even necessity, within biblical criticism. They do so by engaging with literary theory, correcting false images of their disciplines, and, in theology, pressing the need to still speak of God's actions in history. Historical critics have adjusted their methodologies as a response to some demands of the critiques they have accepted. These include the desire to welcome new voices in historical readings of the biblical text, embrace uncertainty in historical judgments, and welcome literary readings in concert with (rather than to the exclusion of) historical analysis.

Responses to Issues in Literary Theory

We begin by noting that larger theoretical concerns of literature outside of biblical criticism have emerged in response to New Criticism, the intentional fallacy, and postmodernism. Since the work of Friedrich Schleiermacher, theorists have been aware of the so-called "hermeneutical circle," in which we attempt to understand the complexity of a text's meaning and significance through the author's intention, how that intention is inscribed, and the reader's engagement with the text. Schleiermacher described the hermeneutical circle as, "Each part can be understood only out of the whole to which it belongs, and vice versa.... Only in the case of insignificant texts are we satisfied with what we understand on first reading."[1] Thus, the understanding of a text—or at least a text with a meaning worth taking time to digest—involves a whole network of subjects and lines of inquiry that require effort to understand. The hermeneutical circle has been refined by later theorists, such as Wilhelm Dilthey and Hans Georg Gadamer. Gadamer's *Truth and Method* has become a classic philosophical reading, in part because of the clarity with which he describes the complex understanding of texts within the hermeneutical circle.

Gadamer sees textual understanding as so complex and involving so many "horizons" that we can only determine the goal of writing on a case-by-case basis. Anthony Thiselton writes, "Gadamer's major point . . . is that only as part of the very process of understanding can we tell in each case, and not in advance, what counts as an act or process of understanding."[2] For instance, Gadamer notes that Rankean-style history writing had a

---

1. Quoted in Thiselton, "Biblical Studies," 99.
2. Thiselton, "Biblical Studies," 103.

philosophical *telos* of continuity through time.[3] This continuity then becomes the lens by which we should understand history for this school of thought. But other schools of thought may have different trajectories of understanding history. In biblical criticism, then, under Gadamer's approach, the goal for one's interpretation becomes among the most important criteria for understanding the text rather than an objective, or "scientific" takeaway.[4]

While Gadamer's approach tries to retain a vision for some meaning in a text, it certainly does not provide lucid guidelines for understanding, and some have argued that he does not go far enough in establishing the way interpretation ought to be.[5] Philosopher and literary critic E. D. Hirsch has contended that New Critics like Eliot and Wimsatt have been misread in the subsequent "history of interpretation" of their works.[6] Indeed, these authors dealt with poetry, a genre of literature for which fluidity in interpretation is traditionally more acceptable than in, say, historical narrative. Can we then totally obscure an *intentio operis* in *all* written texts? Hirsch says no. Although he concedes that an author's intention might be lost even to the author himself, the words inscribed in the text using intelligible language do not shift in meaning.[7] Hirsch argues for a distinction between meaning and "significance," the latter being what he thinks most critics mean by "meaning."

> Meaning is that which is represented by a text; it is what the author meant by his use of a particular sign sequence; it is what the signs represent. Significance, on the other hand, names a relationship between that meaning and a person, or a conception, or a situation, or, indeed anything imaginable.[8]

This meaning can surely be multifaceted and complex, but it is stable, contra Derrida and other deconstructionists. It is only what others, even the author herself, does with the text from this point on that attributes significance to it. Yet both the understanding of a text's meaning and the understanding of its significance require ongoing interpretation, all of which may

---

3. Gadamer, *Truth and Method*, 184–85.
4. Thiselton, "Biblical Studies," 103.
5. See Thiselton's comment on discussions between Emilio Betti and Gadamer in which Gadamer only describes understanding as it is, not what it "ought to be or should be." Thiselton, "Biblical Studies," 101.
6. Hirsch, *Validity in Interpretation*, 10–12. Note that Hirsch dedicates this work to Wimsatt and seems at pains to stress his personal understanding of Wimsatt's work here.
7. Hirsch, *Validity in Interpretation*, 8–9.
8. Hirsch, *Validity in Interpretation*, 8.

appear certain, but such certainty is immanently unattainable.[9] It is then validity for Hirsch, not certainty, that is required in our interpretations of any text.[10]

Author and literary critic Umberto Eco has also contended that the *intentio operis* serves a helpful function for written texts. He acknowledges that a text does not necessarily have to contain one "repressive"[11] meaning, but neither can it mean anything we wish.[12] A text must rather balance between a "dialectic of openness and form, initiative on the part of the interpreter and contextual pressure."[13] Although it is not the primary focus of his work, Eco points to the Bible as a classic example of this kind of text, in which a biblical passage may have "every possible meaning," leading to the threefold and fourfold senses canonized by the church. But this multiplicity of meaning had to be "tamed" in pointing to Christ, so as not to mean whatever one wishes.[14]

Many biblical interpreters have also not been willing to go to the extremes as some New Critics about authorial intention. Jochen Flebbe, for one, concurs that *intentio operis* may have a wide range of meaning and may never be fully grasped. What it does, however, is to set limits on interpretation.[15] Oda Wischmeyer notes that since Barthes's proclamation of the death of the author, the concept of author has not died, but the "significance of the text has flourished."[16] What remains of the author is a recognition that an author "is defined by the text he produces" although we can still speak of a text "without mentioning their authors."[17] Nevertheless, texts—in particular, "rich literary, philosophical, or scholarly ones"—contain intentions that we may observe through the study of rhetoric with its inscribed (and

---

9. Hirsch, *Validity in Interpretation*, 164.

10. See especially Hirsch, *Validity in Interpretation*, 169–70. Thiselton sees Betti's case for hermeneutics as more refined that Hirsch's, yet still making similar claims. Thiselton, "Biblical Studies" 101.

11. Eco, *Limits of Interpretation*, 21.

12. I find the best summary of Eco's thought in Eco, *Limits of Interpretation*, 45–46.

13. Eco, *Limits of Interpretation*, 21.

14. Eco, *Limits of Interpretation*, 11–12.

15. Flebbe, "And God Was the Text," 48.

16. Wischmeyer, "Author–Text–Intention," 31.

17. Wischmeyer, "Author–Text–Intention," 32.

purposeful) persuasive speech.[18] It is such observations that then urge us to pursue the authorial intentions of these texts, as obscure as they may be.

John Barton has been the most forward in supporting Hirsch's approach to literary readings. He agrees that there should be a division between a static "meaning" (or "meanings") and the significance of the biblical text.[19] Otherwise, we would be left with a "kind of critical nihilism in which communication between people is impossible."[20] Instead, Barton wants to leave room in biblical criticism for understanding texts that were produced in foreign times and places while still being able to plumb their depths for meaning in the present.[21] The split between meaning and significance, then, allows us to have our cake (i.e., critically study the text for the meaning of its original utterances) and eat it too (i.e., allow the text to still speak to readers living after its composition). The former search for an *intentio operis*, according to Barton, does not consist in discovering the "inside of an author's mind," but in comprehending the claims of the text to work as a coherent whole.[22] This investigation of the work as a whole has significant implications for the continued study of traditional historical-critical methodologies, to which we will return in the next chapter.

After a lengthy assessment of literary theories and their impact on biblical exegesis, Kevin J. Vanhoozer defends meaning inscribed in the text, while acknowledging the many directions a text can go. He writes,

> The author is a communicative agent and the text is a communicative act with matter (propositional content) and energy (illocutionary force). Texts also have, like arrows, a certain trajectory and direction (perlocutionary aim). With respect to this third aspect, however, everything hinges on the reader's response.[23]

Vanhoozer approaches reading a text as one does a human. It requires humility to be open to the text's meaning with committed attention. In other words, readers must avoid both "sloth" and "pride" in attentive exegesis.[24] Exegesis thus calls for trust in an author's meaning, allowance for limited trajectories of that meaning, and a reader's thorough engagement with the text.

18. Wischmeyer, "Author–Text–Intention," 39–40.
19. Barton, *Nature*, 86–87.
20. Barton, *Nature*, 87.
21. Barton, *Nature*, 87.
22. Barton, *Nature*, 105–6.
23. Vanhoozer, *Is There a Meaning?*, 367.
24. Vanhoozer, *Is There a Meaning?*, 281–468.

The Place of the Past

Biblical scholars have also attempted to reckon with the distinction put forth by the father of structuralism, Ferdinand de Saussure, between "synchrony" and "diachrony." Whereas synchrony describes the meaning of the whole text, with all its parts existing together and in relation to each other *at a single time*, diachrony describes meaning *through* time.[25] In other words, synchrony studies the meanings of words, sentences, phrases, and so on at the time of the final text's formation, and diachrony studies the change in these meanings over time. In terms of biblical criticism, it would seem that synchrony replaced diachrony as the fashionable method of reading the Bible after the critiques of historical criticism. Alter's literary readings and Childs's canonical criticism, for example, pay close attention to the final literary form of the text and attend to its various linguistic meanings in that single, terminal stage of the text.[26] These recent approaches cohere with Saussure's own preference for the priority of synchronic study. Moreover, Derrida's slogan that "there is nothing outside of the text" supports the concept of a synchronic reading of any text, not merely of the Bible.

In recent years, however, it has become more common for interpreters to claim that biblical criticism needs synchronic readings *alongside of* the diachronic readings of historical criticism which seek to uncover layers of the text and how meanings of its individual words and pericopes developed over time. Krister Stendahl's entry on contemporary biblical theology in the *Interpreter's Dictionary of the Bible* has been influential in this respect, differentiating between, while showing the necessity of, what the text *meant* and what the text *means*.[27] Stendahl writes,

> For the descriptive biblical theologian this is a necessity implied in his own discipline; and whether he is a believer or an agnostic, he demands respect for the descriptive task as an enterprise valid in its own right and for its own sake. For the life of the church such a consistent descriptive approach is a great and promising asset which enables the church, its teaching and preaching ministry, to

---

25. For a helpful and accessible summary of Saussure's approach, see Silva, *Biblical Words*, 35–38; McKnight, *Post-Modern*, 118–21.

26. See Hong, "Synchrony and Diachrony," 526; Long, "Historiography," 146. It should be noted that Brett contends Childs is close to synchrony, but might be better described as "formalist." Brett, *Biblical Criticism in Crisis?*, 114–15.

27. Stendahl, "Biblical Theology, Contemporary," 419–20. Cf. Polzin, "Literary and Historical Criticism," 100; Perdue, *Collapse*, 303–4; Greenstein, "State of Biblical Studies," 22; Stone, "Historical Authenticity," 94. For criticism of the "double vision" of historical readings complementary to the theological, see McKnight, *Post-Modern*, 93–102.

be exposed to the Bible in its original intention and intensity, as an ever new challenge to thought, faith and response.[28]

After all, it is apparent that studying both the final form of the text, a single and final stage of writing, and the changes within the text, with its multiple layers as identified in source, redaction, and form criticism, provides a *complementary* view of the text. To anticipate part of the conclusion, this holistic attitude toward reading the biblical text is appropriate.

Nevertheless, the distinction between these two modes of reading, at least as Saussure envisioned it, has been misunderstood by many biblical scholars. K. P. Hong demonstrates that the difference between these two is not that one deals with time (diachrony) and the other does not (synchrony); rather the issue is the perspective of time.[29] Diachrony reckons with the ways language, and therefore meaning, changes over time; synchrony only considers language within a single frame of time. Hong supports the view of James Barr, whom we mentioned in the previous chapter as a notable critic of the ways in which theologians utilized historical criticism to support biblical theology, contending that historical readings are always involved in *both* synchronic *and* diachronic readings. Unless a text is contemporary to our own world, we must investigate the historical context of the use of language in the past.[30] That is, a historical dimension still exists in a synchronic reading of a biblical text, because we must understand what a word meant at that particular time. It would be incorrect, for example, to assume that the Greek word *agapē*, often translated as "love," appearing frequently in 1 Corinthians 13 holds the same meaning as "love" for us today. Indeed, as has frequently been noted, there were many words in Greek to capture our one English word for "love." Greek used many words to encapsulate the many dimensions of the concept of love, whereas English requires further definition of the concept to understand what is meant in 1 Corinthians 13. To assume a direct transfer of meaning between these two words would be illegitimate. It is imperative, even in a synchronic reading, to understand the meaning of that word in the context in which Paul

---

28. Stendahl, "Biblical Theology, Contemporary," 431.

29. Hong, "Synchrony and Diachrony," 523.

30. Barr, "Synchronic, Diachronic and Historical," 1–14; Hong, "Synchrony and Diachrony," 528. In addition, Barton points out that historical critics did not consciously decide to do diachronic readings over against synchronic readings, as these have more in common than is often suggested. Barton, "Historical-Critical Approaches," 14.

used it.[31] A diachronic reading, by contrast, would merely demonstrate that the concept of "love" has shifted in meaning and would explore the words used to encode it over time.

A helpful corrective to scholarly misperceptions on this distinction and the muddle of literary theories affecting the reading of the Bible appears in Helmut Utzschneider's "Text–Reader–Author." Here, Utzschneider argues that the synchronic/diachronic dichotomy as it has been (mis)understood is really about a trichotomy of intention of the text, authorial intention, and the reader's intention. These concepts, which Utzschneider borrows from Eco, convey that understanding begins with the intention inscribed within the text itself, although texts have authors whose intentions may or may not be clear within the text itself. And the recipient of that meaning is the reader, who brings her own worldviews and assumptions to the text.[32] This does not finish a cycle of understanding, but involves "lecture and relecture," a continuous re-reading to deepen understanding.[33] The "aesthetic" understanding of the text in the form in which the reader encounters it comes first in this process. But this attention to the literary features "provokes further reading," which is "still always historical" in understanding the text's genre, the context of its communication, and reception history.[34] This is to say that reading a biblical text responsibly involves first attention to its literary features, but that such a literary (for some, "synchronic") reading prompts further questions about what the text means for the present reader, what that text meant for the author, the original audience, and all audiences ever since. Textual understanding is then inescapably historical, although our initial readings may not be overtly historical.

A similar view comes from Barton, who has argued that literary and historical readings of the Bible are not as far apart as many have supposed. And, though we may begin with an understanding of text before the reader, we realize that this has its own context. To make sure it makes sense

---

31. Regarding the difficulty of even a synchronic reading, Silva notes, "The principle of contextual interpretation is, at least in theory, one of the few universally accepted hermeneutical guidelines, even though the consistent application of the principle is a notoriously difficult enterprise." Silva, *Biblical Words*, 138.

32. Utzschneider, "Text–Reader–Author," 7–12.

33. Utzschneider, "Text–Reader–Author," 13. This concept has resonance with what Dinkler has described as "diegesis," as opposed to "exegesis." Dinkler describes this as viewing the text and reader as both active agents. Dinkler, "Between Intention and Reception," 72–93.

34. Utzschneider, "Text–Reader–Author," 13–14.

to us in our present context, we necessarily are drawn into the author's.³⁵ "Biblical criticism is a semantic operation in that it is concerned with the meaning of words and phrases," Barton writes. A "word does not have a timeless meaning that is independent of the historical setting in which it is uttered. To that extent and in that sense, biblical criticism is inevitably a historical discipline."³⁶

In further reaction against the final-form readings, biblical critics have also relied on models from communication theories. One recognizable example of this is Jeannine K. Brown's widely-used *Scripture as Communication*, now in its second edition. Brown distinguishes between meaning that is *intended* by the author but not available to the reader and meaning that is *inscribed* by the author in the text and therefore available to the reader.³⁷ The latter is identifiable thanks to theories of communication, such as "speech-act theory" and "relevance theory." Speech-act theory, as formulated by J. L. Austin and John Searle,³⁸ recognizes that words have intended actions implied within them. The words themselves are "locutions" and the intentions are "illocutions." Brown offers the example of telling her class, "You shouldn't wait until the last minute to write your research paper." Not only do (or should!) her students *hear* the words but they should also understand them as *a warning*. Thus, locutionary signs point to an illocutionary, implied reality.³⁹

Relevance theory similarly marries the code (or semiotics) of a locutionary act with inferences of an utterance. That is, communication requires not only language, with all of its semantic and grammatical understandings, but also an "assumed context."⁴⁰ Dan Sperber and Dierdre Wilson, the pioneers of this theory, argue that "there is a gap between the semantic representations of sentences and the thoughts actually communicated by utterances. This gap is filled not by more coding, but by inference."⁴¹

Suppose, for instance, I ask the question, "Have I signed off on that?" This question could have many meanings depending on the context. If I am

---

35. Barton, "Historical Criticism," 3–15; Barton, *Nature*, 101–16.
36. Barton, *Nature*, 102.
37. Brown, *Scripture as Communication*, 12.
38. For further background on this movement, see Vanhoozer, *Is There a Meaning?*, 209–14; Thiselton, "Biblical Studies," 102.
39. Brown, *Scripture as Communication*, 21–22.
40. Brown, *Scripture as Communication*, 24.
41. Sperber and Wilson, *Relevance*, 9.

in my office, I could be speaking to a colleague who needs my signature for a curriculum proposal. If I am at home, the question could refer to whether I have signed my son's school binder so that his teacher knows he has done his homework. If I am with my friends, the statement could be ironic if they have already decided where we are going to eat without consulting me. The location and time of an utterance, not to mention the nonverbal cues and shared social understandings among all present, deeply inform the understanding of speech. John W. Hilber writes, "If speech-act asserts something as true, relevance theory attends to the contextual assumptions that inform the propositional content. The link that enables a listener to know which inferences are intended by the speaker is a contextual relevance."[42]

The implication of these arguments within biblical studies of such communication theories is that it is difficult to dispense with authorial intention. Biblical texts, like all modes of communication, are written to be understood. These understandings may be complex, inferred, and historically situated in contexts beyond our own, but understanding does not have to be impossible. They can become clearer by attempting to understand both what they intend to achieve (speech-act theory) and the cognitive environments in which they are written (relevance theory). Historical criticism, by extension, can aid in these endeavors. By providing background information to the world behind biblical speech, we can more easily understand what an author might intend for a text to accomplish and what such a text meant in its native environment.

As we have seen here, some recent literary and communicative theories have not been satisfied with the fashionable disregard for authorial intention. The critiques of intention may have revealed some holes in what has been, at least in biblical studies, assumed from ancient times and thoroughly promoted in the Renaissance and Reformation. But the uncertainty in authorial intention has not meant, at least for some theorists, its total abolition. Theoretical refinements have helped us understand the complexity of speech, so evident in biblical literature, as well as the boundaries we may place on a text's stability of meaning.

The Fields of Historical Criticism Today

As we have suggested, the critiques against classical historical criticism have not meant the end of the various methodologies found under its

---

42. Hilber, *Old Testament Cosmology*, 10.

umbrella. But neither has historical criticism from its normative period remained static. Researchers have refined the various approaches of historical criticism in different ways since the middle of the twentieth century. Historical criticism has been reassessed from perspectives outside of its western, male, continental origins. Some critics have attempted to jettison the more speculative historical aspects of historical criticism while retaining some of its crucial impulses. Others have doubled down on the value of historical criticism, arguing for historical viewpoints of texts that support the historicity of events rather than viewing them with skepticism. The only field within historical criticism to not have been affected as significantly by critique is textual criticism. Given its reckoning with hard evidence and a few stable rules for evaluating this evidence, it has been the least controversial field for outsiders. Either one finds the development of the text important or not. But the disciplines affected the most by the critiques have been those of higher criticism, which involve more theory or conjecture about the events described in the text and the history of text's composition.

Several scholars have offered differing schemes for the composition of the Pentateuch as Wellhausen outlined in his documentary hypothesis. Some have dated Wellhausen's earlier sources (J and E) as late as the postexilic period. Form critics have pressed the oral backgrounds of the Pentateuchal narratives. Still others contend that a single author is responsible for the Pentateuch with some later supplements. And some have gone in the other direction to assert that the Pentateuch is a collection of fragments.[43] But Wellhausen's theory (building on what others before him had argued) that literary sources underlie the Pentateuch has still held sway and remained dominant over historical criticism. A contributing factor here has been the work of Jeffrey Tigay, who noticed that later versions of the Mesopotamian *Epic of Gilgamesh* were compiled using earlier sources in much the same way Wellhausen had theorized about the Pentateuch.[44] Tigay's introduction of an "external control" to Pentateuchal composition has been difficult to overcome for critics of the source theory.[45]

The loudest voices against Wellhausen's scheme have come in his assertion of a late P document. Jewish scholars such as Yehezekhel Kaufmann,

---

43. For a review of the late-twentieth-century critiques against Wellhausen, see Wenham, "Pondering," 116–44.

44. Tigay, "Introduction," 1–52. To this, we may also add the work of Stephen A. Kaufman on the Qumran Temple Scroll. Kaufman, "Temple Scroll," 29–43.

45. Although indebted to Tigay's work, for a reassessment of the project, see Person and Rezetko, *Empirical Models*.

Israel Knohl, and Moshe Weinfeld have argued for an earlier P document than Wellhausen posited. Kauffmann and Knohl spelled out literary-critical objections to the dependence of the P source on other material as Wellhausen had defined it. Kaufmann demonstrated that P antedates Deuteronomy.[46] Knohl argued meticulously for two separate sources under Wellhausen's P rubric.[47] Weinfeld even demonstrated that Wellhausen's anti-Semitic bias played a role in constructing a late priestly document relative to the charismatic, prophetic sources.[48] Still these scholars do not argue against Wellhausen's literary-critical methodology. Their results instead stem from a disagreement about his conclusions and the influences that may have formed them.

Similarly, post-Holocaust responses emerged within comparative studies. Delitzsch's conclusions about the barbaric view of religion found in the Hebrew Bible in contrast to the more "sophisticated" approaches of the Mesopotamians seemed, in retrospect, to also be fueled by anti-Semitism. This led to a push away from comparing the Old Testament to ancient Near Eastern literature. Not long after Delitzsch, Assyriologist Benno Landsberger contended for scholars to focus on the "conceptual autonomy" of ancient Near Eastern literature instead of drawing such hasty parallels. Decades after World War II and the tragedy of the Holocaust, bolstered in theory by much of Germany's intellectual elite, Landsberger's thesis was translated into English.[49] Later Samuel Sandmel decried the "parallelomania," especially seen in the Biblical Theology Movement of his time, that too quickly sought to draw conclusions between biblical literature and ancient Near Eastern literature.[50] It became painfully clear that comparisons between the Bible and ancient Near Eastern literature were being performed with little methodological care accompanied by disastrous results.

---

46. Kaufmann, *Religion of Israel*. To see the explicit aim of his work set against the prevailing scholarship of the time, see pp. 1–4.

47. Knohl, *Sanctuary of Silence*. For his place among Kaufmann and other critiques, see pp. 1–7.

48. See especially Weinfeld, *Place of the Law*, 3–15. Barton does not agree with this assessment of Wellhausen, but neither does he say why. Barton, *Nature*, 52. For a summary of the impact of the post-Holocaust critiques of Wellhausen, see Arnold and Schreiner, "Graf and Wellhausen," 3:263–65.

49. Landsberger, "Conceptual Autonomy"; in German, see Landsberger, "Eigenbegrifflichkeit," 355–72.

50. Sandmel, "Parallelomania," 1–13.

By the 1970s, however, scholars sought a path forward to balance the strains of "parallelomania" and the opposite phenomenon of "parallelonoia."[51] While Landsberger and Sandmel had made compelling points, it also seems intellectually dishonest to treat biblical and ancient Near Eastern literature in a conceptual and scribal vacuum. Shemaryahu Talmon contended for specific conceptual and linguistic comparisons to combat the general and hasty generalizations of most comparisons.[52] William H. Hallo argued for taking both comparisons and contrasts into account. Hallo's "contextual approach" has become influential in setting the biblical literature against its cognitive environment while simultaneously recognizing how a given culture might uniquely appropriate common concepts from across the ancient literary milieu.[53]

Form criticism has suffered the most among the historical-critical disciplines. It is difficult to find a place in which form criticism exists in the same way Gunkel formulated it. Muilenburg's critique mitigated its more speculative aspects, especially in hypothesizing a *Sitz im Leben* drawn from written sources. For many, the value in form criticism is in its recognition of genres and pericopes. Antony F. Campbell finds the historical focus of form criticism "disturbing," but the value "intrinsic to form criticism is a focus on text before event."[54] The text is more certain than a proposed background of a saying and is thus a more sure footing for discussing the text. From the literary form, scholars can come to a greater acceptance of matters such as structure and genre. Yet some scholars still wish to emphasize the oral background of biblical texts, which contributes to some instability in using traditional biblical criticism to identify a text's component parts.[55] Although some have argued that genre is too elusive, thus complicating the entire enterprise of form criticism,[56] most would agree that one of form

---

51. The latter phrase comes from the chapter in Eilberg-Schwartz, "Beyond Parallel-Anoia," 87–102.

52. Talmon, "Comparative Method," 320–56.

53. Hallo, "Biblical History," 1–26; Hallo, "Compare and Contrast," 1–30. Both Hallo and Talmon have been influential in the following works: Walton, *Ancient Near Eastern Thought*; Hays, *Hidden Riches*; Schreiner and Holland, *Silhouettes*.

54. Campbell, "Form Criticism's Future," 19.

55. Blum, "Formgeschichte," 32–45.

56. Knierim, "Old Testament Form Criticism," 435–68. Longman notes the fluidity of genres, but does not find it impossible to discern. See Longman, "Israelite Genres," 177–95. David B. Schreiner and I have contended for the importance of genre in the ancient Near East and its importance in comparative work, though recognizing a range of genre and the ability of scribes to manipulate genre. Schreiner and Holland, *Silhouettes*, 1–18.

criticism's greatest benefits has been its attention to genre as an essential component of biblical understanding.[57]

Old Testament theology has not experienced quite the existential threat of form criticism since the Biblical Theology Movement's recent critiques, but it does suffer from what W. H. Bellinger Jr. has described as a "shattered spectrum" of approaches.[58] On the one hand, Brueggemann's critiques of historical criticism have led him to compose an Old Testament theology that turns from the question of "What happened?" to "What did they say?" His work focuses on Israel's speech about God as a dialectical testimony. Thus, his approach is not so much about what God says to Israel (or humanity) than it is about what Israel says to itself about God.[59] On the other end of the spectrum, Duane A. Garrett has composed an unapologetically christological reading of the Old Testament. Historical concerns may affect this reading, but the primary interest is theological.[60] Still other approaches, such as those of Bellinger and R. W. L. Moberly, are less ambitious and consider piecemeal themes throughout without locating a center.[61] What these all have in common is a reticence towards confirming much value in the historical aspects of the Old Testament. At best, the role of historical criticism in theology is indefinite, with theologians often acknowledging a need to understand historical context but considering the theological point of the text ultimate. It seems thus that the heyday of the Biblical Theology Movement is past.

But even Perdue, who proclaimed the collapse of history, wishes to retain some importance for history in Old Testament theology. Postmodern and literary theories have been insufficient to construct a faith which is so inextricably tied with history. He writes,

> Thus, history and text belong together. While there are important discussions of the meaning of "history" in reference to a field of knowledge about the past and the methods used to recapture plausible understandings of the past, one should not dispense with history in the theological enterprise of reconstructing major and

---

57. For an excellent and accessible treatment of the role of genre in understanding different parts of the Bible, See McKenzie, *How to Read*.

58. Bellinger, *Introducing Old Testament Theology*, 39.

59. Brueggemann, *Theology*, 117–20.

60. Garrett, *Problem*. The first sentence of his preface, found on p. ix, establishes the christological reading immediately. For a brief summary of historical criticism and Old Testament theology, see pp. 133–36.

61. For Moberly, see Moberly, *Old Testament Theology*.

varied expressions of Israelite and early Jewish faith. To do so is to invent a philosophy (actually revive an old one) in which there is no objective or attainable knowledge and every view is capable of acceptance or rejection.[62]

It remains a struggle for biblical theologians to construct a theoretical apparatus in which history might function for Old Testament theology and no comprehensive work of the likes of Eichrodt's and Von Rad's have appeared since the critiques they received. Protestant Old Testament scholar Lawson G. Stone, however, proposes five rules for reading the Bible historically in the service of theology. First, against the Troeltschian model of analogy, historical study should operate with a "commitment to the truth value of Scripture and to the traditional Protestant, supernaturalist theism." Second, as it regards the historical-critical obsession with the development of the text, "*all stages* are regarded as participating to some degree in divine revelation and inspiration." However, thirdly, privilege for normative theological interpretation in the church lies in the canonical form. Fourthly, if genre dictates that a writer *did not intend* for a reader to believe in the historicity of an event, the reader is not required to take the text as reporting a historical happening. Indeed, to do so would be to misread it. Finally, faith that seeks understanding of the text requires the use of the intellect while depending "radically on the Spirit of God to brood over the church and lead us to truth."[63]

Stone's principles then attempt to balance the gains of historical criticism with a trusting eye toward both the miraculous and the authority of the text. Each stage is attributed some level of inspiration, as Richard Simon long ago proposed (and got in trouble for!). But the final witness of the text for the church is the canonical form that blends together the underlying literary strands. A literary and historical mindset that pays close attention to genre should meet with the reality of dogmatic faith claims. Although many will not agree with the principles as Stone has laid them out, he has straightforwardly demonstrated how we can and should utilize criticism to read for theological truth.

An even more elusive quest for interpreters has been the attempt to utilize archaeology to prove or disprove events of the Bible. Although the apex of the Biblical Theology Movement saw the refinement of archaeological techniques and the discovery of many interesting artifacts, scholars have

62. Perdue, *Reconstructing*, 341.
63. Stone, "Historical Authenticity," 85–86.

recognized that archaeology is limited in what it can and cannot say about the Bible. For one, artifacts uncovered during a dig still need interpretation. They are, after all, "texts" (whether they have inscriptions on them or not) that do not speak fully for themselves. Scholars still must interpret why they are where archaeologists have found them, what function they exist for, and what these might say to the witness of the Bible. Similarly, it is apparent (especially from the Biblical Theology Movement) that, for as much as archaeology relies on the natural sciences, it is not a fully objective discipline and it still incorporates the biases of those who interpret them. On top of these concerns, archaeology has only uncovered a small fraction of the biblical world. Many items archaeologists and biblical scholars would love to find have either been destroyed or lie in parts unknown.

Yet archaeology persists as a significant discipline of the historical-critical paradigm. Indeed, some artifacts, such as the Tel Dan Stele and Hezekiah coins, that contribute to the conversation about the historicity of the Bible continue to be discovered. But biblical archaeology's focus has shifted from an Indiana-Jones-like find to more anthropological ends. Today, archaeologists tend to uncover patterns of daily life for those on the ground in the biblical world since these types of results are more readily available through archaeological research. Archaeologists are able to discern fascinating aspects of life, such as the practice of religion, the structure of society, household roles, and economic interchange.[64] Along the way, archaeologists are sure to stoke the fire of debates about biblical historicity, but it no longer remains the primary aim of what they do.[65]

In a similar vein, life on the ground in the ancient world as seen through the lenses of both anthropology and sociology have had a massive, and still-growing, impact on the interpretation of the Bible. Feminist, womanist, African-American, Latinx, and other such readings of the biblical text subversive to the dominant Western, male criticisms of the Bible have introduced a welcome and much-needed diversity to biblical interpretation. Discussing all of these perspectives would take us too far afield for the current project since much of these subversive readings of the Bible are indebted more to theory than history.[66] But it is worth mentioning that these critiques can sometimes utilize historical data. Carol Meyers, for

---

64. For notable contributions here, see King and Stager, *Life in Biblical Israel*.

65. Cf. Cline, *Biblical Archaeology*, 3–4.

66. For some examples, see Scholz, *Women's Hebrew Bible*; McCaulley, *Reading While Black*; Gutierrez, *We Drink*. For helpful summaries of subversive views, see Perdue, *Reconstructing*, 76–182.

instance, assesses the archaeological and biblical views of women to highlight the roles that women played in the households of ancient Israel.[67] She notes that the modern concept of patriarchy does not encapsulate the significant role that women played in household survival and religious practice, despite the dominance of males in areas such as passing on the family line. Her work then is illustrative of how historical research can inform contemporary theory and do so in a way that evinces the need for broader voices beyond western male ones.

Furthermore, socio-rhetorical criticism has recognized the blending of a text's historical social background with the words on the page. Vernon Robbins describes socio-rhetorical criticism as including the literary and rhetorical features of the text with the sacred, but also features such as the "intertexture" that understands the "phenomena that lie outside the text" like historical and social events, the "social and cultural texture" that witnesses to social dynamics, and the "ideological texture" that "concerns the way the text itself and interpreters of the text position themselves in relation to other individuals and groups."[68] For example, he offers the story of Jesus' healing of a blind man in John 9 to lead the reader to understand that Jesus' engagement with the Pharisees was explicitly countercultural.[69] Whereas the Pharisees are bound up with cultural assumptions of Jesus' sin since he healed on the Sabbath, Jesus later declares in vv. 39 and 41 that the more significant "blindness" lies on his detractors who have denied the true work of God that transcends strict Sabbath observation. In order to understand this passage, as Robbins has presented it, it is necessary to understand not only the literary movement of the text but also its social and historical background, which illuminates this countercultural ideology. Thus, we find in this approach a need to consider the many layers of communication that we have witnessed above, and that the historical background of a text plays into it.

Historical criticism, in this example, is necessary to come to a fuller understanding, especially a theological one, of a biblical passage. Within the New Testament, at least, some historical investigation is inescapable. Within Paul's epistles, historical-critical approaches of social understandings in the Greco-Roman world, grammar, and philology are integral to comprehending Paul's message, which itself has shaped Christian

---

67. See especially Meyers, *Discovering Eve*; Meyers, "Patriarchal Society," 8–27.
68. Robbins, *Texture of Texts*, 3–4, 58–68.
69. Robbins, *Texture of Texts*, 91–94.

theology.⁷⁰ Debates about Paul's intentions and the direct implications for these intentions in Christian theology extend at least as far back as Luther. But studies of the Gospels still retain a historical emphasis. The dominant source-critical theory of Markan priority and the existence of Q have remained for most New Testament scholars.⁷¹ Yet, other theories have also emerged and are gaining steam, such as the idea that Q never existed and that Luke borrowed from Matthew.⁷²

While these studies may seem too speculative for some, the import lies in what they suggest about the trustworthiness of these documents, particularly as they relate the events of the life of Jesus. And the continued search for the historical Jesus continues to be vital. John P. Meier, who has written the most extensive study on the historical Jesus thus far, acknowledges the long-held separation between history and theology in relation to Jesus. For him, historical Jesus study and Christology must proceed along their own lines of inquiry before merging them. Although he does not indicate when such a merger might happen, he is adamant that both are necessary for the faithful.⁷³

Taking another route, Murray A. Rae presses the idea that the Gospels, and especially Luke, do not pretend to function as myth, but rather contend for the historical life of Jesus, including the resurrection. The Jesus of history is inextricably a Christ of faith, no matter how difficult it may be for us to construe this relationship. He writes,

> [Luke] also acknowledges that alternative explanations will be sought, but he particularly emphasizes that the resurrection of Jesus is to be understood as something that happened to Jesus independently of the disciples' faith, that it is to be understood as involving some sort of physical body, and that it takes place on the same terrain of historical occurrence that historians typically investigate. What will not do, however, is the prevailing assumption of secular historiography that the same terrain cannot be the locus of the action of God.⁷⁴

70. For the most recent prominent example of this, see Barclay, *Paul and the Gift*.

71. For contemporary support of the dominant hypothesis, see Stein, *Studying the Synoptic Gospels*.

72. Cf. Goodacre, *Case Against Q*.

73. Meier, *Marginal Jew*, 4:5–6.

74. Rae, *History and Hermeneutics*, 84. The larger section of Rae's argument can be found on pp. 69–84. See also Strawn's use of Rae in supporting Käsemann's second quest and against the critiques of A. K. M. Adam. Strawn, "Docetism." Rae attacks what I find to be the great weakness in Harvey's account of history and faith in the historical Jesus, namely the willingness to take Jesus' life and death seriously, but not the resurrection. Harvey, *Historian and Believer*, 274–75.

Rae then calls for a merger of history and Christology based not only on the claims of orthodox theology but also on the claims of the biblical text itself. Something of the sort is evident in the use of historical criteria such as "the embarrassment factor" to point to the likelihood of the empty tomb tradition.[75] But it appears that work remains to be done in debating the historical life of Jesus and convincing some of the faithful in the line of Luke Timothy Johnson and A. K. M. Adam that it is necessary.

So, as we have seen, the work of classical historical criticism is not finished. Debates still rage over the same issues that nagged scholars in the late nineteenth century. However, the approaches to address historical questions have shifted in significant ways. Historical criticism has opened up its fields of inquiry beyond dominant white male Protestant views, offering new perspectives to old questions. Many of the old solutions to historical problems (such as those we encountered in chapter 4) have been challenged and reconfigured. The impact of historical criticism on the theology of the Bible has even been reconsidered to integrate historical-critical methodologies into the life of faith without neglecting the ultimate purpose of the text. The practice of historical criticism is clearly conversational among many different constituents. And neither can we say many strong consensuses have emerged from such a grand dialectic. Although such a lack of consensus supports historical criticism's detractors, the greater enterprise of historical criticism seems to find its investigations worthwhile for reasons we will detail in the next chapter.

Excursus: Memory

In recent years, scholars have applied the insights of the field of memory studies to the Bible. With origins in the work of sociologist Emile Durkheim,[76] "memory" describes how individuals and cultures construe the past to shape a present identity. The individual's or culture's conception of the past does not

---

75. Harris, *New Testament*, 250–51.

76. For a history of memory studies as it relates to the Bible, see Ro, "Memory and History," 1–17. We have not had occasion to speak much of sociology and the social sciences. In general, early sociological theories set out to provide general principles to understand social movements, whereas history tends to view individual events. Contemporary sociology also includes investigations of "life on the ground" for individuals both in the present and past and has, as we have mention, greatly affected biblical archaeology. For more on sociology and the Bible, see Long, "Historiography," 156–61; Edelman, "Doing History," 295–99.

necessarily have to match how it really happened, but it emphasizes that one's perception of the past affects present conditions and markers of remembering that past appear in places from texts to monuments.

The responsibility for integrating memory studies into biblical studies lies with Egyptologist Jan Assmann. Assmann refines previous memory theories by differentiating between recent memory shared by contemporaries, which he calls "communicative memory," and "collective memory," which reach further in the past and involve both foundational etiologies and biographies.[77] The latter particularly plays a role in the shaping of Israel's identity from slavery in Egypt, which informs Israel's identity in features such as the law, monotheism, and reconstruction after exile. Assmann even finds here the foundation of our modern concept of religion. The book of Deuteronomy, for instance, reveals the residues of this memory most prominently with its repeated commandments to Israel to "remember" the exodus.[78]

The relationship between memory and history is a complicated one. For Assmann, history is a concept that arises from memory and the creation of the law of the people. The order of law influences the order of shaping the past, a past in which not only humans but also the God of the Torah act. He writes,

> It is only possible to reconstruct the past on which memory and history depend through the establishment of binding obligations that bring order, meaning, and cohesion both to the temporal and the social dimensions of the world. That which is remembered is the binding obligation that must never be forgotten. Remembering the past is not the result of instinct, of some innate interest, but of a duty that is part of culture's impact on man. It is from the cultural construct of *iustitia connectiva* that the commemorative imperative arises: "Thou shalt remember. Thou shalt not forget." This is what is solidified into historical meaning in all cultures and in all individuals, each in their own way.[79]

Johannes Unsok Ro similarly states that the relationship between history and memory is unsettled. Some tend to differentiate between the two,

---

77. Assmann, *Cultural Memory*, 34–41. Assmann is also influenced by the work of his wife, Aleida Assmann. See Assmann, "Transformations Between History and Memory."

78. Assmann, *Cultural Memory*, 175–205. See also Assmann, *Moses the Egyptian*, 1–54.

79. Assmann, *Cultural Memory*, 233.

while others wish to integrate them.[80] But, within biblical studies, "the focal point has moved from historical accuracy in the biblical historiography to the society producing the relevant biblical historiography."[81] Thus, biblical scholars focused on memory studies are more likely to skirt around the question of whether an event actually happened or a historical person existed and focus on the purpose for which the community produced the portrait of the past that it did.

A look into a volume on memory studies in Deuteronomy edited by Ro and Diana Edelman reveals that memory is used in myriad ways, from particular themes that were present at the time of recording past events, how past events were remembered, the use of poetics to shape memory, and even the employment of memory to bolster source-critical theories.[82] While it is obvious that memory has many possible applications to biblical studies, its relationship to classical historical criticism is unclear. At the very least, we can aver that it is helpful for us in remembering that the way the past is constructed matters. Whether in the Bible itself or modern historiography, the past often becomes a tool to inform our view of the present. Merely antiquarian concerns have little value for those who attempt to reconstruct the past for a present audience.

Defenses of Historical Criticism

It should be apparent from the preceding analysis that historical criticism has not, and likely will not soon, experience its demise. Practitioners of its various methods still cling to the value of inquiring about the past. In the next chapter, I will provide some guidelines for responsible historical criticism and assess its value. But it is important at this point to consider what defenders of historical criticism have thus far contended in terms of its value and shape in the wake of its various critiques.

The dominant concern among historical critics is that, if we were to lose historical criticism, we would also lose an understanding of the context in which a biblical text was conceived. Historical criticism, at its base, helps us to understand the wide range of the social, political, and scribal world of the Bible. It helps us to understand all manner of issues, including: what

80. Ro, "Introduction," 4-6.
81. Ro, "Introduction," 6.
82. Ro and Edelman, *Collective Memory*. See my review in Holland, Review of *Collective Memory*, 1-5.

life was like for Israel and the Jews under the thumb of various hegemonic rulers; how and why texts were written; what gave meaning to ancient peoples; ancient understandings of various words that may not translate well into target languages, and so on. All of these at once enable readers to understand that the biblical world was not their own. To make sense of the Bible, they must then enter into that world as much as possible to determine whether and how the texts speak to contemporary readers.[83]

This dimension of historical-critical study boosts the descriptive, or "plain," sense of biblical interpretation.[84] The tools that proliferated in the Renaissance, such as grammatical and geographic aids, in addition to the more recent discoveries of archaeology, provide a helpful first step before asking more theoretical, and even theological, questions.[85] Indeed, establishing as much descriptive information as possible before higher reasoning was a feature of biblical exegesis as far back as Origen.

Similarly, the establishment of context creates boundaries for interpretation.[86] This aspect of historical interpretation clearly will not satisfy postmodernists in the Derridean strand who believe that no meaning outside of the text exists. But for others, historical exegesis will help us see that we are not always free to draw meaning from a text in the way we wish. This is not to say that the *only* meaning is inscribed in the historical context of the text, as early Christian interpreters have shown us and as so conservative a critic as Hirsch has even contended.[87] But we cannot read an apple into an orange, and historical criticism can assist us with where the boundaries lie. For example, contemporary impulse suggests reading a personal prosperity message into Jeremiah 29:11, "'For I know the plans I have for you,' says YHWH, 'Plans for your welfare and not for harm, to give you

---

83. Cf. Capetz, "Theology," 471; Keck, "Historical Critical Method," 124; Brown, *Scripture as Communication*, 270; Nissinen, "Reflections," 61; Krentz, *Historical-Critical Method*, 61, 64–65; Dunn, "Biblical Hermeneutics," 65–78.

84. Barton, *Nature*, 101–16; Capetz, "Theology," 467; Stuhlmacher, *Historical Criticism*, 90; Krentz, *Historical-Critical Method*, 63–64.

85. On the order of operations, see John Barton, "Historical Criticism," 5; Barton, *Nature*, 101; Polzin, "Literary and Historical Criticism," 104; Klement, "Modern," 439–59.

86. Cf. Barton, "Historical-Critical Approaches," 17; Joyce, "First Among Equals?," 23–26; Donfried, "Alien Hermeneutics," 25.

87. Among other examples we could note, Hirsch writes, "the historicity of interpretation is quite distinct from the timelessness of understanding." In other words, an author may intend to inscribe something in her context, and it is understood in a different way by later readers. But we are then both emancipated but still "enslaved... by whatever reality it is to which we have chosen to relate his work." Hirsch, *Validity*, 137, 142–43.

a future with hope."[88] But historical criticism can aid us in understanding that this address is communal, not personal, as Jeremiah utilizes the plural form of the second person (not found in standard English) and is writing to a community of exiles. Moreover, this statement concerns a specific moment of exile, to which our contemporary definitions of "welfare" and "hope" may not match. This leaves open the historical critic to caution us as to the viability for reading such a passage for our own (in the case of this passage, often "prosperity") purposes.

Similarly, biblical critics have also stressed the importance of genre.[89] To read a passage like Jeremiah 23 for today, even if not individualistically or in terms of prosperity, is possible because prophecy is by nature a genre open to future fulfillment. The words of prophecy, and poetry in general, are often vague enough and sufficiently open to transcendent intervention in history to welcome more meaning than an author may intend. Other genres, such as genealogies, which have limited application for meaning, should not be read so liberally with regard to meaning, but with a particular goal in mind (usually legitimacy). The identification of genres within biblical text was not only important in many strands of the history of biblical interpretation but is one of the aspects of form criticism still deemed as valid by contemporary biblical scholars. Moreover, historical criticism allows us to understand how genres functioned within their ancient contexts. This enables us to know, for example, what legal prescriptions, creation narratives, biographies, and so on might have aimed to accomplish in the ancient world, giving us more insight into the original purpose of composition for these biblical texts.

From the humanistic point of view, many scholars press that an understanding of the context of the Bible aids us in being more sympathetic to the human side of the Bible. Even the most orthodox reader of the Bible must confess that the Bible did not come directly from heaven but was composed in the hands of human beings. We will return later to what this might mean for inspiration. But for many historical critics, whether faithful or secular, historical criticism enables us to value the human side of biblical composition and the events that it portrays.[90]

88. Translation my own.

89. We have mentioned several of these throughout the history of interpretation, but among modern authors, see Barton, *Nature*, 23–24; Levenson, *Hebrew Bible*, 111; Vanhoozer, *Is There a Meaning?*, 335–50.

90. Cf. Capetz, "Theology," 479–84; Barton, "Historical-Critical Approaches," 17; Stone, "Historical Authenticity," 94.

The Place of the Past

A common critique against historical criticism that we have seen from both the literary and theological sides is that it undermines the unity of the text. In attempting to discover the origins of utterances and literary sources that comprise the text's final form, historical critics have neglected to read the text in its intended form. Although there may be diversity beneath the text, this diversity has proven to be conjectural and irrelevant to what the text ultimately means. But a few scholars contend that discovering the multifaceted origins of the text can bolster views of the text's unity.[91] Doing so can enable us to see the great amount of diversity of thought that was allowable in Israel's and early Christianity's canonical forms, while also demonstrating their interpretational boundaries.

As another example: although it is generally accepted by scholars that Genesis 1:1—2:4a constitutes a separate creation account from that found starting in Genesis 2:4b (because of the varying orders of creation, names for God, and so on), this diversity need not shock readers, especially faithful ones. This is because the commonalities between them—such as the value of humanity, goodness of work, significance of sexuality, and the like—are valued (and are perhaps more important for understanding how Israel conceived of its God) over against the other features of earlier strands of the creation story.

Finally, there are few historical critics remaining who support the positivistic understandings of historical criticism that reigned under thinkers such as Troeltsch.[92] Many historical critics now press that historical readings are open to critique and are always provisional.[93] As new information pours in from archaeology, as new perspectives on historical events emerge from a broader array of thinkers, and as new insights appear from interdisciplinary study, it is certain that views on the biblical past will change. This is perhaps easier to see from hindsight as historical critics have now corrected several of the dominant early views. And critics would be arrogant to assume that their own views will not change.

As we will see in the next chapter, this among many other principles we have alluded to here are common assertion, not only of biblical historical criticism, but historians in general. Unfortunately, biblical scholars have

---

91. Baden, "Tower of Babel," 221–23; Barton, "Historical Criticism," 7; Stone, "Historical Authenticity," 94.

92. A notable exception to this would be John J. Collins. See especially Collins, *Bible After Babel*, 3–16.

93. Cf. Capetz, "Theology," 467; Stuhlmacher, *Historical Criticism*, 83–90; Krentz, *Historical-Critical Method*, 66, 67.

not thoroughly engaged with the philosophy of history common to other areas of historical inquiry. But we will find that many of these impulses are elucidated among historians and philosophers who have reflected on their craft. It is from these that we hope to construct a more thoughtful and responsible historical criticism for the Bible.

7

The Future of Historical Criticism[1]

THUS FAR, WE HAVE established the trajectory of historical criticism from its origins, to its many challenges, to its present practice. We have seen that historical criticism is not without its faults. It often appears confident of past events and causes, as if historians were there when they happened. Its givens sometimes appear so certain as to drive us to indubitable conclusions about the past's relationship to the present and future. Critics, such as those we mentioned in chapter 5, have pointed out that, if historical study functions in this way, it stands on thin ice. They have demonstrated that certainty is far from given in words describing past events, let alone in our knowledge of the events themselves. Moreover, these events do not occur with a sole person, but affect many different people in the time of the events themselves, but also all the way to the present. Who then can claim a dominant perspective?

Yet we have also seen in the previous chapter that inquiry into the world behind the pages of the Bible persists. Archaeologists still dig, source critics still divide the text, and so on. Articulation of the allure of history evades us, however, as historical critics have continued their work without much philosophical grounding.

---

1. Some insights of this chapter also appear in the following: Holland, "Why Bother?," 289–317; Holland, "Wesleyan-Methodist Tradition?," 76–92.

The Future of Historical Criticism

What remains is for us to determine how historical criticism should proceed. If indeed it does not ultimately succumb to its criticisms and is to complement final-form readings, what does the responsible practice of historical criticism look like? Biblical historians have seldom engaged in philosophical reflection, especially across the historical discipline, for their purpose and core values. So here, we engage with the philosophy of history in order to discover the principles that should undergird responsible investigations into the Bible's past. In so doing, some common practices of historical criticism will be defended on philosophical grounds, but we will also see that some common practices should be reassessed.

In particular, historical critics go about their work properly when it is cautious about its conclusions and cognizant of the many perspectives on historical events. Further, history's critics have overlooked commonplace and assumed practices among historians of all stripes, including its use of inferential, rather than certain, knowledge and a complex view toward historical causation.[2] In addition, it will be important to address the purpose for studying history. Discovering a *telos* for the study of history should, ideally, drive the biblical historian to grasp history's place within exegesis. Finally, we will examine what import the philosophy of history might have on the use of historical criticism in biblical theology.

The Cautious Practice of History

In chapter 5, we encountered the claims that historians often operate with an arrogant certainty about the past, supposedly rooted in a positivistic, scientific framework.[3] To assuage some of these objections to historical criticism, we begin with the common assumption that historical study, and by extension historical criticism, functions in the same manner as the natural sciences. Put directly, the accusation of history as a positivistic, scientific discipline is a philosophical straw man. Although rises in the discipline of history correlate to boons in scientific knowledge, whether we speak of ancient Greece or the Enlightenment, such correlation does not lead to

---

2. On the duty of the historian to recognize the complexity of the past, see Fischer, *Historians' Fallacies*, 142–44, 172–75, 200–203.

3. For example, Adam, *Postmodern*, 4; Brueggemann, *Theology*, 8–14; Perdue, *Collapse*, 19–20. Ankersmit, "Historiography and Postmodernism," 137–38; Ankersmit, "Postmodern Reply," 287.

identification. It is not fair to describe historical practice in such a positivistic fashion.

Previously, we reviewed the progenitor of the modern historical method, Leopold von Ranke. His rallying cry of *"wie es eigentlich gewesen"* has certainly drawn the ire of final-form interpreters of the Bible and postmodernists. However, this slogan of Ranke's is not meant to confidently venture that we can gain pure understanding of the past but to set boundaries on fanciful interpretations of the past by carefully respecting the evidence of the past through an organized *Wissenschaft*—a *Wissenschaft* that was determined to be distinct from other forms of knowledge.[4] For Ranke, the gathering of facts is only the starting point for doing history, as he confessed the historical imagination (albeit one grounded in reality) launches from the established reality of the past.[5]

In his magisterial book *That Noble Dream: The "Objectivity Question" and the American Historical Profession*, Peter Novick argues that a certain misperception of German scientific objectivity (*wissenschaftliche Objektivität*), in particular Ranke's, filtered into the burgeoning American historical profession in the late-eighteenth century. This skewed version of historical practice became the standard goal of historians on this side of the Atlantic. He writes,

> If the historian was conscientious, mastered *Quellenkritik* and the auxiliary sciences, avoided the "phantoms" of hypotheses, he could produce a body of reliable atomistic facts which "when justly arranged interpret themselves." The road to ultimate history—the definitive, objective, re-creation of the historical past—was open. And the journey, while arduous, might not be that long.[6]

Surely this depicts the kind of history against which New Critics, postmodernists and those we discovered in chapter 5 argue. But this was *not* the kind of scientific objectivity that Ranke and other historians in Germany had proposed. History, as Ranke had imagined it, was founded more on Hegelian idealism than on a Baconian scientific method or Lockean empirical epistemology. History in the Rankean sense undeniably involves hypotheses—to the extent that Ranke was roundly criticized by positivists

---

4. In their defense of the testimony of the Bible as a legitimate source for historical reconstruction, Provan, Long, and Longman also recognize the distinction between Ranke's program and the positivism introduced by Comte. Provan et al., *Biblical History of Israel*, 21–24, 38–43.

5. On misunderstandings of Ranke, see Iggers, "Introduction," xi–xiv, xxvii.

6. Novick, *That Noble Dream*, 39.

in Germany. And "objectivity" was less about perfect knowledge or "actual facts" of a thing and more about the study of something as phenomenon outside of one's consciousness.[7] It seems that idea of Rankean history as it has been filtered down to us is a shadow of Ranke, infiltrated by positivist philosophies foreign to Ranke himself.[8]

In fact, the connection between the discipline of history and the natural sciences is not assumed by historians, but is very much an ongoing conversation, with practitioners often acknowledging both the convergences and the distinctions. R. G. Collingwood, who worked both as a historian and a philosopher, recognizes that history is a science (*Wissenschaft*) in so far as it is an "organized body of knowledge."[9] For him, history's correlation with science is a matter of defining the latter term. History shares with the natural sciences an interest in evidence and interpretation through the boundaries of a critical method. It deals with the "brute facts" of texts, artifacts, and other "primary" sources. But there is a recognition within history that these sources were not created by monolithic machines. Rather, they are products of human minds, which pushes the historian into more complex realms of thought than a mere examination of primary sources.

For Collingwood, history's interpretations have a different goal than the natural sciences' concern for the physical objects of space and time. History deals in human self-knowledge, which overlaps not only with natural sciences but also with philosophy and art.[10] Patrick Gardiner and Isaiah Berlin are also notable among those thinkers who similarly acknowledge history's intersections with natural science, while underscoring its interest in particular human events, which is opposed to the natural sciences' preoccupation with generalizing rules.[11]

---

7. Novick, *That Noble Dream*, 21–46. Biblical historical criticism also accepts the term "scientific" as it arose in Germany with a similar understanding of the term. See especially De Wette's quote mentioned in Brettler and Arakaky, "Historical-Critical," 211.

8. See also Iggers's argument that Ranke was "little understood in America or Great Britain," in "Introduction," xi–xii.

9. Collingwood, *Idea*, 249. Walsh also appropriates a more general notion of science in Walsh, *Philosophy of History*, 35–37. See also Novick, *That Noble Dream*, 24–25.

10. Collingwood's thoughts on this matter are dense, but particular claims about the relationship between history and science can be found in the following: Collingwood, *Essays*, 48–49, 136; Collingwood, *Idea*, 1–10, 234, 305, 318.

11. Gardiner, *Historical Explanation*, 60. The relationship between history and science is a preoccupation of most of Gardiner's work, but his most essential viewpoints can be seen on pages 28–64. See also Berlin, "Scientific History," 1–31; Walsh, *Philosophy of History*, 18, 25, 30–47.

The Place of the Past

In engagement with biblical exegesis, theologian Van A. Harvey argues that positivistic dimensions of history fail to capture the spirit of historical investigations. Scientific laws cannot neatly describe the sorts of inquiries historians make. "History, like ordinary discourse," he writes, "presupposes much more than the sciences, for the historian makes judgments about men's motives and values, national character, political trends, institutional capabilities, revolutions—none of which, precisely speaking, can be said the be the subject matter of a science."[12]

Biblical historians also wrestle with distinctions and intersections between history and science, though their work does not often leave room for meta-level reflections on the philosophy of history.[13] We fastidiously study the artifacts uncovered by archaeologists and the historical witness of the biblical text, striving to make sense of them while knowing they came about at the hands of humans with complex motivations not unlike our own. To get to know those who created the realia we still have with us today requires a detailed and sympathetic study of those artifacts and texts. To that extent, our work will be scientific. But we must always be on guard against thinking they were created by simplistic minds. Therefore, blanket critiques of historical criticism as rooted in positivistic science do not reflect the actual practice of historians, who view their work as a related, but not identical, body of knowledge to the natural sciences.

Moreover, because historical criticism is a human-centered activity, it is the responsibility of the historical interpreter to treat historical characters as the subjects they are. That is, the historian ought to put forth an effort to understand historical persons and the world in which they lived. As historians, we are in the wrong to presume thoughts and actions of our subjects without first rigorously studying as much as we can about that person and the historical context.[14] We must enter into historical inquiry with fear and

---

12. Harvey, *Historian and Believer*, 80. See Harvey's description of positivistic science, by contrast, on p. 68.

13. Provan et al., *Biblical History*, 42.

14. Berlin, "Scientific History," 26–27. This also strikes at the motivation for Collingwood's influential theory of "re-enactment," in which the historian is called upon to inhabit the particular thought world of a historical subject. Collingwood, *Idea*, 82–102. One can discern this theme throughout Collingwood's *Idea*, but these pages constitute the most concentrated section on re-enactment in this book. Day recognizes similarities between re-enactment and a fully empathetic approach, yet correctly identifies Collingwood's theory as purely rational. Day, *Philosophy of History*, 122. I do not find myself sympathetic to Collingwood's purely rational approach, acknowledging instead the interplay of reason and feelings. Day also stresses that Collingwood has pressed reason too far as a totalizing feature of history. Day, *Philosophy of History*, 128–29.

trembling, recognizing the chasm between ourselves and actors of the past, knowing that we study them and their time from a murky distance but that it is also our duty to allow them to speak as products of their time and as fellow human beings. Mark Day therefore contends the historian must operate with charity, beginning with a default stance of openness to the historical person, assuming her or his reasonableness in acting in or testifying to a historical event. Although historical actors are capable of lying, bias, and irrational behavior, such an open posture provides "constraint on the interpretation of others" while also bearing in mind that further evidence may press the interpreter into skepticism regarding that actor's thoughts or claims.[15]

In recognizing the temporal distance from our historical objects, especially within the discipline of biblical studies where the temporal distance from us to them is so great, it is imperative that we understand our subjects within their own historical contexts. That is, we must rigorously study the thought world and society of biblical authors and characters. We are compelled to know as much Greek, Hebrew, Aramaic, Akkadian, Ugaritic, and hieroglyphics as possible. We must study the political landscape of the ancient Near East and the Greco-Roman world. We must familiarize ourselves with the archaeological data. We are compelled to investigate genres and the expectations genres generate in readers. All the while, we must be cognizant of the limitations of such approaches. The more we can study about the ancient world that gave rise to the Bible, the more responsible we will be as historical critics.

We study these areas of knowledge, not to know the biblical world better than those who lived in it, but to attempt to be sympathetic to them. To construct, as much as we can, the worldview of the ancients is to admit that the particular topic a historian may study does not arise in a vacuum, but within a complex network of understanding. The responsible historian will attempt to make use of the concepts of her or his subjects, not the historian's own subjects.[16] Perdue, who chronicles the "collapse" of historical criticism in Old Testament theology, concedes that historical context assists the interpreter in understanding meaning, and will continue to provide a fruitful dimension of historical-critical study.[17] To my knowledge, only Derrida has

---

15. Day, *Philosophy of History*, 148–49.

16. Day, *Philosophy of History*, 137–44. See also Shoemaker's point in this regard on interpretation of Collingwood's "re-enactment" phenomenon in Shoemaker, "Inference and Intuition," 107. See also Bloch, *Historian's Craft*, 35.

17. Perdue, *Collapse*, 303–4. See also Frei's sentiments along the same lines. Frei finds some appeal in Johann Gottfried von Herder's concept of *Einfühlung* in theological study,

challenged the significance of historical context.[18] But this opens a door to a boundary-less and uncharitable reading, in which individuals and whole societies are dispensable in lieu of twisting their words and world to fit our modern agendas. Thus, many have found at least a search for historical contexts to be *a moral imperative* within the study of history.

The French historian Marc Bloch finds respect towards our historical subjects as foundational, both as a cog of the historiographical method and also to the discipline of history as a whole. He writes,

> When all is said and done, a single word, "understanding," is the beacon of light of our studies. Let us not say that the true historian is a stranger to emotion: he has that, at all events. "Understanding," in all honesty, is a word pregnant with difficulties, but also with hope. Moreover, it is a friendly word. Even in action, we are far too prone to judge. It is so easy to denounce. We are never sufficiently understanding. Whoever differs from us—a foreigner or a political adversary—is almost inevitably considered evil. A little more understanding of people would be necessary merely for guidance, in the conflicts which are unavoidable; all the more to present them while there is yet time. If history would only renounce its false archangelic airs, it would help us to cure this weakness. It includes a vast experience of human diversities, a continuous contact with men. Life, like science, has everything to gain from it, if only these contacts be friendly.[19]

Bloch's statement becomes more profound, and more urgent, when we learn he was later killed by a Nazi firing squad. His death at the hands of those infamous for their "mis-understanding" and perverted use of German history to fit a then-present need underscores how the world needs more understanding, whether with respect to our own time or the past. History is a discipline bound up with human nature,[20] and it is our responsibility as biblical historians to respect the humanness of biblical actors and authors, giving credence to their world and its events.[21]

---

though he is also frustrated that Herder left the concept fully unexplained. Frei, *Eclipse*, 184–92, 321.

18. Clark, *History, Theory, Text*, 130–55.

19. Bloch, *Historian's Craft*, 134–35.

20. Bloch, *Historian's Craft*, 26–27.

21. From the perspective of biblical studies, see a similar sentiment in Krentz, *Historical-Critical Method*, 47.

The Future of Historical Criticism

All of these factors urge the historian to be cautious in making hasty assessments based on historical data. If history writing takes on a confident air, as if writing about some *a priori* or empirical truth, this is less a fundamental flaw of the study of history than an accident of writing. Some of us learned from our teachers to avoid equivocation when we write, so there is often some conflict between historical theory and what is considered by many to be effective writing.[22] The study of history constantly evolves as new evidence arises (and in the case of the Bible, the historical evidence is literally "unearthed"). Still, based on the data we have, it is important to assert in some fashion the events and circumstances of the past. It is a means of giving voice to those who can no longer speak, and we must learn how to fairly give them space to speak. At times we may have to refrain from rushing to judgment and allow the gaps in our knowledge and tensions to remain. On this count, history will not appear as a positivistic science. But if the data coheres logically to a fact of the past, historians are bound to make claims for characters and events of the past.

Interpretation

The aspect of historical criticism that undoubtedly witnesses the most scrutiny within biblical studies is historical interpretation.[23] That we have evidence, testimony, and data concerning the past is doubtful only to the most radical epistemological skeptics. But *making sense* of this information introduces a host of issues.[24] As James M. Banner Jr. writes, knowledge about the past must reckon with "the ineradicable distance between

---

22. Gardiner, though allowing for some room for error in hypotheses elsewhere (see p. 129), asserts that historians should "insist that their formulation represent the *end* of historical inquiry, not that they are stages on the journey toward that end." Gardiner, *Historical Explanation*, 95–96.

23. As mentioned above, there are many essays within V. Philips Long's volume on ancient Israelite historiography dealing with this issue of history writing because of long-running debates between so-called "minimalists" and "maximalists." Many of these essays are found in Long, *Israel's Past*, 142–278.

24. White indicates that the disagreement among historians about causation and about how to interpret data is the difference between history and "the sciences," where there is more agreement on methodology. This is a narrow view of science and assumes more about modern scientific agreement than is true. White's point is to enumerate the different approaches to historical explanation. White, *Metahistory*, 12–13. In some ways, Levin anticipates White's analysis, but he clearly believes that the best history writing combines literary artistry and historical accuracy. Levin, *In Defense*, 1–13.

The Place of the Past

history-as-it-happened and history-as-it-is written."[25] Whose interpretation of historical realia is best? How would we even begin to claim one interpretation as better than another? What about the historian's own biases and worldview? Is the past as neat and tidy as historians tend to make it? Can we even claim we know what a historical author was trying to say?

Earlier, we introduced the seminal work of Hayden White, who argued that historical explanations are influenced by our "linguistic protocols." His work has alerted historians of all stripes as to the worldview that shapes the way we understand the past. Further condemning any ideas of historians telling an objective past, we have discussed postmodernism's insistence that either there is no metanarrative of history to tell, or that only those in power are able to determine the truth of the past. To this, we add the critique of Karl Jaspers, who reminds the historian that she or he is not transcendent above history, but still a part of it.[26] "History is at one and the same time happening and consciousness of this happening, history and knowledge of history,"[27] he writes. Since this is the case, how can the perspective[28] of a historian offer any "pure knowledge" of the past?

Yet, practically speaking, proper historical study should enable us to increase the diversity of scholars, opening up insights onto the interpretation of data of the past from worldview perspectives very different to the western ones that have dominated the academy. Historical study should not be the provenance of only a few elites.[29] Because of the use of modern history, for instance, we are able to tell stories of heroes of our own culture who

25. Banner, *Ever-Changing Past*, 242.

26. Jaspers, *Origin and Goal*, 235–76.

27. Jaspers, *Origin and Goal*, 234.

28. In keeping with much contemporary historical usage, I prefer "perspective" to the more pejorative term "bias." Whereas "perspective," in my view, refers to both a unique viewpoint and a natural restriction of an individual's knowledge, "bias" typically implies some animus on the part of the historian. I would, however, like to acknowledge the input of a treasured colleague W. Cochran Pruett, who informed me of the temporal dimension of these terms. "Bias" refers to a disposition in the present, whereas "perspective" refers to our view from the present to the past. This presses me further to reduce my use of "bias" when speaking about a historian's view of past events, however acknowledging that our present biases are often shaped by certain views of the past. To boot, Harvey concedes the historian's prejudices, but remarks that the nature of historical explanation is too dynamic and "the term 'presuppositions' obscures the plurality of fields and the correspondingly different types of warrants which are implicit in our various claims." Harvey, *Historian and Believer*, 84.

29. For instance, consider the numerous elitist fallacies Fischer lists in Fischer, *Historians' Fallacies*, 224–36.

have subverted the power of their day, such as Jarena Lee, Sojourner Truth, Dr. Martin Luther King Jr.[30] Evans counteracts postmodern claims by noting that they divert "attention away from real suffering and oppression."[31] Indeed, history responsibly done is bound to absorb as many perspectives as possible and, in so doing, should enable us to tell the stories of those who are at the margins, not just the so-called "great men of history."

In the realm of biblical studies, for instance, we are pressed to deal with a people, ancient Israel and the Jews, who confess their existence from an act of liberation from slavery in Egypt and who write from the perspective of a minor player in the sociopolitical world of the ancient Near East, constantly worn down under the hegemony of greater military and political entities.[32] In my estimation, it would be disingenuous for a biblical historian in particular to deny that studying the past in any organized way prevents us from telling the histories of the powerless.[33]

Such a view of history should warn us that only socially dominant perspectives will not suffice. Though the discipline of history is a *Wissenschaft*, it is, as Bloch states, "a science still in travail."[34] And part of the enduring struggle of the discipline of history is that no one work or interpretation of the past can lay claim to the sole understanding of any one historical event. To do so is to commit what David Hackett Fischer calls "the Baconian fallacy," which is (or ought to be!) rejected by every historian.[35] Historians are

30. See also Evans, *Defense*, 128–29. Evans also adds the suffrage movement as an example.

31. Evans, *Defense*, 158. Jenkins counters that postmodernism does not deny the reality of events, only the signification of them through words. Jenkins, "Postmodern Reply," 190. Either way, Evans, in my opinion, strikes at the more pertinent point that, in order to address injustice, we must be able to communicate and understand history in a meaningful way. For a reading sympathetic to Evans, see Zammito, "Historians and Philosophy," 63–84.

32. It is important to note that, within their own society, biblical writers were privileged. But, when writing on behalf of their people, biblical authors were clear that their land was an insignificant one in ancient geopolitics and that they were dependent upon the hands of YHWH for their survival and thriving.

33. In addition to these points, Appleby, Hunt, and Jacob accept that narrative can shape meaning, but do not wholesale concede that the identification of narrative fundamentally negates meaning. They note that postmodernism has in fact crafted its own narrative, thus undermining its more radical claims about narrative and meaning. Appleby et al., *Telling the Truth*, 235–36.

34. Bloch, *Historian's Craft*, 185. Consider also Fischer's "inexact science." Fischer, *Historians' Fallacies*, xxi.

35. Fischer, *Historians' Fallacies*, 4–8.

compelled to seek verification, criticism, and differing viewpoints of their work. One historian's triumphant event may be seen as an act of oppression through the lens of another. One historian's trust in the historical veracity of the exodus event is another's idealized narrative of the postexilic community. Such conversations enable historians to anticipate objections, hone their explanatory reasoning, and perhaps even be persuaded to see the past in a new way.[36] The hermeneutics of historical research requires an ongoing dialogue of the historian with others also familiar with the same evidence to gain a fuller picture of the past. Bloch is thus able to assert, "historical research will tolerate no autarchy."[37]

This process for the historian typically involves the tedious and anxious course of submitting articles to peer-review journals and presenting papers at academic conferences. For historians of the Bible, this means that submitting our articles and monographs to the guild for wider critique and presenting at the Society of Biblical Literature, which is laborious and often much less comfortable than remaining in the echo chambers of the like-minded scholars who attended the same doctoral programs we did or who belong to the same confessions of faith we do. But the insecurities of the historian aside, the input of the scholarly community assists the entire discipline toward a greater understanding of the past. This is not to say there will always be historical consensus after enough conversations (indeed, that will be rare), but that the practice of historiography is, in Day's appropriation of Gadamer, "dialogic."[38] In interacting with historical interpretations in the past and present, historians increase the number of voices providing input and gain clarity from their initial conclusions, which are always provisional.[39]

In their prominent book *Telling the Truth About History*, Appleby, Hunt, and Jacob similarly contend that history requires an epistemological position with "intellectual spirit of democratic scholarship"[40] and that it must be "a shared enterprise in which the community of practitioners acts as a check on the historian."[41] Indeed as a practice heavily dependent

---

36. This comment is inspired by Day, *Philosophy of History*, 21.

37. Bloch, *Historian's Craft*, 47.

38. Day, *Philosophy of History*, 162–66.

39. The understanding of historical conclusions as preliminary appears prominently in Appleby et al., *Telling the Truth*, 284; Collingwood, *Idea*, 248.

40. Appleby et al., *Telling the Truth*, 283.

41. Appleby et al., *Telling the Truth*, 261.

The Future of Historical Criticism

upon interpretation, history is only better for multiple viewpoints. Diversity within the guild will check many of the past pitfalls of the discipline we have already discussed, such as monocausal explanations, Western-only perspectives, and interpretations without evidential support. Such a conception of historical study militates against a charge of arrogance and suggests instead that our views of the past are enriched if we work as a guild rather than individually.

Nicely encapsulating the state of the historical discipline is the recent argument by Banner that "all historians are revisionists—at least in some respects."[42] By "revisionist," Banner does not mean that their conclusions are just a matter of personal opinion, for that they are

> gained through extended reading, research, study, reflection, and criticism. This does not mean that arguments about the past must be confined to academic circles, for many nonacademics have proved themselves deeply versed in various subjects of the past. It does, however, mean that what may be measured against each other as "standard" or "revisionist" histories can legitimately be considered one or the other only when they result either from archival research or from deep, knowledgeable consideration of what historians have earlier written.[43]

Thus it is foundational to history that those who write it do so with a perspective that is limited.[44] But such limitations do not prevent the historian from diligently researching sources and sympathetically constructing the past based on those sources. And neither should the historian believe her or his interpretation is the final one; rather, as Banner argues, rigorously-researched and argued history must remain subject to "revision" by the guild and public. He writes, "all historical stories can—and for historians must—be subject to analysis and critique and therefore to alteration."[45]

---

42. Banner, *Ever-Changing Past*, 10.
43. Banner, *Ever-Changing Past*, 13–14.
44. Fischer writes, "Every historian must learn to live within the limits which his own freely chosen assumptions impose upon him. These assumptions may differ radically from one historian to the next, but they exist, and a historian must learn to respect them. ... No man is free from the logic if his own rational assumptions—unless he wishes to be free from rationality itself." Fischer, *Historians' Fallacies*, xvii.
45. Banner, *Ever-Changing Past*, 262.

Evidence and Boundaries in History Writing

We have seen thus far that historiography must not be an arrogant affair.[46] It necessarily involves a deep engagement with historical actors and their contexts, not assuming or casting aspersions from a safe distance. The writing of history entails the hard work of thorough research and a sympathetic imagination toward the past. It may also include recognition of our present biases and acknowledgement of the perspective from which we write, but it must involve that we can somehow speak meaningfully about the past.

Although White astutely demonstrated the role of interpretation in the historical enterprise, this does not mean that historians are free to interpret as they wish. Rather, the other side of writing history is dealing with the constraints of evidence. Yes, historical evidence does not interpret itself and requires thorough study before it can be fitted into a broader historical picture. But historical evidence—coins, annals, chronicles, inscriptions, archaeological data, testimony, and more—provides boundaries for the conclusions historians can make.[47] Evidence does not permit the historian to use her imagination unfettered. Bloch trenchantly argues, "Explorers of the past are never quite free. The past is their tyrant. It forbids them to know anything which it has not itself, consciously or otherwise, yielded to them."[48]

In traditional historical criticism, we give priority of place to the primary sources, those that are more "evidentially reliable."[49] Of course, this is a difficult judgment for the historian to make and it is a judgment that should not be made rashly.[50] Neither, as we have already suggested,

---

46. Maza notes that contemporary historians assume the critiques of White and the postmodernists, but continue to write about the past as "compelling, fact-based stories." Maza, *Thinking About History*, 233.

47. In an opaque statement, Ankersmit takes the approach that evidence is more like a painter's brushstroke that puts constraints on a historian responding to the discovery of this evidence than it is like a magnifying glass into the past. Ankersmit, "Historiography and Postmodernism," 146. Zagorin's response to Ankersmit on this point is clearer and more in line with what I maintain here. Zagorin, "Historiography and Postmodernism," 272. See also cautions in the interpretation of evidence in Day, *Philosophy of History*, 159–62.

48. Bloch, *Historian's Craft*, 59. See also Collingwood, *Idea of History*, 241, 316; Evans, *Defense of History*, 91; Roberts, *Logic of Historical Explanation*, 265.

49. Day, *Philosophy of History*, 27–29. Also note that this distinction between primary and secondary sources is often mistakenly attributed to Ranke. See Iggers, "Introduction," xxiii–xiv.

50. For an understanding of this issue within Old Testament studies, see Deist, "Contingency, Continuity, and Integrity," 373–90.

should it be done in isolation. But evidence can limit what we say about the events and individuals of the past. We cannot say that an apple was there when the evidence points to an orange. It is the evidence that grounds our interpretations, as flawed as those interpretations may be. David Hackett Fischer writes, "The conventional wisdom of contemporary historiography still consists in the common idea that 'a historian cannot know what *really* happened, but he has a duty to try.'"[51]

For students of the Old Testament, for example, consider the biblical events describing King Hezekiah. We have at our disposal the narratives of 2 Kings 18–20, Isaiah 36–39, alongside Assyrian Annals, archaeological data, and realia such as the so-called "Hezekiah coins."[52] These are real objects and witnesses to events of the late eighth century BCE in Judah, and we must take them into account when studying this particular time and place. They indicate to us the following minimal boundaries for historical interpretation: that a King Hezekiah existed in this period and ruled over Judah, that there were battles between the Judahites and Assyrians during Hezekiah's reign, including an attempted invasion of Jerusalem in 701 BCE, and that foreign imagery and culture bore some semblance of influence on the tiny nation of Judah. It would be a steep uphill climb for a historical interpreter to argue against such facts. The evidence becomes more precarious when we consider testimony of these events. For instance, there are differing versions of why the Assyrian attack on Jerusalem did not end with the destruction of Jerusalem, depending on one's source. We must also recognize that the Judahite scribes further attest a religious reformation in Judah under Hezekiah, a detailed relationship between Hezekiah and the prophet Isaiah, and a diplomatic visit from Babylonian envoys. Finally, the redactors who helped shape the final canonical forms of 2 Kings and Isaiah were not interested in this past event out of simple curiosity but for its contemporary relevance for the post-exilic descendants of those eighth-century Judahites, descendants who had returned from Babylon and built the colony of the Yehud under the reign of the Persian King Cyrus. Interpretations of this data range from the so-called "minimalist" response

---

51. Fischer, *Historians' Fallacies*, 43. This comment appears at the end of his discussion of relativism from pages 40–43.

52. For the Assyrian perspective of Sennacherib's siege of Jerusalem, see *COS* §2.119B. Regarding the archaeological data of Jerusalem in this period, especially the expansion of the city during Hezekiah's reign, see the influential article Broshi, "Expansion of Jerusalem," 21–26. For a recent summary of the realia surrounding Hezekiah that has been discovered in Jerusalem, see Ngo, "King Hezekiah."

The Place of the Past

that, as the testimony is only known from the writings of a later post-exilic groups who used the Judahite story for their own ends, we cannot place much trust in its historical claims,[53] to a hermeneutic of historical trust that the Judahite account of the repulsion of the Assyrian army should be treated with the same respect as Sennacherib's own perspective.[54]

This is but one example of how historians of the Bible must engage in a complex study of primary sources, testimony,[55] archaeological evidence, and their own interpretations. This study must occur in conversation with those of other perspectives and be open to new evidence in order to be valid. This is obviously no straightforward science and rather operates with painstaking deliberation.

And what of the oft-debated question, seen in chapter 5, of whether an interpreter is ever able to discern an author's intention? The concept gains steam under the rubrics of postmodernism, which doubts our ability to make judgments on any author's meaning. In the previous chapter, we have dealt with critiques of the intentional fallacy, and we will not rehash all of those here. But we must revisit one previous point. That is, we must ironically point to a matter of authorial intention to make the counter-claim to objections of authorial intention. As mentioned before, Wimsatt and Beardsley, the progenitors of the idea of the intentional fallacy, were concerned with poetry, a genre of literature that is often *intentionally unintentional*. Poets frequently imbue ambiguity into their writing and allow for degrees of interpretation. This is not so with historical records, which attempt to relay a witness or evidence to actions of the past.

For instance, humanity's earliest writing is found on economic tablets from Mesopotamia. These short tablets describe transactions between parties for trade to keep records for these dealings. Room for interpretation here is minimal. As literary genres, including history, and languages become more complex, surely authors begin to write more that is unintentional in their language and more that can often be misconstrued by later readers. Yet misunderstanding of this kind is a matter of degree, dependent upon literary genre, temporal distance, knowledge of the historical context in which the texts were written, and so on. To aver that we can *never* read

---

53. For example, see Lemche, "History of Ancient Israel," 391–414.
54. For example, see Kitchen, *Reliability*, 50–51.
55. For more on testimony, see Rae, *History and Hermeneutics*, 106–30; Provan et al., *Biblical History of Israel*, 43–49.

intentionality into the text of another author is nonsense.[56] Yes, we must acknowledge our distance from the historical subject and the tendencies toward our own interpretations. But to speak meaningfully about the past and to do so with respect to our subjects, we must assume they intended to communicate meaningfully about the events of their day. This is no simple assumption, and it requires both self-awareness on the part of the historian to realize her or his own worldview and a deep study of the historical subject's worldview.

The Logic of Historical Criticism

Final-form, literary analysis of biblical texts has the distinct advantage of working with materials evident and available to any researcher. The canonical approach, narrative criticism, and postmodern literary criticism all deal with the text as it stands before us and has little-to-no need for getting behind this text.[57] Conversely, the historical-critical approach, in the minds of many in the camps of the former, masquerades as a tactic to achieve certainty about the historical realities to which texts point. And though many final-form interpreters do not completely deny the aims of historical criticism, postmodernists in particular react to what they perceive as historical criticism's search for absolute truth and attempt to poke holes in such epistemological assumptions.[58]

Yet, we must tread lightly in claiming that historical critics search for absolute certainty. This does not fall within the aim of most, if any, practicing historians. Bloch iterates as much when he notes that historical certainty and universality are "questions of degree."[59] Tucker reinforces his argu-

---

56. Day is correct that, when we make sense of a literary product, "we assign meaning and intention together." Day, *Philosophy of History*, 138. Keith Windschuttle similarly critiques White's *Metahistory* by claiming that literary devices do not encroach upon the deepest structures of language. He writes, "White has mistaken the surface for the substance, the decoration for the edifice." Windschuttle, *Killing of History*, 241.

57. Since adherents to these methodologies differ in their approach, I intentionally refrain at this point from using Derrida's rallying cry of there being "nothing outside the text." But perhaps Jenkins's interpretation of this slogan is applicable to all, namely that we cannot pretend to know that the text is pointing to realities beyond itself. Jenkins, "Postmodern Reply," 190.

58. In particular, see Adam, *Postmodern*, 5, 20; Jenkins, "Postmodern Reply," 187–88, 193.

59. Bloch, *Historian's Craft*, 17.

ments with the contention that history writing aims at the best explanation of the evidence at hand.[60] Day contends that historical knowledge is both "underdetermined" and "defeasible."[61] Berlin writes that historical language is necessarily fraught with "such words as plausibility, likelihood, sense of reality, [and] historical sense."[62] Evans asserts, rather bluntly, "No historians really believe in the absolute truth of what they are writing, simply in its probable truth, which they have done their utmost to establish by following the usual rules of evidence."[63] We see that Evans, with his insistence on historians doing "their utmost to establish" the truth, does not want to denigrate the search for historical knowledge. But he concedes that an element of probability is necessarily part and parcel of a historical epistemology. Thus, I think that Evans would agree with the assessment of Keith Jenkins, his postmodern interlocutor, that the truth of history is elusive.[64] Yet he would disagree that it is a futile endeavor. For historians, a well-educated investigation of the past that yields sparse results is more worthwhile than no investigation at all. Surely this is more than mere self-justification on the part of the historian but lies in the initial impulse for her or him to pursue historical studies.

Harvey combats the common view of certainty in historical work by emphasizing the quality of assent in historical judgment. He writes,

> Our assertions and claims . . . cannot simply be classified as either true or false, but have a certain degree of probability attached to them. This degree of probability need not be understood in a mathematical or statistical sense; rather, it can best be viewed as a way of talking about the degree of force a conclusion is believed to have by virtue of the given data and warrants. It reflects the trained judgment of the historian, the degree to which he is prepared to stake his authority on a certain utterance.[65]

Although some historians pressing specifically Bayesian calculations may argue against Harvey's claim that historical judgments are not necessarily

---

60. Tucker, *Our Knowledge*, 254–62.
61. Day, *Philosophy of History*, 148–49. For further explanation of this concept, see Tucker, *Our Knowledge*, 197–99.
62. Berlin, "Scientific History," 30.
63. Evans, *Defense*, 189.
64. Jenkins, "Postmodern Reply," 193.
65. Harvey, *Historian and Believer*, 62. See also his argument for probability on p. 82 against "scientific" conceptions of history.

The Future of Historical Criticism

mathematical, the point for us here is clear: arguments about the past have a probabilistic character that eschews mathematical certainty.

And neither, as we have noted, do historians believe their work is final. They must yield to peer review and the possibility of further evidence. Biblical historian V. Philips Long writes, "Just because *absolute* objectivity is a chimera does not mean that we must resign ourselves to *absolute* subjectivity." Instead, for Long, the plausible or probable nature of historical knowledge is "driven by the larger model of reality that we each embrace."[66] Finally, Collingwood summarizes this process well when he writes,

> No fact ever has been wholly ascertained, but a fact may be progressively ascertained; as the labour of historians goes forward, they come to know more and more about the facts, and to reject with greater and greater confidence a number of mistaken accounts of them; but no historical statement can ever express the complete truth about any single fact. . . . This is perfectly well known to all historians. No historian imagines that he knows any single fact in its entirety, or that any historian ever will.[67]

So if historians do not seek unconditional certainty, with what logic do they proceed? In short, historical logic is inferential.[68] There is not space here to enumerate the depth of this form of logic, as it is at present an entire subset of study for logicians and has gained popularity for researchers working on artificial intelligence.[69] Inferences may take the form of Bayesianism, which seeks to relate the evidence and the hypothesis by proportion

---

66. Long, "Introduction," 9. See also Miller, "Reading the Bible," 357. Also within biblical studies, see Maier, "Truth and Reality," 198.

67. Collingwood, *Essays*, 43. Or, consider the ever-pithy Santayana, who writes, "History is always wrong, and so always needs to be rewritten." George Santayana, *Life of Reason*, 5:237. Biblical historian Baruch Halpern says, "historiography is never accurate." Halpern uses the metaphor of a portrait. The painter will not get every detail correct in capturing reality, but will do his or her best to paint reality from his or her perspective. In the same way, the historian cannot capture the reality of the past in every detail and will be led by an interpretive lens, but must still strive to understand the historical subject as best as possible. Halpern, *First Historians*, 8.

68. Collingwood uses this term as a means of demonstrating how history is a science in that it pieces together data to draw conclusions, but historians are not able to empirically observe the events they describe, as natural scientists do. Collingwood, *Idea*, 50, 251–52, 282. Santayana uses the same term in Santayana, *Life of Reason*, 5:238.

69. For an overview of inferential logic as it is presently practiced, see McClain and Poston, *Best Explanations*.

The Place of the Past

to which they support one another.[70] Inferences also may utilize explanationism, which attempts to explain the evidence from the hypothesis.[71] Or inferences may incorporate abduction, which rules out hypotheses that do not fit the evidence.[72] None of these logical tools offers certainty, but they do assist us in reaching more likely historical propositions.[73]

In practice, historians may or may not be conscious of or intentional about the type of inferential logic they use. But, as they attempt to explain historical phenomena, they will undoubtedly use inference because it is an earnest attempt to be reasonable and pragmatic. Inference is reasonable in that it seeks to make the most sense of the connections between the evidence and testimony.[74] It is pragmatic because it acknowledges that we, and the historical actors we study, exist in real time and space.[75] And in time and space, we often must use the best logic available to us, which is often inferential. In fact, we use inferential logic all the time in real life when we conduct "historical" investigations, such as when we piece together data at hand to find lost car keys or try to discern why the restaurant we used to visit suddenly has a closed sign on the door. Historians formalize this process for events temporally more distant and with fragmented evidence, especially as the temporal distance increases. But this does not mean that our hypotheses are without logical foundation. While this sort of logic will not appease the hardline empiricist, it provides workable rationales for understanding the past.[76]

---

70. Day, *Philosophy of History*, 37–44. For a helpful introduction to Bayesinaism, see Day, *Philosophy of History*, 31–37.

71. Misak, "Peirce and Ramsey," 25–38.

72. For a review of these methods, as well as some other lesser-known logical tools for history, see Day and Radick, "Historiographic Evidence," 87–97.

73. See Fischer's mention that natural scientists "can never assert that an effect will always happen but only that it will probably happen." Fischer, *Historians' Fallacies*, 184.

74. See the discussion of consilience below. Collingwood stresses the importance of the historian's identification with historical actors in his concept of re-enactment. I would not go as far as Collingwood in assuming the transferability of reason between ourselves and historical actors, but I do believe that, in so far as we share a common human nature with historical actors and thoroughly study their historical context and thought world, we might reasonably imagine their actions in history.

75. Gardner especially underscores the practical nature of historical understanding. Gardiner, *Historical Explanation*, 12.

76. See Misak's similar statement about "the solipsist and the skeptic." Misak, "Peirce and Ramsey," 25.

The Future of Historical Criticism

We should note here Day's claim that the historian's judgment of evidence should be "consilient." That is, we ought to account for a wide range of phenomena that converge on a strong conclusions and require the simplest explanation.[77] In other words, we ought to choose the relationship between the evidence at hand that requires the simplest explanation. This tactic yields a more reasonable explanation with less nuance. This is not to deny, as mentioned above, that the past can be messier than our typically monocausal view of the it. That would be the case when evidence from the past is sparse, as if often the case in biblical studies. But our explanations must logically work to cohere many levels of causes, and consilience remains a logical approach in so far as it acknowledges the full range of evidence, whether primary or secondary, and seeks to paint a fuller picture of the events of the past.[78]

To return to the example of Hezekiah's run-in with the neo-Assyrian army, archaeological digs in Jerusalem remain limited, and we have conflicting and rhetorically charged reports of what happened. On the one hand, there are strictures to what we will be able to say about this event, as we have mentioned above. But on the other hand, it is an important inquiry for the guild to pursue due to the bearing it has on various issues, including the redaction of the Deuteronomistic History, the reliability of the Old Testament as Scripture, and what causes mighty empires to fall. And, because of this importance, biblical historians and Assyriologists alike will continue to pursue it. They will closely examine everything from the primary evidence, biblical testimony, our understanding of ancient warfare, ancient religious views about divine causality, and so on. They will do so by drawing conclusions that may appear confident. But these conclusions are not certain; rather, they are inferential, attempting to cohere the evidence with a hypothesis. And they are provisional, subject to critique by the guild and the availability of further evidence.

---

77. Day, *Philosophy of History*, 148–49. This concept, and the related idea of "colligation," trace their origins to the philosopher and scientist William Whewell. For a detailed application of colligation to the philosophy of history, see Roberts, *Logic of Historical Explanation*, 16–37.

78. Roberts writes, "The greatest explanatory power . . . is gained neither by counting more instances nor by manipulation; it is gained by describing the connection between the two terms of the correlation." Roberts, *Logic of Historical Explanation*, 25. For a review of causation in the philosophy of history, see Tucker, "Causation in Historiography," 99; Tucker, "Origins," 220–30; Maza, *Thinking About History*, 157–98.

Thus, we see that the practice of history does not rely on mathematical certainty in its results. Neither does it depend on pure conjecture. Instead, historians must operate with informed knowledge of their subjects to infer hypotheses. Although this may not satisfy those seeking epistemological positivism, it aligns with history's precarious balance between facts and interpretation.

Causation in the Study of History

Another way in which traditional historians have been critiqued for following the rules of modern science is the manner in which historians have sought to find a single cause in historical events. In the same way a chemist seeks to find the chemical that has caused a reaction, the historian, so the thinking goes, seeks the underlying cause to a major historical event.

F. R. Ankersmit, for one, employs Nietzsche's critique of causation in science to demonstrate how historians have viewed causation of events too simply. For Nietzsche, the cause is supposed to be the "primary" event that leads to the "secondary" event, the "effect." However, we can only know the primary by means of the secondary. So if a cause only becomes a cause by means of an effect, it ceased to be primary. In the same way, historians forensically search for causes to events that only become causes once we deem the event important enough.[79] The cause of an event then becomes a construction of the historian, not something that is "out there" to be discovered as if it is some natural, scientific phenomenon.

In contrast to this perception of the historian's work, Patrick Gardiner argues that causation in history is much more complex than is often assumed. He writes,

> Misled by the ambiguities hidden in the word "cause," philosophers have believed that somewhere in every historical situation there is present a factor of a certain type and that, once this factor is pin-pointed, everything else can be seen to follow from it. But this belief is an illusion. The historical process is not like a machine that has to be kept in motion by a metaphysical dynamo behind the scenes. And there are no absolute Real Causes waiting to be discovered by historians with sufficiently powerful magnifying glasses. What do exist are historians writing upon different levels and at different distances, historians writing with different aims

---

79. Ankersmit, "Historiography and Postmodernism," 141–42.

and different interests, historians writing in different contexts and from different points of view. It is not altogether surprising that, when the levels are confused, the contextual distinctions blurred, and the points of view run into one another, contradictions arise and antimonies are created. For when this is done there are no rules according to which they may be settled.[80]

Thus, we see for Gardiner that causation depends on the questions one asks of how an event came to be, as well as the perspective of the historian.[81] This leads to a thicker description of an event than the simple attribution of a single cause. Historians ought to have a better grasp of the complexity of history.

Bloch, for instance, acknowledges that causes can be multiple, and they often deal with human motives not easily observable.[82] Day contends that historians must view causation as a broad phenomenon, not easily attributable to one source.[83] This is because, in part, causation is viewed from varying perspectives (as with Gardiner) and deals with tendencies and capabilities that are not directly perceptible (as Bloch).[84]

For this reason, many practicing historians resist simplistic explanations of historical phenomena. Fischer argues that reducing causation from "complexity to simplicity, or diversity to uniformity" is an objectionable fallacy.[85] Evans claims that historians should be, and have been, "hostile to 'oversimplification,'" as they seek rather to question all narratives, whether those of their peers or even those of past testimonies.[86] Sarah Maza writes, "Historians often avoid putting their money on one type of cause over another, instead explaining how various factors accumulate over time to a point of no return."[87] Thus, it seems that the mischaracterization of history as producing simplistic causation is more about the faults of historians in practice than it is about the way history ought to be done.

In the same way, historians of the Bible ought to defy naïve, overarching explanations for historical phenomena and look ever deeper into

---

80. Gardiner, *Historical Explanation*, 109.
81. See also Gardiner, *Historical Explanation*, 24.
82. Bloch, *Historian's Craft*, 194–95.
83. Day, *Philosophy of History*, 73–76.
84. Day, *Philosophy of History*, 78–79.
85. Fischer, *Historians' Fallacies*, 172.
86. Evans, *Defense*, 126–27.
87. Maza, *Thinking About History*, 173.

the historical world into which they gaze.[88] Returning to our example of Sennacherib's invasion of Jerusalem and subsequent retreat, we must recognize that, even in the primary record, we have different perspectives on the cause of this retreat. The biblical text attributes it to divine intervention (the angel of YHWH killing 185,000 Assyrians); Sennacherib's record attributes the cause to political machinations. How a modern historian assesses the "real cause" (and as we have seen with Gardiner, such a thing cannot exist) will depend on her or his perspective. A hermeneutic of trust will lean towards the biblical account; a hermeneutic of suspicion will prefer Sennacherib's view of *Realpolitik*. But, there are even more alternatives. The cause could be viewed from an economic perspective (the Assyrians were more interested in filling their coffers). The cause could be viewed from a military perspective (the Assyrians were a long way from home and perhaps not adequately resourced to assault Jerusalem much longer). Must only one of these perspectives be correct? Is causation only about divine, political, economic, or military views?

The historian must take all of these into account in viewing the complexity of a past event. Further, historians ought to recognize the complexity that exists, not only in the primary records, but in their own assessments. And historians ought to accept that their interpretation of such a cause is subject to critique from the guild.

The Purpose in Studying History

Before we leave the philosophy of history, it will be pertinent to discuss the goal of history. What is the purpose of studying history anyway? If we can discover a *telos* for this discipline, perhaps it will help us understand the role it plays in our primary area of concern, biblical exegesis.

It could be that history exists for the present, a phenomenon known as "presentism." After all, this undergirds many etiologies from the primeval history of the Bible, to the ancient Greeks, to the study of the "Founding Fathers." Students of history often want to know, "How did we get here?" Doing so creates a sense of identity and aids us in that existential search for our origins.[89] The study of the past was, for the early Greek historian

---

88. Within biblical studies, see Maier, "Truth and Reality," 198–99.
89. Fischer, *Historians' Fallacies*, 315.

Thucydides, only for the present, as it was only possible to write history from one's present location.[90]

R. G. Collingwood hints at the goal of history in presentism when he writes,

> Finally, since the past in itself is nothing, the knowledge of the past in itself is not, and cannot be, the historian's goal. His goal, as the goal of a thinking being, is knowledge of the present; to that everything must return, round that everything must revolve. But, as a historian, he is concerned with one special aspect of the present—how it came to be what it is. In that sense, the past is an aspect or function of the present; and that is how it must always appear to this historian who reflects intelligently on his own work, or in other words, attempts a philosophy of history.[91]

Similarly, knowing the past can assist us in building a better future. The classical statement in this perspective comes from the philosopher George Santayana, who writes, "Those who do not study the past are doomed to repeat it."[92] This motto, emblazoned on a plaque at Auschwitz, reminds us that we must learn from our faults to avoid the pitfalls of the past. Such a view strikes the present writer as an overly negative view of the past, as if the past does not also include fortunate, happy, and even bittersweet events from which we can learn.[93] Yet the point stands that the past can be useful to us in some respect.

For a biblical historian, the events of Sennacherib's invasion are important for the way it informs faith today. What does this passage say about the character of YHWH, who defended Jerusalem and the Davidic dynasty? What does it say about resistance to YHWH's protection of the city? What does it say about God's character in contrast to the ultimate destruction of Jerusalem over a hundred years later at the hands of the Babylonians? Such questions would be the only ones that drive history with the view of presentism.

But presentism can be dangerous if left as the sole purpose for studying history. Doing so can overlook parts of the past that are not relevant

---

90. Momigliano, "Place of Herodotus," 3–4.
91. Collingwood, *Essays*, 139.
92. Santayana, *Life of Reason*, 1:68.
93. Writing from my own theological tradition, see Holland, "Wesleyan-Methodist Tradition," 90–91.

The Place of the Past

to the present, viewing them as superfluous.[94] Only picking out the useful parts of history is disingenuous and single-minded, overlooking the complexity and many perspectives found in the historical record. For as much as we have defended Ranke here, perhaps this critique could be legitimately made of his work seeking to find an ideological spirit behind German history.[95] This was certainly the case for historians in the Nazi era, who sought Aryan origins for the German people and viewed their history as being one of victimhood at the hands of the Jews.[96] Perhaps the most damning critique of presentism, and even utilizing the past for the future, is that our biases can interfere with an honest assessment of the past that may be inconvenient for our present and future aims. In our example of Hezekiah and Sennacherib, it becomes easy for the modern scholar's viewpoint to be shaped by faith commitments only (although these surely play a role) and for them to jump to conclusions.

Would it then be wise to pursue history for its own sake, a phenomenon known as "antiquarianism"? After all, if we are to truly respect the past, we should not study it to glean something from it in a utilitarian fashion.

This approach, however, is more easily dismissed than presentism. A purely antiquarian view toward history quickly falls victim to the question of "so what?" It fails to make the study of history relevant. But more significantly, it negates the idea that the past exists in continuity to today. We do not stand on some distant perch of perfect knowledge from which we can completely and thoroughly view the past. We are still entrenched in history today.[97] To study history for its own sake is well-intentioned but lacks the self-awareness of our present position as both being informed by history and as a part of it.

Presentism is a valiant attempt to explain why history is relevant. Antiquarianism is to be commended in that it holds the past in high regard without leveraging it for our present agendas. But both are incomplete as goals for studying history.

Combining the best of these approaches while discarding their negative weight is Bloch's aforementioned goal of "understanding."[98] If history

---

94. Fischer, *Historians' Fallacies*, 135. See also Clark, *History, Theory, Text*, 19–20.
95. Braw, "Vision as Revision," 47.
96. Bullock, *Hitler*, 224–25.
97. See discussion of Karl Jaspers on p. 136.
98. Similarly, Collingwood summarizes the point of history as "self-knowledge." Collingwood, *Idea*, 10. Fischer aims at thinking historically. Fischer, *Historians' Fallacies*,

becomes a means of understanding the past, we come closer to understanding humanity and how it functions in this world. This is certainly not to argue that history is about discovering universal laws of human behavior. Sure, patterns may emerge, but if the foregoing has told us anything about the guidelines of practicing history, it is that history resists much that is general and simplistic because it is about human actors in space and time. History is "other" in its temporal distance from us. Yet history is also in continuity with us, never ceasing through time. It is crucial to understand, the best we can, how and why the world has changed through time. We do this neither to achieve some agenda, nor to live in the past, but to come to a greater understanding of who we are as humans. The human condition is at the fore of the rationale for studying history. History is, after all, a humanistic discipline.

In studying history, we will find that the past is much more complex than we might initially expect in the same way that our present life is complex. We will also find that events have multiple and sometimes inexplicable causes, unlike the scientific world, due to human factors. We might even find ourselves sympathetic to those who are vastly different from (read, "other" than) us. If our time needs any further reason to study history than this, then I am unaware of it.

We must, therefore, approach the events of 701 BCE in Jerusalem with an attempt to understand as fully as possible why the neo-Assyrian army fled. An intellectually honest historian must try to sympathize with both Hezekiah and Sennacherib, resisting the call to see one as superstitious and the other opportunistic. Their motivations would have been complex. The pressure they felt must have been dire and their explanations for what happened driven by more than we can possibly know. How do we know these things? Because they, like us, are human. These are not the only two historical actors a historical critic would investigate. A historian of the Bible would also be curious about the characters (named or unnamed) in the background of this text, the scribe or scribal community that produced such a text originally and later on in transmission, and the community to which the text was written. These are all of interest to historians and produce an inexhaustible number of questions for inquiry. What we say about them and the events they experienced we must approach with caution,

---

316. John Fea contends for transformation. Fea, *Why Study History*, 123–40. I am sympathetic to these answers, but I prefer Bloch's response to this question as it more accurately entails the existence of the "other" in historical knowledge. These answers contain a tinge of individualism that I do not believe captures the fullness of the rationale for historical study.

acknowledging our own situatedness in history and perspectives, not to mention the limited evidence available to us. And we must do so on the data we *do* have at hand. We may come away unsatisfied with how much we can conclude. And we will do so knowing that our analysis is subject to critique by others immersed in this history. Such is historical practice done, not for our own sake, or even for the sake of historical actors, but to come to a greater understanding of the human condition that unites all of us.[99]

Historical Theory in Biblical Theology

Thus far, we have considered the value of historical criticism for general study of the Bible. But what about those for whom the study of the Bible is also a matter of faith? Are there principles by which the study of history can be constructive for a normative reading of the Bible?

Although biblical theologians have certainly fallen prey to thin notions of understanding history, the critiques of which we have reviewed in chapter 3, this does not mean that biblical theology should be void of history. Rather, a few biblical critics sympathetic to the aims of historical criticism have elucidated many of the tenets of proper historical use of the Bible in theology, as we have outlined here.

Among these is John Barton, who concurs that proper historical study of the Bible is not "positivistic."[100] Neither does historical criticism seek to be objective in the way we often think of distanced, dispassionate objectivity. Rather, for Barton, historical criticism requires "the sense of recognizing their otherness from ourselves."[101] In lieu of the misconceptions of historical practice, Barton contends that biblical criticism in general, and particularly in its historical-critical mode, is "rigorous."[102] Such an examination of the biblical text cannot lead to certain judgments, only

---

99. I wonder if postmodernists could also appreciate this goal of history. If postmodernism is, as I understand it, more about opposition to "objectivist" and "neutral" accounts of history writing than about arguing against anything in the past happening, could they at least agree that the aim to make sense of the human condition is worthwhile, albeit difficult to fully know in its verbal expressions?

100. Barton, *Nature*, 49–52. Similarly, see Collins, *Bible After Babel*, 10.

101. Barton, *Nature*, 59. See also the similar view of Martti Nissinnen, who view historical criticism as "the interplay between times and spaces in the hermeneutical process." Nissinen, "Reflections," 123.

102. Barton, *Nature*, 51, 66.

probable ones, as it functions with a different logic than that of certainty.[103] Similarly, Paul E. Capetz dismisses the idea that historical criticism used in the service of theology is positivistic. Historical work for Capetz is never "objective" in the rational scientific sense, but operates with presuppositions as do all humanistic disciplines.[104] Still Capetz contends for a clear, but related, delineation between history and theology. Students, he argues, must know the distinction between a historical question and a theological one.[105] Historical criticism's value in theology lies in letting the dead speak, particularly in our contemporary conversations.[106] Once we can do the work of understanding what was said in an original utterance of a text, including the context in which it was written and how it was communicated, theology then takes over to relate the ancient utterance to our modern one. Not only does this have value for a better understanding of the biblical text for Capetz, but it also equips students to have a greater appreciation and understanding across any cultural gap or worldview.[107]

Paul Joyce understands history's service to theology in terms of its intellectual, moral, and imaginative challenges. As for the intellectual challenge, historical criticism should provide guardrails on any interpretive directions with which we may wish to understand a text. Morally, the boundaries we discover in historical interpretation can aid us in understanding the ethical constraints of the original context and how such constraints may still be binding on us today. But, thirdly, the boundaries of historical criticism should ignite the contemporary imagination in ways we might not have otherwise done had we remained solely in a modern mindset.[108] "It is intriguing how often hard-nosed historical research will throw up some of the possibilities even more fruitful than those generated by the unbridled roamings of the mind."[109] Thus Joyce concurs with the value of history for creating interpretive boundaries,[110] but that these boundaries stoke, rather than inhibit, our imagination through greater understanding

---

103. Barton, *Nature*, 66.
104. Capetz, "Theology," 470.
105. Capetz, "Theology," 482.
106. Capetz, "Theology," 479–80, 484.
107. Capetz, "Theology," 484.
108. Joyce, "First Among Equals?," 17–27.
109. Joyce, "First Among Equals?," 26.
110. See also Collins, *Bible After Babel*, 10.

of the original location of the text instead of remaining in our own contemporary *Weltanschauung*.

One sees in these reflections the refrain of "understanding." Whether Barton's emphasis on the "otherness" of the biblical world, Capetz's encouragement to "let the dead speak," or Joyce's reminder that study of the original context can provoke a well-informed imagination for theology in the present, these biblical historians concur with the wider historical project that there is value in sympathetically understanding the past, even for theology today. To these we add the voice of Lawson G. Stone, who similarly argues regarding the history of development of the biblical text, "a historical interpreter seeks an awareness of the human community that bequeathed the text to us."[111] Thus, historical criticism "can show to what extent we are listening to the text, and, by sharpening the specific profile of a biblical text, can provide a basis for criticizing our biblical-theological statements."[112] Our attention to the historical background and development of a text is then a moral duty as readers to a text's historical actors and those who produced the text.[113] We may not make of a text as we wish, and historical study will certainly constrain us in this regard. But this is exactly the kind of moral virtues that history should produce in its students as they seek to understand others.

Perhaps lost in the minutiae of all of the details about which historical critics argue, understanding remains at the center of historical criticism. It is easy to see how many theologians view historical arguments as useless to present theological claims while historians contend for minor readings of Aramean inscriptions and the like. But some biblical critics have suggested the positive ways in which historical criticism can offer a deeper understanding of the texts that can open up fresh theological meaning for many of them. Historical criticism can establish the parameters of understanding the biblical text more clearly before we try to draw theological judgments from it. And it can further provide the tools to understand both the characters spoken of in the text and those who produced the text.

---

111. Stone, "Historical Authenticity," 94.
112. Stone, "Historical Authenticity," 88.
113. Joyce, "First Among Equals?," 23.

The Enduring Study of the Past

This chapter has attempted to show why interpreters of the Bible need not be wary of studying the Bible's past. Yes, historical criticism has been reckless at times, but this does not mean we should throw out the proverbial baby with the bathwater. The critiques of historical criticism over the last several decades should, instead of eradicating the discipline, press it to be refined.

We have suggested here that several principles should guide the work of historians, particularly in the realm of biblical history. Those of us who are historians should apply caution to our work, understanding that our conclusions, however well researched, cannot aspire to final and total knowledge. We must have awareness of our perspectives, being certain only of the fact that we will not see the past in the same way as others. Therefore, we must introduce our ideas to a broad and diverse community of historians to continue the conversation about the events of the past and their value. We must become more cognizant of the logic we use, knowing that it is not with some kind of epistemological certainty that we operate. Instead, our conclusions should be reliant upon inferential and consilient reasoning. We must resist simplistic causality, being aware of the complexity of the past and all reality. Finally, we should keep the goal of the discipline in mind to constantly impress upon ourselves why "understanding" of those in the past guides our investigations. If we engage history in this way, this ought to press us towards a more responsible reading of the past.

We have also suggested that viewing the past with historical responsibility might prove of some value for biblical theology. Specifically, an understanding of the events and characters of the biblical past leads us toward greater knowledge of God and the human condition now. In the final chapter, we will conclude with some further reflections on historical criticism's role in theology, and the discipline of biblical exegesis as a whole.

8

Conclusion

THIS BOOK HAS ATTEMPTED to examine the various dimensions of historical-critical study of the Bible. Historical criticism is concerned with myriad questions about the origins of the text and the events the text describes. These questions concern matters such as who wrote the compositions, how they were assembled into the form we have now, what the oral backgrounds of the texts might have been, what the world looked like when the texts were composed, whether the events happened the way they are described, and even whether its characters existed in space and time.

We have found that such questions do not yield simple answers. In first sketching an outline of its origins, we discovered that only a few of our contemporary historical interests were relevant in the past. There is certainly a historical impulse in the Bible itself, the ancient Near East, and in Greco-Roman historiography. But neither would we describe their drive to understand the past as having the same precision, or even goals, that many modern historians possess. Even this ancient curiosity to understand the past faded into the background for well over a millennium. The medieval period witnesses to very few investigations of the past, let alone those of the kind for which contemporary historians strive. It is not until the Renaissance that historical interests reemerge. These interests were compounded by the ensuing reaction against ecclesial authority in the Reformation, leading ultimately to some very skeptical conclusions about historical readings during

Conclusion

the Enlightenment. Very rapidly, the Bible became not only a treasured book for the sacred, but an artifact subject to critical examination for all.

In the boom of historical criticism in the late nineteenth and early twentieth centuries, historical questions about the Bible passed critical examination for some, particularly in the Biblical Theology Movement. But for others, such as Troeltsch, historical study demanded that traditional, orthodox conclusions submit to a rigid, often skeptical, view of history. On the one hand, the dominance of historical-critical study of the Bible in this period proved so strong that it became difficult for exegetes to put the proverbial toothpaste back in the tube. Historical criticism in some sense was here to stay, no matter how much its critics complained. On the other hand, the eager way in which historical-critical study was conducted in this period left itself open to censure. Historical criticism had become such a fetish among scholars that they became prone to overemphasize their conclusions in determining the meaning of a text, and especially so for understanding its theological import.

Historical criticism then elicited strong reaction both from within religious circles and from without. From within the church and synagogue, the objection became essentially whether historical criticism was a viable approach to speak about God. The methods, it was said, did not match the source. Its questions were illegitimate ones to apply to a source that exists to serve the faithful. From outside of religious concerns, the study of literature became subject to dense interrogations about the ability of any text to bear a fixed meaning. And the study of history was plagued with assertions that knowledge of the past is too unstable to pursue and that historians themselves bring more bias to the past than they are aware. Critiques from both fields, literature and history, had seamless import to the Bible, which is, in an Enlightenment view, a text from and about the past like any other.

In the previous two chapters, we suggested that many historical critics have rightly seen the critiques against them as an overcorrection. A crucial factor has been the need to cling to some sense of an author's intended meaning in a text. This intention inscribes a historical testimony into the text, yielding a source that should be valuable for historians. Many within literary theory since the peak of deconstructionism's popularity have attempted to show how readings of texts will consider that an author can, and often does, write with some meaning in mind, and moreover that the responsible reader will pay attention to these meanings. For the purposes of historical study, if intended meanings are to be found, it becomes imperative that the historian understand as much about the world of the author as possible to determine that meaning. Thus, the knowledge of historical context is indispensable. We should also add to this historical understandings of language and grammar to clarify how the author viewed her language to communicate intended ideas.

But more than literary quibbling, historians have tried to demonstrate that their craft has been misunderstood. Although most historians operate intuitively and without conscious application of theory, they generally resist seeing their work as positivistic. Historical work does not aim for certainty as much as it does understanding. And understanding of historical subjects is not easily attained. It involves drawing provisional conclusions using inferential logic to interpret historical facts. It involves the historian's own perspective, but one that is in dialogue with others. It is not a field that will produce simple and efficient answers. But it should produce worthwhile ones.

As indicated in the introduction, the fact that historical criticism continues in the wake of strong critiques has led us to a situation in which practitioners of biblical exegesis are at a standstill. Interpreters find themselves working on one side of the divide more than the other, if not exclusively so. And as we often find in such situations, scholars have talked past, and sometimes down to, one another. As someone who has been educated in and worked on each side of this divide, I hoped to bring some healing to this rift. I do not pretend to have solved any issues. But in the interest of continuing the conversation and of constructing a fruitful biblical exegesis, I have attempted to be as sympathetic as possible to both sides and fill in gaps on what has recently been the side more bereft of theory, historical criticism. It is appropriate at this point then to complete my objective and offer some conclusions on what historical criticism offers biblical exegesis.

At stake in the critiques against historical criticism has been a historical captivity of the text. For literary critics, the reader and the text itself are freed for wider meaning than a historical author can determine. For theologians, a Bible put in the service of history fails to do much to serve the church today. But we have seen that historians also view their work as liberative. They wish to free the original meaning of the text to speak before we get to explore what it might mean for us today. This was of particular concern to the Reformers and many in the humanistic vein who followed them.

So it seems that scholars are in agreement that freedom in reading is a good thing. But whom are we freeing when we read? Is it the text, the church,

Conclusion

the reader, or the author? The answer is "yes." *All* of these can be freed in a reading, depending on the questions we ask. Helmut Utzschneider's application of Umberto Eco, which we encountered in chapter 6, rings pertinently here. Depending on which question we bring to a text's meaning, we are bound to get different answers.[1] Although one will occasionally hear that a student is asking the "wrong" question about a text, a stance of free inquiry will not regard this as a valid response. All questions about texts, especially an "open"[2] texts such as the Bible, should be fair game in the name of academic freedom. In the Christian tradition, we must take seriously Jesus' addition to Deuteronomy 6:5, in which he contends we should love God with our minds (Matt 22:37; Mark 12:30; Luke 10:37). Historical questions asked of texts do not pretend to restrict meaning to what the author intended in his or her context, but they should produce answers that both yield a historical answer and demonstrate boundaries on meaning.

By way of example, consider the story of Naaman the Syrian's healing in 2 Kings 5. From a historical perspective, we could ask a number of questions. Did this really happen? What was the nature of Naaman's skin disease? What were the geopolitical dynamics of the conflict of the Syro-Ephraimite War? Who was the author of this story? Was it originally narrated by the author of the Deuteronomistic History or did it come from a different source? Who was his audience, and why did he produce this story? From these we could launch an investigation with a large range of answers about historicity, realities of the ancient Near East, redaction theories, ancient Israelite religion, and so on.

But there are, of course, other legitimate questions we can ask as well. From a literary perspective, we could examine the congruences between this story and the other miracles of the Elijah-Elisha cycles, not to mention Jesus' miracles. We could study repeated words, gaps in the narrative, characterization, and more. From a theological perspective, we could ask what canons of the rule of faith apply here, not to mention whether and how this narrative prefigures baptism. Although some might object to jumping past the historical situation, the baptismal functions of cleansing and doing

---

1. Similar sentiments are noted on Stone, "Historical Authenticity," 92; Capetz, "Theology," 467; Hong, "Synchrony and Diachrony," 538; Barton, "Historical-Critical Approaches," 18; Keck, "Historical Critical Method," 123; Nissinen, "Reflections," 35–36; Wischmeyer, "Author–Text–Intention," 24.

2. Thiselton borrows the concept of the Bible as an "open" text to describe it as a text that "sets the mind going in different directions" even though its possible meanings have limitations. Thiselton, "Future of Biblical Interpretation," 3–4.

something simple but humbling to receive relief (5:13) have clear analogues in a theological setting despite whatever incongruities there might be between the practice of Christian baptism and this ancient Israelite story. It is not then that the question is right or wrong but *proper to a given field of inquiry*. Each discipline will work with its own set of assumptions and methods regarding the same object, the Bible.

The historical-critical approaches limit us from arguing that a passage like 2 Kings 5 can be taken to mean whatever we want it to mean. It sets a strong, though admittedly broad, framework on matters ranging from how ancient Israel viewed the efficacy of divine healing, to relations between officials in wartime of the ancient world, to prominent indicators that different traditions of miraculous healers have been brought into the canon of 1–2 Kings. These boundaries do not intend to provide *strictures* on the questions the interpreter may ask. Rather, they provide *structure* to what other interpretations may do.[3]

So we cannot expect a historical question to directly affect the theological if they lie in different fields of inquiry. Or can we? Is there any intersection between the two? Although we have just divided the historical from the theological, as have Gabler and so many modern critics, this need not be the case. While it is necessary to pursue lines of inquiry in both historical and theological issues regarding the Bible, they are not mutually exclusive. One overlooked piece of this division is that the Bible represents the earliest witness to tradition.[4] The theological tradition after the writing of Scripture that reflects on it continues the conversation. Both the Bible and later theological tradition need interpretation, and they can, within a Gadamerian framework of hermeneutics, easily be seen as mutually informed horizons of interpretation.

As noted throughout our history of historical criticism, the "literal" or "plain" meaning of a biblical text, which often included the forerunners of contemporary historical-critical concerns, had to be established before drawing theological points from the Bible. Origen, for instance, searched for the best text to exegete. Eusebius considered the issue of authorship. Antiochenes pressed the importance of genre. Even though the literal sense of the Bible collapsed as the Renaissance wore on into the Reformation, it nonetheless has been commonplace in Christian hermeneutics to determine the meaning(s) inscribed in a biblical text before applying it to the

---

3. See a similar sentiment in Bell, *Ruled Reading and Biblical Criticism*, 123.
4. See also Bell, *Ruled Reading and Biblical Criticism*, 103.

Conclusion

faith of one's own day. Calvin's argument that the *mens scriptoris* is already theological is helpful in some places (i.e., Paul's letters or the Deuteronomistic Historian) more than others (i.e., Song of Solomon). But almost all exegetes can agree that the plain sense of the text has ordinal, even if not theological, priority. Historical criticism is a gift to deepen our understanding of this dimension of the biblical text. Exegetes have long contended that we must understand what words meant in their context, what sociopolitical factors play into what an author may write, and the genre to which a text belongs. It would be inappropriate for us to use 2 Kings 5, for instance, to support our own theory of baptism without first detailing what the event of Naaman's washing and healing meant in its original context. To do otherwise is theologize on something other than the basis of Scripture. This is not to say that all historical exegetes will come up with the same conclusions about this event of washing and that all theologians will come to the same theological doctrines from it. Instead, the "letter" constructs the apparatus on which the theological may play.[5]

Another dimension to theological readings of the Bible in which historical criticism may be of aid is in comprehending the human side of divine revelation. In some ways, Troeltsch's concept of analogy leads us in this direction, although I do not wish to assume that the worldview of the ancients was wholly the same as our own. And this is exactly the point. Judeo-Christian interpretation of the Bible traditionally makes space for the human element in divine inspiration. It is humans who dictated, wrote, edited, copied these works we now include in the canon. A theological approach does not, or at least should not, assume ill will on the part of these human agents. These are individuals who have composed their texts after some experience of the divine—the same divine being the synagogue and church confess today. This human experience is valued by God from the outset of Scripture (Gen 1:26–27). Particularly in the Christian tradition, it is valued in the person and work of God made flesh and the God who, though God began human history in a Garden (Gen 2–3), returns in the last times to us with all the marks of human history intact (Rev 21–22). Human history matters to God, and the humanistic elements of historical investigation, though they may have gone awry in the eyes of many traditional believers, provide the tools for a sympathetic understanding of those who encountered the living God.

---

5. See also Stanglin, *Letter and Spirit*, 207–10, 213–14; Barton, *Nature*, 69–116.

The Place of the Past

Neither should we fear, then, of what we may find in our historical investigations. Much as we use standard language and phrases (i.e., academic rhetoric and technical terms), composition techniques (i.e., word processing software), and assuming an entire worldview (i.e., my own white, male, Western, Methodist one), it should not surprise us that a biblical author or redactor would employ genres and redactional techniques to compose a biblical text. If historical investigation does not match our expectations of how an event is narrated in the biblical text, this ought to push us to ask what the author was aiming for rather than expecting their mode of historiography to match ours, denying the factual evidence, or even rejecting our faith altogether. It ought to press us towards a deep examination of our canons of interpretation. It ought to produce a "faith seeking understanding." Lawson G. Stone has similarly detected a "moral and spiritual cowardice" in running from historical-critical examinations of the Bible in a theological setting.[6] Reckoning with the conundrums and puzzles of historical criticism indeed requires a willingness to enter into questions that challenge a willful naiveté. It requires us to encounter data that challenges our presuppositions. It requires us to enter into conversations with historians of other perspectives. It requires us to sometimes say, "I don't know." But it also requires us to take a long, serious gaze into the fascinating and edifying lives of biblical authors and characters, as well as the worlds they inhabited.

---

6. Stone, "Historical Authenticity," 89.

Bibliography

Adam, A. K. M. *What Is Postmodern Biblical Criticism?* GBS. Minneapolis: Fortress, 1995.
Aichele, George, et al. "An Elephant in the Room: Historical-Critical and Postmodern Interpretations of the Bible." *JBL* 128 (2009) 383–404.
Aichele, George, et al., eds. *The Postmodern Bible*. New Haven: Yale University Press, 1997.
Albrektson, Bertil. *History and the Gods: An Essay on the Idea of Historical Events as Divine Manifestations in the Ancient Near East and Israel*. Lund: CWK Gleerup, 1967.
Alter, Robert. *The Art of Biblical Narrative*. New York: Basic, 1981.
———. *The Art of Biblical Poetry*. 2nd ed. New York: Basic, 1985.
———. *Canon and Creativity: Modern Writing and the Authority of Scripture*. New Haven: Yale University Press, 2000.
Ankersmit, F. R. "Historiography and Postmodernism." *HistTh* 28 (1989) 137–53.
———. "Reply to Professor Zagorin." *HistTh* 29 (1990) 275–96.
Appleby, Joyce, et al. *Telling the Truth About History*. New York: Norton, 1994.
Arnold, Bill T., and David B. Schreiner. "Graf and Wellhausen, and Their Legacy." In *A History of Biblical Interpretation*. Vol. 3, *The Enlightenment Through the Nineteenth Century*, edited by Alan J. Hauser and Duane F. Watson, 252–73. Grand Rapids: Eerdmans, 2017.
Arnold, Bill T., and David B. Weisberg. "A Centennial Review of Friedrich Delitzsch's 'Babel und Bibel' Lectures." *JBL* 121 (2002) 441–57.
Assmann, Aleida. "Transformations Between History and Memory." *SocRes* 75 (2008) 49–72.
Assmann, Jan. *Cultural Memory and Early Civilization: Writing, Remembrance, and Political Imagination*. Cambridge: Cambridge University Press, 2011.
———. *Moses the Egyptian*. Cambridge: Harvard University Press, 1997.
Attridge, Harold W. "Historiography." In *Jewish Writings of the Second Temple Period: Apocrypha, Pseudepigrapha, Qumran Sectarian Writings, Philo, Josephus*, edited by Michael E. Stone, 157–84. CRINT 2. Philadelphia: Fortress, 1984.
———. "Josephus and His Works." In *Jewish Writings of the Second Temple Period: Apocrypha, Pseudepigrapha, Qumran Sectarian Writings, Philo, Josephus*, edited by Michael E. Stone, 185–232. CRINT 2. Philadelphia: Fortress, 1984.
Baden, Joel S. "The Tower of Babel: A Case Study in the Competing Methods of Historical and Modern Literary Criticism." *JBL* 128 (2009) 209–24.

Bibliography

Baird, William. "An Overview of Historical Criticism." In *A History of Biblical Interpretation*. Vol. 3, *The Enlightenment Through the Nineteenth Century*, edited by Alan J. Hauser and Duane F. Watson, 96–119. Grand Rapids: Eerdmans, 2017.

Bakhos, Carol. "Jewish Midrashic Interpretation in Late Antiquity an the Early Middle Ages." In *A History Biblical Interpretation*. Vol. 2, *The Medieval Through the Reformation Periods*, edited by Alan J. Hauser and Duane F. Watson, 113–40. Grand Rapids: Eerdmans, 2009.

Banner, James M., Jr. *The Ever-Changing Past: Why All History Is Revisionist History*. New Haven: Yale University Press, 2021.

Barclay, John M. G. *Paul and the Gift*. Grand Rapids: Eerdmans, 2017.

Barr, James. *Comparative Philology and the Text of the Old Testament*. Oxford: Oxford University Press, 1968.

———. "Story and History in Biblical Theology: The Third Nuveen Lecture." *JR* 56 (1976) 1–17.

———. "The Synchronic, the Diachronic and the Historical: A Triangular Relationship?" In *Synchronic or Diachronic? A Debate on Method in Old Testament Exegesis*, edited by Johannes C. De Moor, 1–14. OtSt. Leiden: Brill, 1995.

Barthes, Roland. *Image—Music—Text*. Edited and translated by Stephen Heath. New York: Hill and Wang, 1977.

Barton, John. "Historical-Critical Approaches." In *The Cambridge Companion to Biblical Interpretation*, edited by John Barton, 9–20. Cambridge: Cambridge University Press, 1998.

———. "Historical Criticism and Literary Interpretation: Is There Any Common Ground?" In *Crossing the Boundaries: Essays in Biblical Studies in Honour of Michael D. Goulder*, edited by Stanley E. Porter et al., 3–15. BibInt 8. Leiden: Brill, 1994.

———. *The Nature of Biblical Criticism*. Louisville: Westminster John Knox, 2007.

Bell, Matthew T. *Ruled Reading and Biblical Criticism*. JTISup 18. University Park, PA: Eisenbrauns, 2019.

Bellinger, W. H., Jr. *Introducing Old Testament Theology: Creation, Covenant, and Prophecy in the Divine Human Relationship*. Grand Rapids: Baker Academic, 2022.

Berlin, Isaiah. "The Concept of Scientific History." *HistTh* 1 (1960) 1–31.

Bloch, Marc. *The Historian's Craft*. Delhi: Aakar, 2017.

Blum, Erhard. "Formgeschichte—A Misleading Category? Some Critical Remarks." In *The Changing Face of Form Criticism for the Twenty-First Century*, edited by Marvin A. Sweeney and Ehud Ben Zvi, 32–45. Grand Rapids: Eerdmans, 2003.

Braaten, Carl E., and Robert W. Jenson. "Introduction: Gospel, Church, and Scripture." In *Reclaiming the Bible for the Church*, edited by Carl E. Braaten and Robert W. Jenson, ix–xii. Grand Rapids: Eerdmans, 1995.

Braw, J. D. "Vision as Revision: Ranke and the Beginning of Modern History." *HistTh* 46 (2007) 77–91.

Brett, Mark G. *Biblical Criticism in Crisis?* Cambridge: Cambridge University Press, 1991.

Brettler, Mark Zvi, and Matthew Arakaky. "On the Term 'Historical-Critical.'" *ZAW* 136 (2024) 206–18.

Bright, John. *A History of Israel*. 3rd ed. Philadelphia: Westminster, 1981.

Broshi, Magen. "The Expansion of Jerusalem in the Reigns of Hezekiah and Manasseh." *IEJ* 24 (1974) 21–26.

Brown, Jeannine K. *Scripture as Communication: Introducing Biblical Hermeneutics*. 2nd ed. Grand Rapids: Baker Academic, 2021.

Bibliography

Brueggemann, Walter. *Theology of the Old Testament: Testimony, Dispute, Advocacy.* Minneapolis: Fortress, 1997.
Bullock, Alan. *Hitler: A Study in Tyranny.* Abridged ed. New York: Harper Perennial, 1991.
Burke, Peter. "Ranke the Reactionary." In *Leopold von Ranke and the Shaping of the Historical Discipline,* edited by Georg G. Iggers and James M. Powell, 36–44. Syracuse, NY: Syracuse University Press, 1990.
Butterfield, Herbert. *The Origins of History.* New York: Basic, 1981.
Campbell, Antony F. "Form Criticism's Future." In *The Changing Face of Form Criticism for the Twenty-First Century,* edited by Marvin A. Sweeney and Ehud Ben Zvi, 15–31. Grand Rapids: Eerdmans, 2003.
Capetz, Paul E. "Theology and the Historical-Critical Study of the Bible." *HTR* 104 (2011) 459–88.
Chestnut, Glenn F. "Eusebius." *ABD* 2:673–76.
Childs, Brevard S. *Biblical Theology in Crisis.* Philadelphia: Westminster, 1970.
———. *Introduction to the Old Testament as Scripture.* Philadelphia: Fortress, 1979.
———. "On Reclaiming the Bible for Christian Theology." In *Reclaiming the Bible for the Church,* edited by Carl E. Braaten and Robert W. Jenson, 1–17. Grand Rapids: Eerdmans, 1995.
Clark, Elizabeth A. *History, Theory, Text: Historians and the Linguistic Turn.* Cambridge: Harvard University Press, 2004.
Clements, Ronald E. *One Hundred Years of Old Testament Interpretation.* Philadelphia: Westminster, 1976.
Cline, Eric H. *Biblical Archaeology: A Very Short Introduction.* Oxford: Oxford University Press, 2009.
Clines, David J. A. "Historical Criticism: Are Its Days Numbered?" In *Exegetical Day of the Finnish Exegetical Society,* 1–20. Helsinki, 2007.
Cogan, Mordechai. *The Raging Torrent: Historical Inscriptions from Assyria and Babylonia Relating to Ancient Israel.* Jerusalem: Carta, 2008.
Collingwood, R. G. *Essays in the Philosophy of History.* Austin, TX: University of Texas Press, 1965.
———. *The Idea of History.* Mansfield Centre, CT: Martino, 2014.
Collins, John J. *The Bible After Babel: Historical Criticism in a Postmodern Age.* Grand Rapids: Eerdmans, 2005.
Day, Mark. *The Philosophy of History.* London: Continuum, 2008.
Day, Mark, and Gregory Radick. "Historiographic Evidence and Confirmation." In *A Companion to the Philosophy of History and Historiography,* edited by Aviezer Tucker, 87–97. Chichester: Wiley-Blackwell, 2011.
Deist, Ferdinand. "Contingency, Continuity, and Integrity in Historical Understanding." In *Israel's Past in Present Research: Essays in Ancient Israelite Historiography,* edited by V. Philips Long, 373–90. SBTS 7. Winona Lake, IN: Eisenbrauns, 1999.
Derrida, Jacques. *Of Grammatology.* Translated by Gayatri Chakravorty Spivak. Baltimore: John Hopkins University Press, 1976.
Descartes, René. *Discourse on Method.* Translated by John Veitch. London: Dent, 1960.
Dimant, Devorah. "Qumran Sectarian Literature." In *Jewish Writings of the Second Temple Period: Apocrypha, Pseudepigrapha, Qumran Sectarian Writings, Philo, Josephus,* edited by Michael E. Stone, 483–550. Philadelphia: Fortress, 1984.
Dinkler, Michal Beth. "Between Intention and Reception: Textual Meaning-Making in Intersubjective Perspective." In *Exegesis Without Authorial Intention? Interdisciplinary*

Bibliography

Approaches to Authorship and Meaning, edited by Clarissa Breu, 72–93. BibInt 172. Leiden: Brill, 2019.

Donfried, Karl P. "Alien Hermeneutics and the Misappropriation of Scripture." In *Reclaiming the Bible for the Church*, edited by Carl E. Braaten and Robert W. Jenson, 19–45. Grand Rapids: Eerdmans, 1995.

Dunn, James D. G. "Biblical Hermeneutics and Historical Responsibility." In *The Future of Biblical Interpretation: Responsible Plurality in Biblical Hermeneutics*, edited by Stanley E. Porter and Matthew R. Malcolm, 65–78. Milton Keynes: Paternoster, 2013.

———. "The Quest for the Historical Jesus and Its Implications for Biblical Interpretation." In *A History of Biblical Interpretation*. Vol. 3, *The Enlightenment Through the Nineteenth Century*, edited by Alan J. Hauser and Duane F. Watson, 300–318. Grand Rapids: Eerdmans, 2017.

Durant, Will, and Ariel Durant. *The Story of Civilization VII: The Age of Reason Begins*. New York: Simon and Schuster, 1961.

Eco, Umberto. *The Limits of Interpretation*. Bloomington: Indiana University Press, 1990.

Edelman, Diana. "Clio's Dilemma: The Changing Face of History-Writing." In *Congress Volume: Oslo 1998*, edited by Andre Lemaire and Magne Saebo, 247–55. VTSup 80. Leiden: Brill, 2000.

———. "Doing History in Biblical Studies." In *Israel's Past in Present Research: Essays on Ancient Israelite Historiography*, edited by V. Philips Long, 292–303. SBTS 7. Winona Lake, IN: Eisenbrauns, 1999.

Eichrodt, Walther. *Theology of the Old Testament: Volume I*. Translated by J. A. Baker. Philadelphia: Westminster, 1961.

———. *Theology of the Old Testament: Volume II*. Translated by J. A. Baker. London: Bloomsbury, 1967.

Eilberg-Schwartz, Howard. "Beyond Parallel-Anoia: Comparative Inquiry and Cultural Interpretation." In *The Savage in Judaism: An Anthropology of Israelite Religion and Ancient Judaism*, 87–102. Bloomington: Indiana University Press, 1990.

Evans, Richard J. *In Defense of History*. New York: Norton, 1997.

Fea, John. *Why Study History? Reflecting on the Importance of the Past*. Grand Rapids: Baker, 2013.

Fischer, David Hackett. *Historians' Fallacies: Toward a Logic of Historical Thought*. New York: Harper & Row, 1970.

Fish, Stanley. *Is There a Text in This Class? The Authority of Interpretive Communities*. Cambridge: Harvard University Press, 1980.

Flebbe, Jochen. "'And God Was the Text': An Essay on Intentio Operis and the Bible as the Word of God." In *Exegesis Without Authorial Intention? Interdisciplinary Approaches to Authorship and Meaning*, edited by Clarissa Breu, 43–55. BibInt 172. Leiden: Brill, 2019.

Foucault, Michel. "Madness in Society." In *The Essential Foucault: Selections from Essential Works of Foucault, 1954–1984*, edited by Paul Rabinow and Nikolas Rose, 370–76. New York: New, 1994.

———. "What Is an Author?" In *Aesthetics, Method, and Epistemology*, translated by James Faubion and Robert Hurley, 205–22. New York: New, 1998.

Fox, Robin Lane. "Thucydides and Documentary History." *ClQ* 60 (2010) 11–29.

Frampton, Travis L. "Spinoza and His Influence on Biblical Interpretation." In *A History of Biblical Interpretation*. Vol. 3, *The Enlightenment Through the Nineteenth Century*,

Bibliography

edited by Alan J. Hauser and Duane F. Watson, 120–50. Grand Rapids: Eerdmans, 2017.

Frei, Hans W. *The Eclipse of Biblical Narrative: A Study in Eighteenth and Nineteenth Century Hermeneutics*. New Haven: Yale University Press, 1974.

Gabler, Johann P. "An Oration on the Proper Distinction Between Biblical and Dogmatic Theology and the Specific Objectives of Each." In *Old Testament Theology: Flowering and Future*, edited by Ben C. Ollenburger, 497–506. SBTS 1. Winona Lake, IN: Eerdmans, 2004.

Gadamer, Hans-Georg. *Truth and Method*. New York: Crossroad, 1984.

Garbini, Giovanni. *History and Ideology in Ancient Israel*. Translated by John Bowden. London: SCM, 1988.

Gardiner, Patrick. *The Nature of Historical Explanation*. Oxford: Oxford University Press, 1961.

Garrett, Duane A. *The Problem of the Old Testament: Hermeneutical, Schematic, and Theological Approaches*. Downers Grove, IL: IVP Academic, 2020.

Gilkey, Langdon B. "Cosmology, Ontology, and the Travail of Biblical Language." *JR* 41 (1961) 194–205.

Gonzalez, Justo L. *The Story of Christianity*. Vol. 1, *The Early Church to the Dawn of the Reformation*. New York: HarperSanFrancisco, 1984.

Goodacre, Mark. *The Case Against Q: Studies in Markan Priority and the Synoptic Problem*. Harrisburg, PA: Trinity, 2002.

Grabbe, Lester. *A History of the Jews and Judaism in the Second Temple Period*. Vol. 2, *The early Hellenistic Period (335–175 BCE)*. London: T&T Clark, 2008.

———. "Who Were the First Real Historians? On the Origins of Critical Historiography." In *Did Moses Speak Attic? Jewish Historiography and Scripture in the Hellenistic Period*, edited by Lester Grabbe, 156–81. Sheffield: Sheffield Academic, 2001.

Grayson, A. Kirk. *Assyrian and Babylonian Chronicles*. Winona Lake, IN: Eisenbrauns, 2000.

Green, Joel B. *Seized by Truth: Reading the Bible as Scripture*. Nashville: Abingdon, 2007.

Greenstein, Edward L. "The State of Biblical Studies, or, Biblical Studies in a State Book." In *Essays on Biblical Method and Translation*, 3–27. Providence, RI: Brown Judaic Studies, 2003.

Gunkel, Hermann. "'Fundamental Problems of Hebrew Literary History." In *What Remains of the Old Testament and Other Essays*, 57–69. New York: Macmillan, 1928.

———. *Genesis*. Translated by Mark E. Biddle. Macon, GA: Mercer University Press, 1997.

Gutierrez, Gustavo. *We Drink from Our Own Wells: The Spiritual Journey of a People*. Maryknoll, NY: Orbis, 2003.

Hallo, William W. "Biblical History in Its Near Eastern Setting: The Contextual Approach." In *Scripture in Context: Essays on the Comparative Method*, edited by Carl D. Evans et al., 1–26. PTMS 34. Pittsburgh: Pickwick, 1980.

———. "Compare and Contrast: The Contextual Approach to Comparative Literature." In *The Bible in Light of Cuneiform Literature: Scripture in Context III*, edited by William W. Hallo et al., 1–30. Lewiston, NY: Edwin Mellen, 1990.

Halpern, Baruch. *The First Historians: The Hebrew Bible and History*. San Francisco: Harper & Row, 1988.

Bibliography

Harris, Robert A. "Medieval Jewish Biblical Exegesis." In *A History Biblical Interpretation*. Vol. 2, *The Medieval Through the Reformation Periods*, edited by Alan J. Hauser and Duane F. Watson, 141–71. Grand Rapids: Eerdmans, 2009.

Harris, Stephen L. *The New Testament: A Student's Introduction*. 9th ed. New York: McGraw-Hill, 2020.

Harvey, Van A. *The Historian and the Believer: The Morality of Historical Knowledge and Christian Belief*. Philadelphia: Westminster, 1966.

Hayes, John H. "The History of the Study of Israelite and Judean History: From the Renaissance to the Present." In *Israel's Past in Present Research: Essays in Ancient Israelite Historiography*, edited by V. Philips Long, 7–42. SBTS 7. Winona Lake, IN: Eisenbrauns, 1999.

Hayes, John H., and Carl R. Holladay. *Biblical Exegesis: A Beginner's Handbook*. Louisville: Westminster John Knox, 2007.

Hays, Christopher B. *Hidden Riches: A Sourcebook for the Comparative Study of the Hebrew Bible and Ancient Near East*. Louisville: Westminster John Knox, 2014.

Heinen, Sandra. "Exegesis Without Authorial Intention? On the Role of the 'Author Construct' in Text Interpretation." In *Exegesis Without Authorial Intention? Interdisciplinary Approaches to Authorship and Meaning*, edited by Clarissa Breu, 7–23. BibInt 172. Leiden: Brill, 2019.

Hendel, Ronald. "Mind the Gap: Modern and Postmodern in Biblical Studies." *JBL* 133 (2014) 422–43.

Hilber, John W. *Old Testament Cosmology and Divine Accommodation*. Eugene, OR: Cascade, 2020.

Hirsch, E. D., Jr. *Validity in Interpretation*. New Haven: Yale University Press, 1967.

Holland, Drew S. "Is There a Place for Historical Criticism in the Wesleyan-Methodist Tradition?" *WTJ* 58 (2023) 76–92.

———. "The Form and Function of the Source Citations in 1–2 Kings." *ZAW* 130 (2018) 559–70.

———. Review of *Collective Memory and Collective Identity: Deuteronomy and the Deuteronomistic History in Their Context*, edited by Johannes Unsok Ro and Diana Edelman. *RBL* December (2023) 1–5.

———. "They Are Written Right There: An Investigation of Royal Chronicles as Sources in 1–2 Kings." PhD diss., Asbury Theological Seminary, 2018.

———. "Why Bother with Historical Criticism? Lessons for Biblical Studies from the Philosophy of History." *AsTJ* 77 (2022) 289–317.

Holland, Tom. *Dominion: How the Christian Revolution Remade the World*. New York: Basic, 2021.

Hong, Koog P. "Synchrony and Diachrony in Contemporary Biblical Interpretation." *CBQ* 75 (2013) 521–39.

Huizinga, Johann. "A Definition of the Concept of History." In *Philosophy and History: Essays Presented to Ernst Cassirer*, edited by Raymond Klibansky and H. J. Paton, 1–10. Gloucester, MA: Peter Smith, 1963.

Icke, Peter P. *Frank Ankersmit's Lost Historical Cause*. London: Routledge, 2012.

Iggers, Georg G. "The Image of Ranke in American and German Historical Thought." *HistTh* 2 (1962) 17–40.

———. "Introduction." In Leopold von Ranke, *The Theory and Practice of History*, edited by George G. Iggers, xi–xlv. London: Routledge, 2010.

Jaspers, Karl. *The Origin and Goal of History*. New Haven: Yale University Press, 1953.

Bibliography

Jenkins, Keith. *On "What Is History?" From Carr and Elton to Rorty and White.* London: Routledge, 1995.

———. "A Postmodern Reply to Perez Zagorin." *HistTh* 39 (2000) 181–200.

Jenson, Robert W. "Hermeneutics and the Life of the Church." In *Reclaiming the Bible for the Church*, edited by Carl E. Braaten and Robert W. Jenson, 89–105. Grand Rapids: Eerdmans, 1995.

Jodock, Darrell. "Biblical Interpretation in the Work of F. C. Baur and the Tübingen School." In *A History of Biblical Interpretation*. Vol. 3, *The Enlightenment Through the Nineteenth Century*, edited by Alan J. Hauser and Duane F. Watson, 170–91. Grand Rapids: Eerdmans, 2017.

Johnson, Luke Timothy. *The Real Jesus: The Misguided Quest for the Historical Jesus and the Truth of the Traditional Gospels.* New York: HarperSanFrancisco, 1996.

Jongkind, Dirk. "The Text and Lexicography of the New Testament in the Eighteenth and Nineteenth Centuries." In *A History of Biblical Interpretation*. Vol. 3, *The Enlightenment Through the Nineteenth Century*, edited by Alan J. Hauser and Duane F. Watson, 274–99. Grand Rapids: Eerdmans, 2017.

Joyce, Paul. "First Among Equals? The Historical-Critical Approach in the Marketplace of Methods." In *Crossing the Boundaries: Essays in Biblical Studies in Honour of Michael D. Goulder*, edited by Stanley E. Porter et al., 17–27. BibInt 8. Leiden: Brill, 1994.

Käsemann, Ernst. "The Problem of the Historical Jesus." In *Essays on New Testament Themes*, translated by W. J. Montague, 15–47. SBTS 41. London: SCM, 1964.

Kaufman, Stephen A. "The Temple Scroll and Higher Criticism." *HUCA* 53 (1982) 29–43.

Kaufmann, Yehekel. *The Religion of Israel: From Its Beginnings to the Babylonian Exile.* Translated by Moshe Greenberg. New York: Schocken, 1972.

Keck, Leander E. "Will the Historical Critical Method Survive? Some Observations." In *Orientation by Disorientation: Studies in Literary Criticism and Biblical Literary Criticism*, edited by Richard A. Spencer, 115–27. Eugene, OR: Wipf and Stock, 1980.

Keener, Craig S. *Christobiography: Memory, History, and the Reliability of the Gospels.* Grand Rapids: Eerdmans, 2019.

Kelley, Donald R. "Mythistory in the Age of Ranke." In *Leopold von Ranke and the Shaping of the Historical Discipline*, edited by Georg G. Iggers and James M. Powell, 3–20. Syracuse, NY: Syracuse University Press, 1990.

Keuss, Jeffrey F. "David Friedrich Strauss and Ludwig Feuerbach: The Rise of Sturm und Drang in Biblical Scholarship." In *A History of Biblical Interpretation*. Vol. 3, *The Enlightenment Through the Nineteenth Century*, edited by Alan J. Hauser and Duane F. Watson, 192–210. Grand Rapids: Eerdmans, 2017.

King, Philip J., and Lawrence E. Stager. *Life in Biblical Israel.* Edited by Douglas A. Knight. LAI. Louisville: Westminster John Knox, 2001.

Kitchen, Kenneth A. *On the Reliability of the Old Testament.* Grand Rapids: Eerdmans, 2003.

Klement, Herbert H. "Modern Literary-Critical Methods and the Historicity of the Old Testament." In *Israel's Past in Present Research: Essays in Ancient Israelite Historiography*, edited by V. Philips Long, 439–59. SBTS 7. Winona Lake, IN: Eisenbrauns, 1999.

Knierim, Rolf. "Old Testament Form Criticism Reconsidered." *JBL* 95 (1976) 435–68.

Knohl, Israel. *The Sanctuary of Silence: The Priestly Torah and the Holiness School.* Minneapolis: Fortress, 1995.

Krentz, Edgar. *The Historical-Critical Method.* Reprint, Eugene, OR: Wipf and Stock, 2002.

Bibliography

Kümmel, Werner Georg. *The New Testament: The History of the Investigation of Its Problems*. Edited by S. McLean Gilmour and Howard C. Kee. Nashville: Abingdon, 1972.

Landsberger, Benno. *The Conceptual Autonomy of the Babylonian World*. MANE. Malibu: Undena, 1976.

———. "Die Eigenbegrifflichkeit der Babylonischen Welt." *Islamica* 2 (1926) 355–72.

Legaspi, Michael C. "The Term 'Enlightenment' and Biblical Interpretation." In *A History of Biblical Interpretation*. Vol. 3, *The Enlightenment Through the Nineteenth Century*, edited by Alan J. Hauser and Duane F. Watson, 73–95. Grand Rapids: Eerdmans, 2017.

———. "What Ever Happened to Historical Criticism?" *JRS* 9 (2007) 1–11.

Lemche, Niels Peter. "Is It Still Possible to Write a History of Ancient Israel?" In *Israel's Past in Present Research: Essays in Ancient Israelite Historiography*, edited by V. Philips Long, 391–414. SBTS. Winona Lake, IN: Eisenbrauns, 1999.

Levenson, Jon D. *The Hebrew Bible, the Old Testament, and Historical Criticism*. JCBS. Louisville: Westminster John Knox, 1993.

Levin, David. *In Defense of Historical Literature: Essays on American History, Autobiography, Drama, and Fiction*. New York: Hill and Wang, 1967.

Lim, Johnson Teng Kok. "Historical Critical Paradigm: The Beginning of an End." *AsJT* 14 (2000) 252–71.

Linnemann, Eta, and Robert W. Yarbrough. *Historical Criticism of the Bible: Methodology or Ideology? Reflections of a Bultmannian Turned Evangelical*. Grand Rapids: Kregel, 2001.

Long, V. Philips. "Historiography of the Old Testament." In *The Face of Old Testament Studies: A Survey of Contemporary Approaches*, edited by David W. Baker and Bill T. Arnold, 145–75. Grand Rapids: Baker Academic, 1999.

———. "Introduction." In *Windows into Old Testament History: Evidence, Argument, and the Crisis of "Biblical Israel,"* edited by V. Philips Long et al., 1–22. Grand Rapids: Eerdmans, 2002.

———, ed. *Israel's Past in Present Research*. SBTS 7. Winona Lake, IN: Eisenbrauns, 2002.

Longman, Tremper, III. "Israelite Genres in Their Ancient Near Eastern Context." In *The Changing Face of Form Criticism for the Twenty-First Century*, edited by Marvin A. Sweeney and Ehud Ben Zvi, 177–95. Grand Rapids: Eerdmans, 2003.

———. "Literary Approaches to Old Testament Study." In *The Face of Old Testament Studies: A Survey of Contemporary Approaches*, edited by David W. Baker and Bill T. Arnold, 97–115. Grand Rapids: Baker Academic, 1999.

Lyotard, Jean-Francois. *The Postmodern Condition*. Edited by Brian Massumi and Geoffrey Bennington. Minneapolis: University of Minnesota Press, 1984.

Maier, Gerhard. "Truth and Reality in the Historical Understanding of the Old Testament." In *Israel's Past in Present Research: Essays in Ancient Israelite Historiography*, edited by V. Philips Long, 192–206. SBTS 7. Winona Lake, IN: Eisenbrauns, 1999.

Mayeski, Mary A. "Early Medieval Exegesis: Gregory I to the Twelfth Century." In *A History Biblical Interpretation*. Vol. 2, *The Medieval Through the Reformation Periods*, edited by Alan J. Hauser and Duane F. Watson, 86–112. Grand Rapids: Eerdmans, 2009.

Maza, Sarah. *Thinking About History*. Chicago: University of Chicago Press, 2017.

McCall, J. Holly. "Pulaski Holds Weekend Equality March." *Tennessee Lookout*, August 17, 2020.

Bibliography

McCaulley, Esau. *Reading While Black: African American Biblical Interpretation as an Exercise in Hope*. Downers Grove, IL: IVP Academic, 2020.

McClain, Kevin, and Ted Poston, eds. *Best Explanations: New Essays on Inference to the Best Explanation*. Oxford: Oxford University Press, 2017.

McGrath, Alister E. "Reclaiming Our Roots and Vision: Scripture and the Stability of the Christian Church." In *Reclaiming the Bible for the Church*, edited by Carl E. Braaten and Robert W. Jenson, 63–88. Grand Rapids: Eerdmans, 1995.

McKenzie, Steven L. *How to Read the Bible: History, Prophecy, Literature: Why Modern Readers Need to Know the Difference and What It Means for Faith Today*. Oxford: Oxford University Press, 2005.

McKnight, Edgar V. *The Post-Modern Use of the Bible*. Nashville: Abingdon, 1988.

Meier, John P. *A Marginal Jew: Rethinking the Historical Jesus*. Vol. 4, *Law and Love*. New York: Doubleday, 2009.

Meyers, Carol. *Discovering Eve: Ancient Israelite Women in Context*. Oxford: Oxford University Press, 1991.

———. "Was Ancient Israel a Patriarchal Society?" *JBL* 133 (2014) 8–27.

Millard, A. R. "Israelite and Aramean History in Light of Inscriptions." *TynBul* 41 (1990) 261–75.

Miller, J. Maxwell. "Reading the Bible Historically: The Historian's Approach." In *Israel's Past in Present Research: Essays in Ancient Israelite Historiography*, edited by V. Philips Long, 356–72. SBTS 7. Winona Lake, IN: Eisenbrauns, 1999.

Misak, Cheryl. "Peirce and Ramsey: Truth, Pragmatism, and Inference to the Best Explanation." In *Best Explanations: New Essays on Inference to the Best Explanation*, edited by Kevin McCain and Ted Poston, 25–38. Oxford: Oxford University Press, 2017.

Moberly, Walter L. *Old Testament Theology: Reading the Hebrew Bible as Christian Scripture*. Grand Rapids: Baker Academic, 2013.

Momigliano, Arnaldo. *The Classical Foundations of Modern Historiography*. Berkeley: University of California Press, 1990.

———. "The Place of Herodotus in the History of Historiography." *History* 43.147 (1958) 1–13.

Moore, Stephen D. "Watch the Target: A Post-Postmodernist Response to Ronald Hendel." *JBL* 133 (2014) 444–50.

Moore, Stephen D., and Yvonne Sherwood. *The Invention of the Biblical Scholar: A Critical Manifesto*. Minneapolis: Fortress, 2011.

Mowinckel, Sigmund. *The Psalms in Israel's Worship*. Translated by D. R. Ap-Thomas. Nashville: Abingdon, 1962.

Muilenburg, James. "Form Criticism and Beyond." *JBL* 88 (1969) 1–18.

Murphy, Frederick J. *Early Judaism: The Exile to the Time of Jesus*. Peabody, MA: Hendrickson, 2002.

Murray, Stuart. "Biblical Interpretations Among the Anabaptist Reformers." In *A History Biblical Interpretation*. Vol. 2, *The Medieval Through the Reformation Periods*, 403–27. Grand Rapids: Eerdmans, 2009.

Ngo, Robin. "King Hezekiah of the Bible: Royal Seal of Hezekiah Comes to Light." *Bible History Daily*, March 2021. https://www.biblicalarchaeology.org/daily/news/king-hezekiah-in-the-bible-royal-seal-of-hezekiah-comes-to-light/.

Bibliography

Nissinen, Martti. "Reflections on the 'Historical-Critical' Method: Historical Criticism and Critical Historicism." In *Prophetic Divination: Essays in Ancient Near Eastern Prophecy*, edited by Martti Nissinen, 29–52. BZAW 494. Berlin: de Gruyter, 2019.

Norris, Richard A., Jr. "Augustine and the Close of the Ancient Period." In *A History of Biblical Interpretation*. Vol. 1, *The Ancient Period*, edited by Alan J. Hauser and Duane F. Watson, 380–407. Grand Rapids: Eerdmans, 2003.

Noth, Martin. *The Deuteronomistic History*. JSOTSup 1. Sheffield: JSOT, 1981.

———. *Überlieferungsgeschichtliche Studien*. Tübingen: Max Niemeyer, 1957.

Novick, Peter. *That Noble Dream: The "Objectivity Question" and the American Historical Profession*. Cambridge: Cambridge University Press, 1998.

Ocker, Christopher. "Scholastic Interpretation of the Bible." In *A History Biblical Interpretation*. Vol. 2, *The Medieval Through the Reformation Periods*, edited by Alan J. Hauser and Duane F. Watson, 254–79. Grand Rapids: Eerdmans, 2009.

Ollenburger, Ben C. "Old Testament Theology before 1933." In *Old Testament Theology: Flowering and Future*, edited by Ben C. Ollenburger, 3–11. SBTS 1. Winona Lake, IN: Eisenbrauns, 2004.

Partner, Nancy F. "Historicity in an Age of Reality-Fictions." In *A New Philosophy of History*, edited by Frank Ankersmit and Hans Kellner, 21–39. Chicago: University of Chicago Press, 1995.

Perdue, Leo G. *The Collapse of History: Reconstructing Old Testament Theology*. OBT. Minneapolis: Fortress, 1994.

———. *Reconstructing Old Testament Theology: After the Collapse of History*. OBT. Minneapolis: Fortress, 2005.

Person, Raymond F., Jr., and Robert Rezetko, eds. *Empirical Models Challenging Biblical Criticism*. AIL 25. Atlanta: SBL, 2016.

Pitkin, Barbara. "John Calvin and the Interpretation of the Bible." In *A History Biblical Interpretation*. Vol. 2, *The Medieval Through the Reformation Periods*, edited by Alan J. Hauser and Duane F. Watson, 341–71. Grand Rapids: Eerdmans, 2009.

Placher, William C. *A History of Christian Theology: An Introduction*. Louisville: Westminster John Knox, 1983.

Polzin, Robert M. "Literary and Historical Criticism of the Bible: A Crisis in Scholarship." In *Orientation by Disorientation: Studies in Literary Criticism and Biblical Literary Criticism*, edited by Richard A. Spencer, 99–114. Eugene, OR: Pickwick, 1980.

Powell, Mark Allan. *Jesus as a Figure in History: How Modern Historians View the Man from Galilee*. Louisville: Westminster John Knox, 1998.

Prickett, Stephen. *Words and The Word: Language, Poetics, and Biblical Interpretation*. Cambridge: Cambridge University Press, 1986.

Provan, Iain W., et al. *A Biblical History of Israel*. 2nd ed. Louisville: Westminster John Knox, 2003.

Rad, Gerhard von. *Old Testament Theology*. Vol. 2, *The Theology of Israel's Historical Traditions*. Translated by D. M. G. Stalker. New York: Harper & Row, 1962.

———. *Old Testament Theology*. Vol. 2, *The Theology of Israel's Prophetic Traditions*. Translated by D. M. G. Stalker. New York: Harper & Row, 1965.

Rae, Murray A. *History and Hermeneutics*. London: T&T Clark, 2005.

Ramban. *Commentary on Torah by Ramban (Nahmanides)*. Translated by Charles B. Chavel. New York: Shilo, 1971–76. https://www.sefaria.org/Ramban_on_Genesis?tab=contents.

Bibliography

Redford, Donald B. *Pharaonic King-Lists, Annals, and Day-Books: A Contribution to the Study of the Egyptian Sense of History*. SSEA 4. Mississauga, ON: Benben, 1986.

Reno, R. R. *The End of Interpretation: Reclaiming the Priority of Ecclesial Exegesis*. Grand Rapids: Baker Academic, 2022.

Rentdorff, Rolf. "The Paradigm Is Changing: Hopes and Fears." In *Israel's Past in Present Research: Essays in Ancient Israelite Historiography*, edited by V. Philips Long, 51–68. SBTS 7. Winona Lake, IN: Eisenbrauns, 1999.

Reventlow, Henning Graf. *History of Biblical Interpretation*. Vol. 1, *From the Old Testament to Origen*. Translated by Leo G. Perdue. SBLRBS 50. Atlanta: SBL, 2009.

———. *History of Biblical Interpretation*. Vol. 2, *From Late Antiquity to the End of the Middle Ages*. Translated by James O. Duke. SBLRBS 61. Atlanta: SBL, 2009.

———. *History of Biblical Interpretation*. Vol. 3, *Renaissance, Reformation, Humanism*. Translated by James O. Duke. SBLRBS 62. Atlanta: SBL, 2010.

———. *History of Biblical Interpretation*. Vol. 4, *From the Enlightenment to the Twentieth Century*. Translated by Leo G. Perdue. SBLRBS 63. Atlanta: SBL, 2010.

Ricouer, Paul. *Time and Narrative*. Edited by Kathleen McLaughlin and David Pellauer. Chicago: University of Chicago Press, 1984.

Ro, Johannes Unsok. "Memory and History: An Introduction." In *Collective Memory and Collective Identity: Deuteronomy and the Deuteronomistic History in Their Context*, edited by Johannes Unsok Ro and Diana Edelman, 1–17. BZAW 534. Berlin: de Gruyter, 2021.

Ro, Johannes Unsok, and Diana Edelman, eds. *Collective Memory and Collective Identity*. BZAW 534. Berlin: de Gruyter, 2021.

Robbins, Vernon K. *Exploring the Texture of Texts: A Guide to Socio-Rhetorical Interpretation*. Harrisburg, PA: Trinity, 1996.

Roberts, Clayton. *The Logic of Historical Explanation*. University Park, PA: Pennsylvania State University Press, 1996.

Rogerson, J. W. "Wilhelm De Wette and His Contemporaries." In *A History of Biblical Interpretation*. Vol. 3, *The Enlightenment Through the Nineteenth Century*, edited by Alan J. Hauser and Duane F. Watson, 236–51. Grand Rapids: Eerdmans, 2017.

Römer, Thomas. *The So-Called Deuteronomistic History*. London: T&T Clark, 2007.

Rummel, Erika. "The Renaissance Humanists." In *A History Biblical Interpretation*. Vol. 2, *The Medieval Through the Reformation Periods*, edited by Alan J. Hauer and Duane F. Watson, 280–98. Grand Rapids: Eerdmans, 2009.

Sanders, James A. "Textual Criticism of the Hebrew Bible: Masoretes to the Nineteenth Century." In *A History of Biblical Interpretation*. Vol. 3, *The Enlightenment Through the Nineteenth Century*, edited by Alan J. Hauser and Duane F. Watson, 211–35. Grand Rapids: Eerdmans, 2017.

Sandmel, Samuel. "Parallelomania." *JBL* 81 (1962) 1–13.

Santayana, George. *The Life of Reason or, The Phases of Human Progress: All Five Volumes- Complete and Unabridged*. Monee, IL: Pantianos Classics, 2021.

Scholz, Susanne. *Introducing the Women's Hebrew Bible*. IFT 19. London: T&T Clark, 2007.

Schreiner, David B., and Drew S. Holland. *Silhouettes of Scripture: Considering the Contextual Approach with Form Criticism*. Lanham, MD: Lexington, 2023.

Shoemaker, Robert G. "Inference and Intuition in Collingwood's Philosophy of History." *Monist* 53 (1969) 100–115.

Bibliography

Silva, Moises. *Biblical Words and Their Meaning: An Introduction to Lexical Semantics.* Grand Rapids: Zondervan, 1994.

Smith, George. "The Chaldean Account of the Deluge." *Transactions of the Society of Biblical Archaeology* 2 (1873) 213–34. https://www.sacred-texts.com/ane/chad/chad.htm.

Smith, James K. A. *Who's Afraid of Postmodernism? Taking Derrida, Lyotard, and Foucault to Church.* CPC. Grand Rapids: Baker Academic, 2006.

Sperber, Dan, and Deirdre Wilson. *Relevance: Communication and Cognition.* 2nd ed. Oxford: Blackwell, 1995.

Stanglin, Keith D. *The Letter and Spirit of Biblical Interpretation: From the Early Church to Modern Practice.* Grand Rapids: Baker Academic, 2018.

Stein, Robert H. *Studying the Synoptic Gospels: Origin and Interpretation.* Grand Rapids: Baker, 2001.

Steinmetz, David C. "The Superiority of Pre-Critical Exegesis." *ThTo* 37 (1980) 27–38.

Stendahl, Krister. "Biblical Theology, Contemporary." *The Interpreter's Dictionary of the Bible: An Illustrated Encyclopedia*, edited by George Arthur Buttrick et al., 1:418–32. Nashville: Abingdon, 1962.

Sterling, Gregory E. *Shaping the Past to Define the Present: Luke-Acts and Apologetic Historiography.* Grand Rapids: Eerdmans, 2023.

Stone, Lawson G. "On Historical Authenticity, Historical Criticism, and Biblical Authority: Reflections on the Case of the Book of Joshua." *AsTJ* 57 (2002) 83–96.

———. "Redaction Criticism: Whence, Whither, and Why? Or, Going Beyond Source and Form Criticism Without Leaving Them Behind." In *A Biblical Itinerary: In Search of Method, Form and Content*, edited by Eugene E. Carpenter, 77–90. JSOTSup. Sheffield: JSOT, 1997.

Strawn, Brent A. "Docetism, Käsemann, and Christology: Can Historical Criticism Help Christological Orthodoxy (and Other Theology) After All?" In *The Incomparable God: Readings in Biblical Theology*, edited by Collin Cornell and M. Justin Walker, 329–48. Grand Rapids: Eerdmans, 2023.

Stuhlmacher, Peter. *Historical Criticism and Theological Interpretation of Scripture.* Translated by Roy A. Harrisville. Philadelphia: Fortress, 1977.

Talbert, Charles H. *Reading Acts: A Literary and Theological Commentary.* Macon, GA: Smith & Helwys, 2005.

Talmon, Shemaryahu. "The 'Comparative Method' in Biblical Interpretation—Principles and Problems." In *Congress Volume: Göttingen, 1977*, edited by Walther Zimmerli, 320–56. VTSup 29. Leiden: Brill, 1991.

Thiselton, Anthony. "Biblical Studies and Theoretical Hermeneutics." In *The Cambridge Companion to Biblical Interpretation*, edited by John Barton, 95–113. New York: Cambridge University Press, 1998.

———. "The Future of Biblical Interpretation and Responsible Plurality in Hermeneutics." In *The Future of Biblical Interpretation: Responsible Plurality in Biblical Hermeneutics*, edited by Stanley E. Porter and Matthew R. Malcolm, 1–15. Milton Keynes: Paternoster, 2013.

Thompson, Mark D. "Biblical Interpretation in the Works of Martin Luther." In *A History Biblical Interpretation.* Vol. 2, *The Medieval Through the Reformation Periods*, edited by Alan J. Hauser and Duane F. Watson, 299–318. Grand Rapids: Eerdmans, 2009.

Thompson, Thomas L. "Historiography (Israelite Historiography)." *ABD* 3:206–12.

Bibliography

Tigay, Jeffrey H. "Introduction." In *Empirical Models for Biblical Criticism*, edited by Jeffrey H. Tigay, 1–20. Philadelphia: University of Pennsylvania Press, 1985.

Tov, Emmanuel. *Textual Criticism of the Hebrew Bible*. 3rd ed. Minneapolis: Fortress, 2011.

Troeltsch, Ernst. *Religion in History*. Translated by James Luther Adams and Walter F. Bence. Minneapolis: Fortress, 1991.

Tucker, Aviezer. "Causation in Historiography." In *A Companion to the Philosophy of History and Historiography*, edited by Aviezer Tucker, 99–108. Chichester: Wiley-Blackwell, 2011.

———. "Origins: Common Causes in Historiographic Reasoning." In *A Companion to the Philosophy of History and Historiography*, edited by Aviezer Tucker, 220–30. Chichester: Wiley-Blackwell, 2011.

———. *Our Knowledge of the Past*. Cambridge: Cambridge University Press, 2004.

Tucker, Gene M. *Form Criticism of the Old Testament*. GBS. Philadelphia: Fortress, 1971.

Utzschneider, Helmut. "Text–Reader–Author: Towards a Theory of Exegesis: Some European Viewpoints." *JHebS* 1 (1997) 1–22.

Van der Spek, R. J. "Berossus as a Babylonian Chronicler and Greek Historian." In *Studies in Ancient Near Eastern World View and Society: Presented to Marten Stol on the Occaision of His 65th Birthday, 10 November 2005, and His Retirement from the Vrije Universiteit Amsterdam*, edited by R. J. Van der Spek, 277–318. Bethesda, MD: CDL, 2008.

Vanhoozer, Kevin J. *Is There a Meaning in This Text? The Bible, the Reader, and the Morality of Literary Knowledge*. Grand Rapids: Zondervan, 1998.

Van Seters, John. *In Search of History: Historiography in the Ancient World and the Origins of Biblical History*. Winona Lake, IN: Eisenbrauns, 1997.

Walsh, W. H. *Philosophy of History: An Introduction*. 2nd ed. New York: Harper Torchbooks, 1967.

Walton, John H. *Ancient Near Eastern Thought and the Old Testament: Introducing the Conceptual World of the Hebrew Bible*. Grand Rapids: Baker, 2006.

Weinfeld, Moshe. *The Place of the Law in the Religion of Ancient Israel*. VTSupp. Leiden: Brill, 2004.

Wellhausen, Julius. *Prolegomena to the History of Israel*. Atlanta: Scholar's, 1994.

Wengert, Timothy. "Biblical Interpretation in the Works of Philip Melanchthon." In *A History Biblical Interpretation*. Vol. 2, *The Medieval Through the Reformation Periods*, edited by Alan J. Hauser and Duane F. Watson, 319–40. Grand Rapids: Eerdmans, 2009.

Wenham, Gordon J. "Pondering the Pentateuch: The Search for a New Paradigm." In *The Face of Old Testament Studies: A Survey of Contemporary Approaches*, edited by David W. Baker and Bill T. Arnold, 116–44. Grand Rapids: Baker, 1999.

The Westminster Confession of Faith. 1647. 3rd ed. Atlanta: Committee for Christian Education and Publications, 1990.

White, Hayden. *Metahistory: The Historical Imagination in Nineteenth-Century Europe*. Baltimore: Johns Hopkins University Press, 1973.

Wimsatt, W. K., Jr., and Monroe C. Beardsley. "The Intentional Fallacy." In *The Verbal Icon: Studies in the Meaning of Poetry*, edited by W. K. Wimsatt, 1–18. Lexington, KY: University of Kentucky Press, 1954.

Windschuttle, Keith. *The Killing of History: How Literary Critics and Social Theorists Are Murdering Our Past*. New York: Free, 1996.

Bibliography

Wischmeyer, Oda. "Author–Text–Intention: A Case Study on the Letter of James." In *Exegesis Without Authorial Intention? Interdisciplinary Approaches to Authorship and Meaning*, edited by Clarissa Breu, 24–42. BibInt 172. Leiden: Brill, 2019.

Wolters, Al. "The Text of the Old Testament." In *The Face of Old Testament Studies: A Survey of Contemporary Approaches*, edited by David W. Baker and Bill T. Arnold, 19–37. Grand Rapids: Baker, 1999.

Yeago, David S. "The New Testament and the Nicene Dogma: A Contribution to the Recovery of Theological Exegesis." *ProEccl* 3 (1994) 152–64.

Young, Frances M. "Alexandrian and Antiochene Exegesis." In *A History of Biblical Interpretation*. Vol. 1, *The Ancient Period*, edited by Alan J. Hauser and Duane F. Watson, 334–54. Grand Rapids: Eerdmans, 2003.

———. *Biblical Exegesis and the Formation of Christian Culture*. Peabody, MA: Hendrickson, 1997.

Younger, K. Lawson, Jr. "The Underpinnings." In *Israel's Past in Present Research: Essays in Ancient Israelite Historiography*, edited by V. Philips Long, 304–45. SBTS 7. Winona Lake, IN: Eisenbrauns, 1999.

Zagorin, Perez. "Historiography and Postmodernism: Reconsiderations." *HistTh* 29 (1990) 263–74.

Zammito, John. "Historians and Philosophy of Historiography." In *A Companion to the Philosophy of History and Historiography*, edited by Aviezer Tucker, 63–84. Chichester: Wiley-Blackwell, 2011.

Subject Index

Abraham Ibn Ezra, 31, 33, 44
Acts of the Apostles, 22–23, 28, 72
Albright, William Foxwell, 66, 75
Allegory, 24–25, 28, 35, 42, 47, 78, 95n71
Anagogical Reading, 35
Analogy of Scripture, 24, 33–34, 45, 48–49
Annals, 13, 140, 141
Antiochene Exegesis, 28–30, 162
Antiquarianism, 10–11, 13, 16n22, 20–21, 27, 41–44, 54, 57–58, 62, 65, 95, 123, 152
Aquinas, Thomas, 37, 96
Archaeology, x, 56–57, 59–60, **65–67**, 74–75, 117–18, 121n76, 124, 126, 133 *see* Historical Criticism, Methodologies
Aristotle, 30, 51, 65
Arminianism, 49
Artifacts, 54, 58, 65, 117–18, 131–32, 159
Ashurbanipal, 65
Astruc, Jean, 53, 67n10, 69
Augustine of Hippo, 34–35, 47
Authorial Intention, ix–x, 29, 35, 37, 47, 50, **80–81**, 83–84, 88, 92, 99–100, 104–12, 120, 142–43, 163
Autopsy, 16–17, 23

Bacon, Francis, 51, 130, 137
Barth, Karl, 74
Bauer, G.L., 69n16
Baur, Ferdinand Christian, 72–73
Behistun Inscription, 65

Bible
    Authors of, x, 3, 5, 8, 24, 27, 29, 30, 38, 42, 52, 54, 56, 57, 62, **83–85**, 92, 133–34, 162, 164
    Complutensian Polyglot, 43
    Contradictions in, 5, 26, 48, 53
    Criticism, 52, 64
    as History Book, 2
    Telos of, 22, 26, 34, 46, 98
Biblical Theology Movement, 8, 64, **75–76**, 79, **91–99**, 109, 114, 116–18, 159
Biography, 22–23, 43, 122, 125
Boundaries in Reading, x, 30, 122, 124, 126, 130–31, 134, **140–43**, 155, 161–62
Bultmann, Rudolf, 73–74

Calvin, John, **46–50**, 80, 163
Canonical Approach, *see* Childs, Brevard
Carter, Howard, 65
Cassian, John, 35
Champollion, Jean-François, 65
Christ, *see* Jesus of Nazareth
Chronicles, x, 13–14, 27, 140
Chrysostom, John, 28
Cicero, 27n73
Clermont-Ganneau, Charles, 66
Coherence, 18, 24, 29–30, 107, 135, 147
Civil War, U.S., 1–2
Coins, 43, 118, 140–41

Subject Index

Comparative Studies, 65–66, 114–15
    see Historical Criticism,
    Methodologies
Comte, August, 130n4
Continental Philosophy, 80, see also
    Postmodernism
Coulanges, Foustel de, 59n88
Courcelles, Étienne de, 49
Cyrus the Great, 17, 141

Davis, Sam, 1–2
Dead Sea Scrolls, 66–67
Delitzsch, Friedrich, **65–66**, 114
Descartes, René, 51
Deuteronomistic History, 11, 14, 16, 71, 147, 161
De Wette, W.M.L., 69, 102n104, 131n7
Diachronic Readings, 7–8, 108–10
Diodore of Tarsus, 28–29
Dionysius of Alexandria, 24
Docetism, 74, 120n74
Duhm, Bernhard, 69n20
Durkheim, Emile, 121

Egypt, 12–13, 65, 76n51, 122, 137
Eichorn, Johann Gottfried, 54
Eliot, T.S., 80, 105
Epic of Gilgamesh, 65
Episcopus, Simon, 49
Erasmus, **42–43**, 67
Eusebius of Caesarea, 25, **27–28**, 40, 162
Ewald, Heinrich, 57–58, 69

Facts, 3, 16, 18–21, 27, 36, 57, 59, 61, 67, 74, 80, 82, 99, 130–31, 135, 140n46, 141, 145–46, 148, 160, 164
Feminist Readings, 118–19
Final-Form Readings, 5–8, 71, 82–83, 93, 96–99, 101, 103, 108–9, 111, 126, 129, 130, 141, 143
Form Criticism, 4, 70–71, 84, 113, 115–16, 125, see also Historical Criticism, Methodologies
Formalism, see New Criticism
Funk, Robert, 74–75

Genre, 11, 12, 15, 23, 28, 29, 36–37, 48, 70, 105, 110, 115–17, 125, 133, 142, 162–63
Geography, 16, 27, 43, 45, 50, 54, 57, 63
Giotto, 43
Gospels, 22–23, 25, 27, 68, 70–71, 72–75, 97, 120
Graf, Karl Heinrich, 69
Griesbach, Jakob, 68
Grotius, Hugo, 52n53

Hecataeus, 16–17, 21
Hegel, G.W.F., 130
Hellanicus, 16, 21
Herder, Johann Gottfried, 70, 134n17
Hermeneutics, 49, 104, 138, 142, 150, 162–63
Herodotus, 11, 15, **17–18**, 19, 21, 40
Hezekiah, 118, 141, 147–49, 152–53
Higher Criticism, 54, 68–71, 84, 103, 113
Historia, 26, 28–29, 36
Historical Background, 8, 26–29, 44, 70, 100–101, 112–13, 115, 119, 153, 156, 158
Historical Criticism
    Consensus, 4–5
    Definition, 4
    Methodologies, 4, 6, 8, 44, 50, 62–63, **64–78**, 94, 96–97, 102, **112–21**
Historical Jesus, see Jesus of Nazareth
Historiography, see History Writing
History Writing,
    in Ancient Near East, 3, 12–16, 133, 158
    Analogy, 60, 117, 163
    Causation, 11, 19–21, 60–61, 90, 128, 147, **148–150**, 153
    Certainty in, 88, 99, 104, 105–6, 128–29, 143–48, 154–55, 157
    Definition, 10–12
    Early Christianity, 22–30
    in the Enlightenment, 5, 8, 40–41, **51–63**, 85, 88, 91, 99, 129–30, 158–59
    Erasmus of Rotterdam, **42–43**, 67
    Evidence, 9, 18–19, 89, 100–101, 113, 131, 133, 135, **140–43**, 144–47, 153–54, 164

180

Subject Index

Goal of, 36, 129, **150–54**
Greco-Roman World, 3, 16–21, 22–24, 133, 150–51, 158
Historiography, 10
  in Jewish Exegesis, 30–34
  Judgment, 15, 18, 60–61, 100–101, 104, 132, 140, 143, 147, 154, 156
  Logic, 9, 18, 51, 135, 139n44, **143–148**, 154–55, 157, 160
  in Medieval Christian Interpretation, 31, **34–39**, 57, 158
  Renaissance, **40–45**, 45–48, 50, 56–57, 62, 112, 162
  Revision in, 60, 139
  as Scientific, 5, 41, 99–100, 105, 129–32, 144n65, 148, 155
  Sources, 3, 15–16, 18, 22–23, 27–28, 42, 58–60, 68–69, 71, 72, 84, 89, 95, 113–15, 126, 131, 139, 140–42, 149, 159, 161
Holocaust, 88n38, 114
Holtzmann, Heinrich Julius, 68–69
Holy Spirit, 23, 46, 48, 52, 55, 72, 117
Homer, 16
Humanism, 125, 132–33, 152–53, *see also* History Writing, Renaissance

Iconography, 12
Illyricus, Matthias Flacius, 48–49
Inscriptions, 12, 15n18, 43, 65, 66, 118, 140, 156
Irenaeus of Lyons, 24
Iron Age, 13–16
Islam, 30, 31

Jericho, 66, 101
Jerome, 24, 37, 43
Jesus of Nazareth, 22–23, 24, 26–29, 37, 46–47, 64, 70–71, **72–75**, 91, 96–97, 106, 119–21, 161
Jesus Seminar, 74–75
Josephus, **21**, 28, 67
Judaism, **30–34**, 96

Kenyon, Kathleen, 66
King Lists, 12, 13
Ku Klux Klan, 1

Lachmann, Karl, 68nn11,13
Late Bronze Age, 12–13
Latinx Readings, 118
Layard, Austen Henry, 65
Lessing, Gotthold Ephraim, 55, 79
Linguistics, *see* Philology
Literal Exegesis, x, 5, 26–29, 33–38, 40, 42, 45–49, 63, 95–96, 162–63
Locke, John, 130
Lower Criticism, *see* Textual Criticism
Luther, Martin, 25n60, **45–46**, 48, 58, 96, 120

Megiddo, 66
Melanchthon, Philip, 45, 46n27
Memory, 9, 50n43, 57, 76n51, 90, **121–23**
Mens Scriptoris, see Authorial Intention
Merneptah Stele, 66
Mesopotamia, 13–14, 19, 65, 113–14
Michaelis, Johann David, 69–70
Moabite Stone, 66
Mommsen, Theodor, 58–59
Morality, 22, 25–26, 53n59, 65, 134, 155–56, 164 *see also* Tropological reading

Napoleon, 65
Narrative, 3, 12, 28, 33, 36, 48, 55, 58, 84, 87, 94–95, 100–102, 137n33, 141, 143, 149, 161
Nazis, 74, 134, 152
Nebrija, 43–44
New Criticism, x, 80, 91–92, 94, 96, 103–6, 130
Ngo, Robin, 141n52
Nicholas of Lyra, 37–38
Nietzsche, Friedrich, 85n26, 148

Origen of Alexandria, 24, **25–27**, 28, 34, 40, 44, 55, 67, 124, 162

Palestine Exploration Fund, 65
Papias of Hierapolis, 25
Paul, 25, 29, 55, 101, 109–10, 119–20, 163
Perspicuity, 45, 49–50
Petrarch, 42–43
Petrie, William Matthew Flinders, 66

Subject Index

Philology, x, 31, 36, 37–38, 40, 43, 52, 56, 57, 62, 69, 76, 83, 108, 115, 119, 133
Plain sense, *see* Literal Exegesis
Plato, 25, 30
Plutarch, 18, 27n73, 28
Polybius, 19–21, 40
Positivism, 59–61, 129–32, 135, 148, 154, 160
Postmodernism, x, 3–5, 8, 82n17, 85–88, 89–90, 92, 94, 96, 99, 103, 104, 116, 124, 136–37, 142, 143–44, 154n99
Pottery Typology, 66
Presentism, 150–52
Pulaski, TN, 1–2

Quadriga, 35, 46
Qur'an, 30

Rabbinic Exegesis, 29, **30–33**, 34, 38
Ramban, 32–33
Ranke, Leopold von, **58–59**, 104–5, 130–31, 152
Rashbam, 32–33
Rashi, 31–32
Rawlinson, Henry, 65
Reader-Response, 81–82
Redaction Criticism, 6, 71, 96, 109, 147, 161, *see* Historical Criticism, Methodologies
Reformation, 41, **45–51**, 57, 62–63, 78, 97n86, 112, 141, 158–59, 162
Reimarus, Hermann Samuel, 55
Relevance Theory, 111–12
Robinson, Charles, 65
Roman Catholicism, 41, 45, 46n27, 50–51, 52–53
Rosetta Stone, 65
Rule of Faith, 24, 34, 161

Saadia ben Joseph, 31
Saussure, Ferdinand de, 86, 108–9
Scholasticism, 38, 41, 65
Schleiermacher, Friedrich, 104
Schumacher, Gottlieb, 66
Schweitzer, Albert, 73, 74

Semler, Johann Salomo, 53
Sennacherib, x, 5, 141–42, 150–53
Shishak/Shoshenq, 66
Siloam Inscription, 66
Simon, Richard, **52–53**, 67, 69, 117
Smith, George Adam, 66
Socinus, Faustus, 49
Socio-Rhetorical Criticism, 119
Source Criticism, 68–70, 113–14, *see* Historical Criticism, Methodologies
Speech-Act Theory, 112–13
Spinoza, Benedict (Baruch) de, 51–52
Spiritual Sense, 5, 28, 34–35, 37–38, 42, 45–46, 63
Stratigraphy, 66
Strauss, David Friedrich, 68, 72
Suetonius, 27n73
Synchronic Readings, 7–8, 108–10

Tel Dan Stele, 118
Textual Criticism, 6–7, 25–26, 28–30, 52, 62, 64, 66, **67–68**, 113, *see also* Historical Criticism, Methodologies
Theodore of Mopsuestia, 28
Theological exegesis, 4, *see also* Spiritual Sense
Thucydides, 11, **18–19**, 21, 22, 30, 36, 40, 59, 150–51
Tradition, 4–6, 11, 13, 17–18, 25, 28, 31–33, 34, 38, 42–44, 45, 51–57, 70, 76–77, 93, 96, 121, 159, 162–63
Trivium, 36–37
Tropological reading, 22, 24–25, 34–35, 38, 48
Tutankhamun, 65

Valla, Lorenzo, 42–43, 62
Victorenes, 37–38
Voltaire, 54–55

Warren, Charles, 65
Weisse, Christian Hermann, 68–69
Wellhausen, Julius, x, **69–70**, 113–14
Weltanschauung, *see* Worldview
Westminster Confession of Faith, 45

Subject Index

Whewell, William, 147n77
Wilke, Christian Gottlieb, 68, 70
Wimsatt, W.K., 80, 84, 105, 142
Witter, Bernhard, 53
Womanist Readings, 118

Worldview, 9, 34n96, 50, 52, 54, 81, 89, 91–92, 100–101, 110, 118–19, 133, 136, 143, 155–56, 163–64
Wright, G. Ernest, 75–76, 98n93

Author Index

Adam A.K.M, 4n5, 85n25, **86–87**, 88, 99n98, 120n74, 121, 129n3, 153n58
Aichele, George, 4n5, 85, 86n27, 88n38, 99n98
Albrektson, Bertil, 98n93
Alter, Robert, 4, **82–83**, 84n24, 108
Ankersmit, F.R., 88n38, **89–90**, 129n3, 140n47, 148
Appleby, Joyce, 90n51, 137n33, 138
Arakaky, Matthew, 4n4, 54n62, 69n16, 131n7
Arnold, Bill T., 65n4, 69nn17–18, 114n48
Assmann, Aleida, 122n77
Assmann, Jan, 50n43, **122**
Attridge, Harold W., 16n21, 21nn45,50
Austin, J.L., 111

Baden, Joel, 6n12, 126n91
Baird, William, 53n60, 54n61, 73n35
Bakhos, Carol, 30n84
Banner, James M., Jr., 135–36, 139
Barclay, John M.G., 120n70
Barr, James, 92n58, **94–95**, 98n93, 109
Barthes, Roland, 80–81, 84, 106
Barton, John, 6n12, 29–30, 41nn1–2, 48n35, 50n45, 52n55, 60nn93,95, 61–62, 64n1, 79n1, 107, 109n30, **110–11**, 114n48, 124nn84–86, 125nn89–90, 126n91, **154–155**, 156, 161n1, 163n5
Beardsley, Monroe C., 80, 84, 142

Bell, Matthew T., 24n55, 85n25, 162nn3–4
Bellinger, W.H., Jr. 116
Berlin, Isaiah, 131
Betti, Emilio, 105n5, 106n10
Bloch, Mark, 133n16, 134, 137–38, 140, 143, 149, 152, 153n98
Blum, Erhard, 115n55
Braaten, Carl E., 41n1
Braw, J.D., 58n83, 59n86,88,91, 152n95
Brett, Mark G., 93–94, 95n74, 108n26
Brettler, Mark Zvi 4n4, 54n62, 69n16, 131n7
Bright, John, 75–76
Broshi, Magen, 141n52
Brown, Jeannine K., 111, 124n83
Brueggemann, Walter, 41n1, 57n77, 76nn48,51, 84n24, 98n96, 99n98, 116, 129n3
Bullock, Alan, 152n96
Burke, Peter, 59
Burr, Kevin B., xi, 18n30, 27n73
Butterfield, Herbert, 14, 16n26, 17n27

Campbell, Antony F., 115
Capetz, Paul E., 98n92, 124nn83–84, 125n90, 126n93, **155–56**, 161n1
Chestnut, Glenn F., 27n72
Childs, Brevard, 4, **92–94**, 95n74, 97, 98n93, 100–101, 108
Clark, Elizabeth A., 58n83, 59n87, 86n32, 88n38, 134n18, 152n94
Clements, Ronald E., 69n20, 70n25, 77–78

Author Index

Cline, Eric, 65n2, 66nn5–6, 101n103, 118n65
Clines, David J.A., 6n11
Cogan, Mordecai, 14
Collins, John J., 41n2, 60n93, 61, 85n26, 126n92, 154n100, 155n110
Collingwood, R.G., 58n80, **131–133**, 138n39, 140n48, 145–46, 146n74, 151, 152n98

Day, Mark, 59n90, 89n42, 132n14, 133, 138nn36,38, 140nn47,49, 143n56, 144, 146nn70,72, 147n77, 149
Deist, Ferdinand, 61n100, 140n50
Derrida, Jacques, 85n26, **86–87**, 101, 105, 124, 133–34, 143n57
Dilthey, Wilhelm, 104
Dimant, Devorah, 67n7
Dinkler, Michal Beth, 110n33
Donfried, Karl P., 124n86
Dunn, James D.G., 72n33, 96n79, 124n83
Durant, Ariel and Will, 51n47

Eco, Umberto 82n17, **106**, 110, 161
Edelman, Diana, 11–12, 121n76, 123
Eichrodt, Walter, 76, 117
Evans, Richard J., 58nn80,82–83, 88n38, 137, 140n48, 144, 149

Fea, John, 153n98
Fischer, David Hackett, 59n88, 129n2, 136n29, 137nn34–35, 139n44, 141, 146n73, 149, 150n89, 152nn94,98
Fish, Stanley, 81–82
Flebbe, Jochen, 106
Foucault, Michel, 3, 13, 19, **81**, 84, 85n26, 87
Fox, Robin Lane, 19n36
Frampton, Travis L., 52nn50–51
Frei, Hans W., 36, 46n27, **94–95**, 98n94, 101, 133n17

Gabler, Johann P., 49, **56–57**, 162
Gadamer, Hans-Georg, **104–5**, 138, 162
Garbini, Giovanni, 15n20

Gardiner, Patrick, 131, 135n22, 146n75, 148–50
Garrett, Duane A., 116
Gilkey, Langdon B., 92, 95
Goodacre, Mark, 120n72
Gonzalez, Justo L., 41n3, 42nn4–5, 46n27
Grabbe, Lester L., 11, 15–16, 18n34, 19nn39–42, 21n50
Grayson, A. Kirk, 14
Green, Joel B., 6n11
Greenstein, Edward L., 6n11, 108n27
Gunkel, Hermann, 70–71, 115
Gutierrez, Gustavo, 118n66

Hallo, William W., 11, 115
Halpern, Baruch, 15, 145n67
Harris, Robert A., 31nn35–38, 32
Harris, Stephen L., 121n75
Harvey, Van A., 59n86, 60n93, 61, 74nn39–40, 75n44, 120n74, 132, 136n28, 144–45
Hayes, John H., 42nn6–7,9, 43–44, 46n24, 48n37, 49n40, 50, 52n55, 53nn56,58, 54nn61,64,65, 55, 57nn78–79, 58n81, 69n20, 70n23, 72
Hays, Christopher B., 115n53
Heinen, Sandra, 83–84
Hendel, Ronald, 85
Hilber, John W., 112
Hirsch, E.D., 82n17, **105–6**, 124
Holladay, Carl R., 70n23, 72
Holland, Drew S., 13nn7–11, 19n37, 65n3, 115nn53,55, 123n82, 128n1, 151n93
Holland, Tom, 2n3
Hong, Koog P., 108n26, 109, 161n1
Huizinga, Johan, 10–12, 14–15

Icke, Peter P., 90n50
Iggers, Georg, 58–59, 61n99, 130n5, 131n8, 140n49

Jenkins, Keith D., 86n30, 88n38, **89–90**, 137n31, 143nn57–58, 144
Jenson, Robert W., 41n1, 55n68
Jodock, Darrell, 72nn33–34, 73n35

Author Index

Johnson, Luke Timothy, **96–99**, 121
Jongkind, Dirk, 11n68
Joyce, Paul, 6n12, 124n6, 155–56

Käsemann, Ernst, 74
Kauffmann, Yehezekhel, 113–14
Kaufman, Stephen A., 113n44
Keck, Leander E., 41n1, 101n102, 124n83, 161n1
Keener, Craig S., 22, 23n52
Kelley, Donald R., 18n35, 59n91
Keuss, Jeffrey F., 72nn32–33
King, Philip J., 118n64
Kitchen, Kenneth A., 142n54
Klement, Herbert H., 124n85
Knierim, Rolf, 115n56
Knoll, Israel, 114
Krentz, Edgar, 41n2, 52n50, 53nn59,60, 54n61, 55n70, 60n93, 61n97, 62, 124nn83–84, 126n93, 134n21
Kümmel, Werner Georg, 25nn58–60, 48nn36,38, 53n60, 70, 68nn11–13, 69, 70n22, 72n33, 73nn35–36

Landsberger, Benno 114–15
Legaspi, Michael C., 51–52, 53n60, 54nn61,64, 61n100, 100
Lemche, Niels Peter, 142n53
Levenson, Jon D., 6n12, 33, 41n1, 61n101, 91, **95–96**, 125n89
Lim, Johnson Teng Kok, 99–100
Linnemann, Eta, 41n1, 91n52
Long, V. Philips, 61n101, 108n26, 121n76, 130n4, 135n23, 145
Longman III, Tremper, 80n4, 82n16, 84n24, 115n56, 130n4
Lyotard, Jean-Francois, 3, **87**, 90, 100

Maier, Gerhard, 145n66, 150n88
Mayeski, Mary A., 34, 36
Maza, Sarah, 140n46, 147n78, 149
McCauley, Esau, 118n66
McClain, Kevin, 145n69
McGrath, Alister, 49n43
McKenzie, Steven L., 116n57
McKnight, Edgar V., 60n93, **82**, 86n28, 96n75, 108nn25,27

Meier, John P., 120
Meyers, Carol, 118–19
Millard, A.R., 15n15
Miller, J. Maxwell, 61n100, 145n66
Misak, Cheryl, 146nn71,76
Moberly, R.W.L., 116
Momigliano, Arnoldo, 14n14, 16, 17n28, 18nn31,33, 19nn36, 39, 151n90
Moore, Stephen D., 49n43, 85n26
Mowinckel, Sigmund, 70
Muilenburg, James, 4, 84n24, 99n96, **115**
Murphy, Frederick J., 67n7
Murray, Stuart, 46n27

Nissinen, Martti, 41n1, 59n88, 88, 124n83, 154n101, 161n1
Norris, Richard A., 34n98, 35n102
Noth, Martin, 15n18, 70n24, 71
Novick, Peter, 130–31

Ocker, Christopher, 35n104, 36n108, 37nn9,10,12,13, 38n116
Ollenburger, Ben C., 56nn74–75

Partner, Nancy, 90
Pelikan, Jaroslav, 98n91
Perdue, Leo G., 41n1, 57n77, 61n101, 76n51, 85n26, 86n30, 87nn35–36, **98–99**, 108n27, 116–17, 118n66, 129n3, 133
Person, Raymond F., 113n45
Pitkin, Barbara, 47nn28–29, 31, 48
Placher, William, 41n3
Polzin, Robert, 108n27, 124n85
Poston, Ted, 145n69
Powell, Mark Allan, 72n33, 73nn36–38, 74nn39,43, 75n44
Prickett, Stephen, 57n77, 83, 99

Rad, Gerhard von, **76**, 98n93, 117
Radick, Gregory, 146n72
Rae, Murray A., 22n51, 52n50, 55n67, 74nn 39–40,43, 75n44, 120, 142n55
Redford, Donald B., 12n6
Reno, R.R., 4n9, 6n11, 27, 46n27, **97–98**, 100

187

Author Index

Rentdorff, Rolf, 69n20, 76n51
Reventlow, Henning Graf, 24n55, 27n69,
　28n76, 31nn87–88, 32n91, 34n98,
　36nn106,108, 37–38, 42n10,
　45n22, 46n24, 47n29, 48nn33–34,
　52, 53nn57,59, 54n61, 55n70,
　57n79, 69nn16,19,20, 71n27,
　72n33, 73n35, 102n104
Rezetko, Robert, 113n45
Ricouer, Paul, 89n40
Ro, Johannes Unsok, 121n76, 122–23
Robbins, Vernon, 119
Roberson, J.W., 69n16
Roberts, Clayton, 140n48, 147nn77–78
Römer, Thomas, 71n30
Rummel, Erika, 42nn6,10, 43nn14–16, 44

Sanders, James A., 67n10
Sandmel, Samuel, 114–15
Santayana, George, 89n41, 145nn67–68,
　151
Scholz, Sussane, 118n66
Screiner, David B., 13n10, 65n3, 69nn17–
　18, 115nn53,56
Searle, John 111
Sherwood, Yvonne, 49n43
Shoemaker, Robert, 133n16
Silva, Moises, 86n28, 108n25, 110n31
Smith, George, 65
Smith, James K.A., 87n35
Speck, R.J. van der, 14n13
Sperber, Dan, 111
Stager, Lawrence E., 118n54
Stanglin, Keith D., 5–6, 24, 25nn61–63,
　26n66, 28nn75,78, 29n79, 35–36,
　37nn112–113, 38, 42, 45n23,
　46nn25–26, 47, 48nn43–44, 49–
　50, 50nn50,52, 55nn68–69, 163n5
Stein, Robert H., 120n71
Steinmetz, David C., 6n11, 95n71
Stendahl, Krister, 108–9
Sterling, Gergory E., 16n26, 22n51, 28

Stone, Lawson G., 71, 108n27, 117,
　125n90, 126n91, **156**, 161n1, 164
Strawn, Brent A., 6n12, 120n74
Stuhlmacher, Peter, 41n2, 49, 52n55,
　53n57, 55, 60n92, 61, 124n84,
　126n93

Talbert, Charles H., 23n53
Talmon, Shermeryahu, 115
Thiselton, Anthony, 104, 105nn4–5,
　106n10, 111n38, 161n2
Thompson, Mark D., 46
Thompson, Thomas L., 16n22
Tigay, Jeffrey, 113
Tov, Emmanuel, 67nn8,10, 68n11
Troeltsch, Ernst, **60–62**, 117, 126, 159, 163
Tucker, Aviezer, 143–44, 147n78
Tucker, Gene M., 71n27

Utzschneider, Helmut, 110, 161

Van Seters, John, 10–12, 14–15, 20–21
Vanhoozer, Kevin J., 81n13, 107, 111n38

Walsh, W.H., 58n80, 85, 131nn9,11
Walton, John H., 115n53
Weinfeld, Moshe, 114
Weisberg, David B., 65n4
Wengert, Timothy, 45n22
Wenham, Gordon J., 70, 113n43
White, Hayden, **89**, 100, 135n24, 136, 140
Wilson, Dierdre, 111
Windschuttle, Keith, 143n56
Wischmeyer, Oda, 106–7, 161n1
Wolters, Al, 67nn9–10

Yeago, David S., 6n11, 41n1, 46n27,
　96–97, 100
Young, Francis M., 16n24, 24n56, 25–26,
　27nn71,73, 28n77, 29
Younger, Lawson K., 11n4

Zagorin, Perez, 140n47

Ancient Document Index

Genesis
1:1—2:4a   126
2:4b   126
1   26–27
1:26–27   2, 163
2–3   163
2:5   32
3   2
3:15   47
6–9   65
33:4   31

Exodus
13:9   32

Deuteronomy
6:5   161
6:8   32
6:20–25   76

Joshua
2–6   102

1 Kings
22   102n104

2 Kings
5   161–63

5:13   162
18–20   141
19:35–37   5

Proverbs
7:22   26

Isaiah
36–39   141
37:36–38   5

Jeremiah
29:11   124–25

Matthew
10:7–10   26
16:20   26
22:37   161

Mark
12:30   161

Luke
3:22   72
10:37   161

John
20:31   71

Ancient Document Index

1 Corinthians
2:4 — 55
13 — 109

Philippians
2:10–11 — 96n79

1 Peter
3:18–21 — 24

Revelation
21–22 — 163

www.ingramcontent.com/pod-product-compliance
Lightning Source LLC
Chambersburg PA
CBHW031427150426
43191CB00006B/435